SCIENTIFIC RESEARCH METHODOLOGY

CONCEPTS AND QUALITY

ENV BOOKS SERIES

SCIENTIFIC RESEARCH METHODOLOGY

CONCEPTS AND QUALITY

Editor

Dr. Pawan Kumar 'Bharti'

Society for Environment, Health
Awareness of Nutrition & Toxicology (SEHAT)
B-225/5D, Top Floor, Subhash Gali, Road No. 7, Block B
Ashok Nagar, Shahdara
Delhi-110 093
(India)

&

Dr. Prasann Kumar

Assistant Professor
Department of Agronomy, School of Agriculture
Lovely Professional University, Jalandhar - 144 411
(Punjab) (India)

DPH

DISCOVERY PUBLISHING HOUSE PVT. LTD.
INDIA

Published by:
Namit Wasan

DISCOVERY PUBLISHING HOUSE PVT. LTD.
4383/4B, Ansari Road, Darya Ganj
New Delhi-110 002 (India)
Phone : +91-11-23279245; 23253475; 43596065
E-mail : discoverybooksindia@gmail.com
discoverypublishinghouse@gmail.com
namitwasan9@gmail.com
web : www.discoverypublishinggroup.com

***First Edition:* 2019**

ISBN: 978-93-86841-95-7

Scientific Research Methodology: *Concepts and Quality*

Printed at:
Infinity Imaging Systems
Delhi

PREFACE

Research is a logical and systematic search for new and useful information on a particular topic. Research is important both in scientific and nonscientific fields. In our life new problems, events, phenomena and processes occur every day. Practically, implementable solutions and suggestions are required for tackling new problems that arise. Scientists have to undertake research on them and find their causes, solutions, explanations and applications.

The research is broadly classified into two main classes:

1. Fundamental or basic research and
2. Applied research.

Basic and applied researches are generally of two kinds: normal research and revolutionary research. In any particular field, normal research is performed in accordance with a set of rules, concepts and procedures called a paradigm, which is well accepted by the scientists working in that field. In addition, the basic and applied researches can be quantitative or qualitative or even both.

The present book updates the subject content of scientific research, concepts and related issues, research ethics, research methodology, statistical tools, scientific writing in research, collaborative and sustainable research.

Thanks are due to publisher and contributors from various institutions and universities.

The book will be helpful for the researchers, academia working in the field of scientific research, concepts and related issues, research ethics, research methodology, statistical tools, scientific writing in research, collaborative and sustainable research.

Editors
(envbooks@gmail.com)

CONTENTS

Scientific Research Methodology : *Concepts and Quality*
***Edited by:* and Dr. Pawan Kumar 'Bharti' and Dr. Prasann Kumar**
ISBN: 978-93-86841-95-7
***Edition:* 2019**
***Published by:* Discovery Publishing House Pvt. Ltd., New Delhi (India)**

1 Introduction

Research conducted for the purpose of contributing towards science by the systematic collection, interpretation and evaluation of data and that, too, in a planned manner is called scientific research: a researcher is the one who conducts this research. The results obtained from a small group through scientific studies are socialised, and new information is revealed with respect to diagnosis, treatment and reliability of applications. The purpose of this review is to provide information about the definition, classification and methodology of scientific research.

Before beginning the scientific research, the researcher should determine the subject, do planning and specify the methodology. In the Declaration of Helsinki, it is stated that 'the primary purpose of medical researches on volunteers is to understand the reasons, development and effects of diseases and develop protective, diagnostic and therapeutic interventions (method, operation and therapies). Even the best proven interventions should be evaluated continuously by investigations with regard to reliability, effectiveness, efficiency, accessibility and quality'.

The questions, methods of response to questions and difficulties in scientific research may vary, but the design and structure are generally the same.

Scientific research can be classified in several ways. Classification can be made according to the data collection techniques based on causality, relationship with time and the medium through which they are applied.

According to data collection techniques:

- Observational
- Experimental

According to causality relationships:

- Descriptive
- Analytical

According to relationships with time:

- Retrospective

- Prospective
- Cross-sectional

According to the medium through which they are applied:

- Clinical
- Laboratory
- Social descriptive research

Another method is to classify the research according to its descriptive or analytical features. This review is written according to this classification method.

I. Descriptive research
   - Case series
   - Surveillance studies

II. Analytical research
   - Observational studies: cohort, case control and cross- sectional research
   - Interventional research: quasi-experimental and clinical research

Descriptive Research: in this type of research, the participant examines the distribution of diseases according to their place and time in society. It includes case reports, case series and surveillance studies.

Case Report: it is the most common type of descriptive study. It is the examination of a single case having a different quality in the society, e.g. conducting general anaesthesia in a pregnant patient with mucopolys accharidosis.

Case Series: it is the description of repetitive cases having common features. For instance; case series involving interscapular pain related to neuraxial labour analgesia. Interestingly, malignant hyperthermia cases are not accepted as case series since they are rarely seen during historical development.

Surveillance Studies: these are the results obtained from the databases that follow and record a health problem for a certain time, e.g. the surveillance of cross-infections during anaesthesia in the intensive care unit.

Analytical Scientific Research: the most important difference of this and the descriptive research is the presence of a comparison group. They are categorised as observational and interventional research.

Observational Research: the participants are grouped and evaluated according to a research plan or protocol. Observational research is more attractive than other studies: as necessary clinical data is available, coming to a conclusion is fast and they incur low costs. In observational studies, the factors and events examined by the researcher are not under the researcher's control. They cannot be changed when requested. All the variables, except for the examined factor or event, cannot be kept constant. Randomisation can be restrictedly used in some cases. It might not be always possible to apparently and completely detect a cause and effect relationship. The results are considerably similar to real-life situations since the events are examined as they are and special conditions are not created. Since the repetition of the observed cases is impossible most of the times, it may not be possible to recreate the same conditions.

Moreover, some studies may be experimental. After the researcher intervenes, the researcher waits for the result, observes and obtains data. Experimental studies are, more often, in the form of clinical trials or laboratory animal trials.

Analytical observational research can be classified as cohort, case-control and cross-sectional studies.

Cohort Studies (Prospective, Retrospective and Ambidirectional): A cohort is a group formed by patients having common characteristics. A cohort study is the one in which a group of patients is followed-up in time, e.g. comparison of academic performances of children (who underwent anaesthesia in their neonatal period) in their adolescence.

Firstly, the participants are controlled with regard to the disease under investigation. Patients are excluded from the study. Healthy participants are evaluated with regard to the exposure to the effect. Then, the group (cohort) is followed-up for a sufficient period of time with respect to the occurrence of disease, and the progress of disease is studied. The risk of the healthy participants getting sick is considered an incident. In cohort studies, the risk of disease between the groups exposed and not exposed to the effect is calculated and rated. This rate is called relative risk. Relative risk indicates the strength of exposure to the effect on the disease.

Cohort research may be observational and experimental. The follow-up of patients prospectively is called a prospective cohort study. The results are obtained after the research starts. The researcher's following-up of cohort subjects from a certain point towards the past is called a retrospective cohort study. Prospective cohort studies are more valuable than retrospective cohort studies: this is because in the former, the researcher observes and records the data. The researcher plans the study before the research and determines what data will be used. On the other hand, in retrospective studies, the research is made on recorded data: no new data can be added.

In fact, retrospective and prospective studies are not observational. They determine the relationship between the date on which the researcher has begun the study and the disease development period. The most critical disadvantage of this type of research is that if the follow-up period is long, participants may leave the study at their own behest or due to physical conditions. Cohort studies that begin after exposure and before disease development are called ambidirectional studies. Public healthcare studies generally fall within this group, e.g. lung cancer development in smokers.

Case-Control Studies: these studies are retrospective cohort studies. They examine the cause and effect relationship from the effect to the cause. The detection or determination of data depends on the information recorded in the past. The researcher has no control over the data.

Cross-Sectional Studies: in cross-sectional studies, the patients or events are examined at a particular point in time. Prevalence studies (the percentage of a population having a disease at a certain time) are the ones in which the diagnosis and disease mechanism are detected and the cause and effect relationship is examined at the same level.

Cross-sectional studies are advantageous since they can be concluded relatively quickly. It may be difficult to obtain a reliable result from such studies for rare diseases.

Cross-sectional studies are characterised by timing. In such studies, the exposure and result are simultaneously evaluated. While cross-sectional studies are restrictedly used in studies involving anaesthesia (since the process of exposure is limited), they can be used in studies conducted in intensive care units.

Interventional Research (Experimental Studies): in this type of research, there is a control group aimed to be tested. The researcher decides upon which effect the participant will be exposed to in this study. Post-intervention, the researcher waits for the result, observes and obtains the data. Interventional studies are divided into two: quasi-experimental and clinical research.

Quasi-Experimental Research: they are conducted in cases in which a quick result is requested and the participants or research areas cannot be randomised, e.g. giving hand-wash training and comparing the frequency of nosocomial infections before and after hand wash.

Clinical Research: they are prospective studies carried out with a control group for the purpose of comparing the effect and value of an intervention in a clinical case. Clinical study and research have the same meaning. Drugs, invasive interventions, medical devices and operations, diets, physical therapy and diagnostic tools are relevant in this context.

Clinical studies are conducted by a responsible researcher, generally a physician. In the research team, there may be other healthcare staff besides physicians. Clinical studies may be financed by healthcare institutes, drug companies, academic medical centres, volunteer groups, physicians, healthcare service providers and other individuals. They may be conducted in several places including hospitals, universities, physicians' offices and community clinics based on the researcher's requirements. The participants are made aware of the duration of the study before their inclusion. Clinical studies should include the evaluation of recommendations (drug, device and surgical) for the treatment of a disease, syndrome or a comparison of one or more applications; finding different ways for recognition of a disease or case and prevention of their recurrence.

Clinical Research

In this review, clinical research is explained in more detail since it is the most valuable study in scientific research.

Clinical research starts with forming a hypothesis. A hypothesis can be defined as a claim put forward about the value of a population parameter based on sampling. There are two types of hypotheses in statistics.

H0 hypothesis is called a control or null hypothesis. It is the hypothesis put forward in research, which implies that there is no difference between the groups under consideration. If this hypothesis is rejected at the end of the study, it indicates that a difference exists between the two treatments under consideration.

H1 hypothesis is called an alternative hypothesis. It is hypothesised against a null hypothesis, which implies that a difference exists between the groups under consideration. For example, consider the following hypothesis: drug A has an analgesic effect. Control or null hypothesis (H0): there is no difference between drug A and placebo with regard to the analgesic effect. The alternative hypothesis (H1) is applicable if a difference exists between drug A and placebo with regard to the analgesic effect.

The planning phase comes after the determination of a hypothesis. A clinical research plan is called a protocol. In a protocol, the reasons for research, number and qualities of participants, tests to be applied, study duration and what information to be gathered from the participants should be found and conformity criteria should be developed.

The selection of participant groups to be included in the study is important. Inclusion and exclusion criteria of the study for the participants should be determined. Inclusion criteria should be defined in the form of demographic characteristics (age, gender, etc.) of the participant group and the exclusion criteria as the diseases that may influence the study, age ranges, cases involving pregnancy and lactation, continuously used drugs and participants' cooperation.

The next stage is methodology. Methodology can be grouped under subheadings, namely, the calculation of number of subjects, blinding (masking), randomisation, selection of operation to be applied, use of placebo and criteria for stopping and changing the treatment.

Scientific research is the systematic investigation of scientific theories and hypotheses.

In science, the people who create such hypotheses are researchers. Most researchers work for companies or academic institutions. Many of them, but not all, have a PhD in an appropriate field related to their research. For example, a person conducting research on a new drug may have a PhD in chemistry - a PhD in history probably wouldn't do much good.

Anyways, scientific researchers try to answer the many questions we have about how the world works. But a lot of their work doesn't really have to do with the questions at the forefront of our minds.

I mean, yes, we're all fascinated with knowing whether or not there may be life on other planets, but for many reasons such research isn't as common as finding out whether or not a drug you never heard of has a potentially dangerous side effect.

We may not think about this kind of research very often, but it impacts us or people we know far more so than the search for life on other planets. Until, of course, we find out we're not alone in this universe and are potentially going to be invaded by little green men.

The Scientific Method

Furthermore, scientists don't just come up with explanations about the world around us willy-nilly. Not even close. Scientists use the scientific method, a process that helps construct an accurate depiction of our universe and its processes, in order to answer whatever question they may have!

What this means is, researchers observe the world around them, formulate potential explanations for the phenomena they observe, test their hypotheses out with experiments, and analyze their results to see if they were right or wrong.

The key thing about the scientific method is that it carries no prejudice, meaning you don't even have to believe whatever it is the researcher wrote or said! Using the scientific method, you can repeat the experiment to find out for yourself whether or not the other researcher's assertions are true. This is a key factor that separates science from dogma!

The other important part of scientific research is that a hypothesis must be falsifiable. A falsifiable hypothesis or theory is one where an experiment or another discovery can prove it to be wrong, untrue, and false. This is another critical factor that separates science from the world of religion, astrology, and pseudoscience.

If I was to say that Bigfoot exists but always hides when humans are around and leaves no evidence behind, that, in the words of Penn and Teller, is bologna! There is no way to disprove such a statement and it is therefore unscientific.

Overall, scientific research helps people come up with rational, objective, testable, and disprovable questions and methods that help us explain the world and its ever-changing nature.

In science, you don't have to believe anything. You are free to test it out for yourself and prove or disprove anything you want in an objective and unbiased manner.

In the field of science, it is important to move away from the looser meaning and use it only in its proper context. Scientific research adheres to a set of strict protocols and long established structures.

Often, we will talk about conducting internet research or say that we are researching in the library. In everyday language, it is perfectly correct grammatically, but in science, it gives a misleading impression. The correct and most common term used in science is that we are conducting a literature review.

Types of Scientific Research

Research is a logical and systematic search for new and useful information on a particular topic. Research is important both in scientific and nonscientific fields. In our life new problems, events, phenomena and processes occur every day. Practically, implementable solutions and suggestions are required for tackling new problems that arise. Scientists have to undertake research on them and find their causes, solutions, explanations and applications.

The research is broadly classified into two main classes:

1. Fundamental or basic research and
2. Applied research.

Basic and applied researches are generally of two kinds: normal research and revolutionary research. In any particular field, normal research is performed in accordance with a set of rules, concepts and procedures called a paradigm, which is well accepted by the scientists working in that field. In addition, the basic and applied researches can be quantitative or qualitative or even both (mixed research).

1. Fundamental or basic research: Basic research is an investigation on basic principles and reasons for occurrence of a particular event or process or phenomenon. It is also called theoretical research. Study or investigation of some natural phenomenon or relating to pure science are termed as basic research. Basic researches sometimes may not lead to immediate use or application. It is not concerned with solving any practical problems of immediate interest. But it is original or basic in character. It provides a systematic and deep insight into a problem and facilitates extraction of scientific and logical explanation and conclusion on it. It helps build new frontiers of knowledge. The outcomes of basic research form the basis for many applied research.

Basic research

- Seeks generalization
- Aims at basic processes
- Attempts to explain why things happen
- Tries to get all the facts
- Reports in technical language of the topic

2. Applied research: In an applied research one solves certain problems employing well known and accepted theories and principles. Most of the experimental research, case studies and inter-disciplinary research are essentially applied research. Applied research is helpful for basic research. A research, the outcome of which has immediate application is also termed as applied research. Such a research is of practical use to current activity.

Applied research

- Studies individual or specific cases without the objective to generalize
- Aims at any variable which makes the desired difference
- Tries to say how things can be changed
- Tries to correct the facts which are problematic
- Reports in common language

Basic and applied research, further divided into three types of research bearing some characteristics feature as follows:

Quantitative research

- It is numerical, non-descriptive, applies statistics or mathematics and uses numbers.
- It is an iterative process whereby evidence is evaluated.
- The results are often presented in tables and graphs.
- It is conclusive.
- It investigates the what, where and when of decision making.

Qualitative research

- It is non-numerical, descriptive, applies reasoning and uses words.
- Its aim is to get the meaning, feeling and describe the situation.
- Qualitative data cannot be graphed.
- It is exploratory.
- It investigates the why and how of decision making.

Mixed research

- Mixed research-research that involves the mixing of quantitative and qualitative methods or paradigm characteristics. Nature of data is mixture of variables, words and images.

Other types of research

Exploratory Research

Exploratory research might involve a literature search or conducting focus group interviews. The exploration of new phenomena in this way may help the researcher's need for better understanding, may test the feasibility of a more extensive study, or determine the best methods to be used in a subsequent study. For these reasons, exploratory research is broad in focus and rarely provides definite answers to specific research issues.

The objective of exploratory research is to identify key issues and key variables.

Descriptive research

The descriptive research is directed toward studying "what" and how many off this "what". Thus, it is directed toward answering questions such as, "What is this?".

Explanatory research

Its primary goal is to understand or to explain relationships.

It uses correlations to study relationships between dimensions or characteristics off individuals, groups, situations, or events.

Explanatory research explains (How the parts of a phenomenon are related to each other).

Explanatory research asks the "Why" question.

Longitudinal Research

Research carried out longitudinally involves data collection at multiple points in time. Longitudinal studies may take the form of:

Trend study-looks at population characteristics over time, e.g. organizational absenteeism rates during the course of a year

Cohort study-traces a sub-population over time, e.g. absenteeism rates for the sales department;

Panel study-traces the same sample over time, e.g. graduate career tracks over the period 1990 – 2000 for the same starting cohort.

While longitudinal studies will often be more time consuming and expensive than cross-sectional studies, they are more likely to identify causal relationships between variables.

Cross-sectional Research

One-shot or cross-sectional studies are those in which data is gathered once, during a period of days, weeks or months. Many cross-sectional studies are exploratory or descriptive in purpose. They are designed to look at how things are now, without any sense of whether there is a history or trend at work.

Action research

Fact findings to improve the quality of action in the social world

Policy-Oriented Research

Reports employing this type of research focus on the question 'How can problem 'X' be solved or prevented ?'

Classification research

- It aims at categorization of units in to groups
- To demonstrate differences
- To explain relationships

Comparative research

- To identify similarities and differences between units at all levels

Causal research

- It aims at establishing cause and effect relationship among variable

Theory-testing research

- It aims at testing validity of a unit

Theory-building research

- To establish and formulate the theory

Last of all, it is needless to say that scientific research helps us in many ways:

- A research problem refers to a difficulty which a researcher or a scientific community or an industry or a government organization or a society experiences. It may be a theoretical or a practical situation. It calls for a thorough understanding and possible solution.
- Research provides basis for many government policies. For example, research on the needs and desires of the people and on the availability of revenues to meet the needs helps a government to prepare a budget.
- It is the fountain of knowledge and provide guidelines for solving problems.
- Only through research inventions can be made; for example, new and novel phenomena and processes such as superconductivity and cloning have been discovered only through research.
- It is important in industry and business for higher gain and productivity and to improve the quality of products.
- Research leads to a new style of life and makes it delightful and glorious.
- It leads to the identification and characterization of new materials, new living things, new stars, etc.
- Mathematical and logical research on business and industry optimizes the problems in them.

- Social research helps find answers to social problems. They explain social phenomena and seek solution to social problems.

REFERENCES

Akan H. Bilimsel Araþtýrmalarda Planlama ve Tasarým. Ankem Dergisi. 2014;28:101–4.

Akan H. Bilimsel Yayýnlarda Taraf Tutma Saðlýk Bilimlerinde Süreli Yayýncýlýk. 2008:89–95.

Bekiroðlu N. Biyoistatistik. The web site: http://docplayer.biz.tr/2029485-Biyoistatistik-nural-bekiroglu-ph-d-giris.html.

Clinicaltrial. Submit studies. The web site: https://clinicaltrials.gov.

Healthwise Staff. Plasebo and Sham Treatment Myhealth. The web site: https://myhealth.alberta.ca/Health/pages/conditions.aspx.

http://www.businessdictionary.com/definition/scientific-research.html

https://explorable.com/what-is-research

https://innspub.net/types-of-scientific-research/

https://study.com/academy/lesson/what-is-scientific-research.html

https://www.ncbi.nlm.nih.gov/pmc/articles/PMC5019873/

Klinik araþtýrmalar Derneði. Helsinki Bildirgesi. 2016. The web site: http://www.klinikarastirmalar.org.tr/icerik.phpid=1304.

Lotte Gluud L. Bias in Clinical Invervention. Am J Epidemiol. 2006;163:493–501. http://dx.doi.org/10.1093/aje/kwj069. [PubMed]

Öcek Z. Epidemiyoloji. The web site: http://dent.ege.edu.tr/dosyalar/kaynak/116.

Özdemir O. Randomizasyon. In: Özdemir O, editor. Medikal Ýstatistik. 1. Baský Ýstanbul: Ýstanbul Medikal Yayýncýlýk; 2006. p. 20.

Özkan S. Ýlaçlarla yapýlan gözlemsel çalýþmalar. In: Akan H, Ýlbars H, Ömeroðlu Çetinkaya N, editors. Klinik Araþtýrmalar Kitabý-2014 1 Baský. Ankara: Bilimsel Týp Yayýnevi; 2014. pp. 205–9.

Sessler D, Imrey PB. Clinical Research Methodology 3: Randomized Controlled Trials. Anesth Analg. 2015;121:1052–64. http://dx.doi.org/10.1213/ANE.0000000000000862. [PubMed]

Scientific Research Methodology : *Concepts and Quality*
Edited by: and Dr. Pawan Kumar 'Bharti' and Dr. Prasann Kumar
ISBN: 978-93-86841-95-7
Edition: 2019
Published by: Discovery Publishing House Pvt. Ltd., New Delhi (India)

2

Collaborative Research

Need for Sustainable Research

[1]Prasann Kumar and [2]Shweta Pathak

GRAPHICAL ABSTRACT

Keywords: Advance, Biological, Collaborative, Research, Sustainable.

Introduction

1. Examples of Possible Collaborations

Collaborative research is any research project that is carried out by at least two people.

- Sharing an instrument/equipment.
- Between faculty and student/s.
- Interdisciplinary work i.e. within the departments of the same university.
- Between universities of the same country.

[1] Department of Agronomy, School of Agriculture, Lovely Professional University, Jalandhar, Punjab, 144411, India

[2] Department of Plant Physiology, I.Ag. Sci., BHU., Varanasi, 221005, U.P., India

- Between different laboratories and universities.
- Between university and industry.
- Between universities of different countries.

Between universities and industries of different countries (Figure 2.1)

Fig. 2.1: Research in collaboration
(Source: Based on review of literature, 2018)

1. What is collaborative research?

"Collaborative Research" as an umbrella term for methodologies that actively involve communities and policy makers in the research process from start to finish.

This means that university researchers, community-based organizations, and policy makers will work together to:

- formulate the problem.
- undertake the research.
- obtaining and interpreting the results.
- distribute the research findings.

Fig. 2.2: Contract for research
(Source: Based on review of literature, 2018)

2. Examples of collaborative research
   - A mechanical engineer working with a physician for developing a new surgical device.
   - A social scientist working with a physician on tobacco-control initiative.
   - A pharmaceutical industry working with a university for the development of some drugs.
   - Chemistry department of any university working with an Iron and Steel company.

Fig. 2.3: Examples of collaborative research
(Source: Based on review of literature, 2018)

Fig. 2.4: Examples for collaborative research
(Source: Based on review of literature, 2018)

Collaboration has been intrinsic to the research process for the past 50 years, but collaboration per se usually refers to researchers who work within the same discipline, either within an institution or in different institutions. When a biochemist solves the crystal structure of a protein for a molecular biologist working on the regulation of the protein, that is a collaboration within the biological sciences. Multidisciplinary research is a form of collaborative research that involves researchers working across disciplines, either within an institution or in different institutions. A physician working with an engineer to manufacture a new imaging device, or an epidemiologist working with a political scientist on a tobacco-control initiative, is an example of a cross-disciplinary research project. When the pharmaceutical industry works with a medical center to perform a clinical trial of a new drug, it is a collaboration across industry and academia. Each of these interactions creates different expectations and requires a variety of modes of communication to ensure that the collaboration is successful.

3. Skills/attributes required for collaborative research
   - Genuine interest
   - Hard work
   - Dedication
   - Honesty
   - Transparency
   - Confidence
   - Strong communication skill
   - Flexibility
   - Stress and anger management
   - Being considerate

Outcome: Gain in knowledge, monitory gain, enjoyment

Fig. 2.4a: Honesty is the first chapter in the collaboration
(Source: Based on review of literature, 2018)

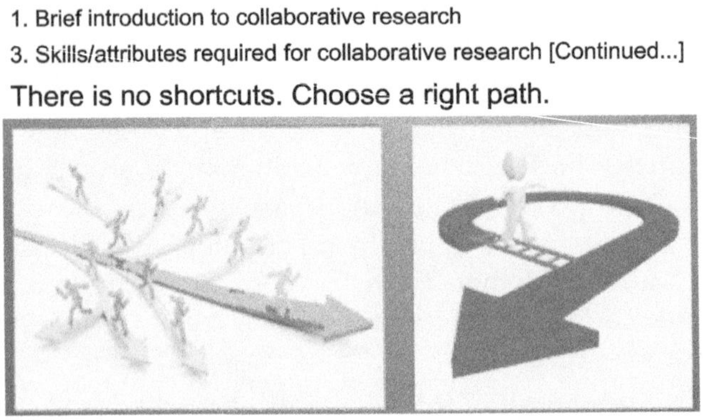

Fig. 2.5: Introduction to collaborative research
(Source: Based on review of literature, 2018)

Importance of Communication

Collaborative research creates different expectations. Communication is the key to success.

Fig. 2.6: Importance of social networking sites
(Source: Based on review of literature, 2018)

Fig. 2.7: Importance of social networking sites
(Source: Based on review of literature, 2018)

Importance of Communication

(*i*) Do not assume anything discuss openly.

(*ii*) Exchange of data, personnel (any skilled personnel e.g. a researcher, a technician) or any materials should take place only after the establishment of formal collaboration.

(*iii*) Researchers need to communicate effectively, whether the other person is across the hall or on the other side of the globe.

(*iv*) Communication is particularly important in collaborations between academia and industry.

(*v*) Special requirements should be discussed on the publication of material or on the invention and patents.

(*vi*) An academic-industrial project must be resolved early on if the research may not be published in a timely fashion.

(*vii*) Also, patent lawyers, technology-transfer administrators, and marketing personnel from industry need to establish a common ground for communication.

Discussing Everyone's Role in Advance, While Understanding that the Research May Evolve

(*i*) Parties in a collaboration should define goals in such a way that they could not have been established without the collaboration. Setting goals leads to expectations and outcomes.

(*ii*) Requirement of a coordinator - As multiple laboratories or groups of researchers may be involved, coordinating the effort among the participants requires management (and communication).

(*iii*) When a research project changes direction, how that will impact participants needs to be addressed.

(*iv*) Authors may be added or eliminated.

(*v*) Finally, researchers have to determine when a collaboration is over.

Difficulties with authorship generally arise when expectations differ between team members. Research team leaders should initiate discussions about authorship from the very beginning of a project and throughout a project. A team should either agree to implement these guidelines as written, or should agree on and record an alternative set of principles and processes. Expectations about each team member's contribution to research and publication should be made explicit.

Discussing Authorship in Advance

But with authorship comes responsibility, so collaborators need to determine how they will deal with the differing expertise levels and available resources of each author.

- Knowledge of the subject: e.g. persons having more experience have more responsibilities.
- Available resources e.g. literature, lab facilities, various software for simulation, time.
- Who will actually write the manuscript and be responsible for the input from collaborators has to be established. If the research changes direction, someone expecting authorship might be disappointed, so the evolution of a project has to be considered.
- Finally, who will be included in acknowledgments?

Fig. 2.8: Discussion with authorship is in advance
(Source: Based on review of literature, 2018)

Discussing Data and Material Management in Advance

Transfer of materials among collaborators is subject to so-called "material transfer agreements," or MTAs, developed by administration offices. They include:

- Limits on the use of the material, usually for non-commercial research purposes.
- Prohibitions on the redistribution of the material.
- Conditions of use, including prohibitions of use in animals or humans.
- Conditions for publication, usually with provisions that the manuscript must be seen by the donor before submission for publication.
- The issue of the return of unused material.

Fig. 2.9: Data material and management
(Source: Based on review of literature, 2018)

Discussing Intellectual Property Issues in Advance

All investigators want to be able to protect results that might have potential commercial application. Disclosing results early could prevent collaborators from being able to obtain patent protection. All parties should know of institutional and granting-agency policy regarding intellectual property and patent procedures. Managers entering into collaborative research agreements MUST utilize the skills of a competent and experienced Intellectual Property lawyer as they plan, structure, negotiate and implement their relationships.

Managing Accountability

Each institution has to abide by certain regulations, policies, and laws. Researchers working with animals, humans, or hazardous substances have to conform to the appropriate regulations, policies, and laws. E.g. regulations regarding use of hazardous materials, confidentiality of data,confidentiality of materials used, confidentiality of process applied e.g. for preparation of some materials.

Types of Agreements

1. Agreement between sponsors and prime awardee.
2. Agreement between sub recipient and prime awardee.
3. Teaming agreements: e.g. the team may agree to have a scientific advisory board.
4. Collaboration agreement: if collaborators from one institution will be using the facilities of the other institution, collaboration agreements may include the typical provisions of a Facility Use Agreement.

5. Intellectual property agreement: The basic issue covered is ownership of the intellectual property (i.e. who owns what, and under what conditions). Other items addressed would be license rights between the parties, and perhaps provisions on sharing costs and income related to the protection and licensing of intellectual property.
6. It all begins with the benefits of collaboration. Here is a list of 20 of the most obvious.
7. Higher impact publications: A good scientific work requires a combined effect of several good scientists. This leads to the publication of the papers in journal of high impact factor. There is a direct correlation between the number of authors and impact factor.
8. More creativity: Chances of generation creative ideas increases.
9. Future: Collaborations are always filled with potential. Those you collaborate with today will think of you tomorrow when they are putting together a 20 million euro grant proposal.
10. Less work: Done well, collaboration means less work for everyone without compromising on results.
11. Criticism: Criticism from the other collaborators helps in achieving perfection. Debating ideas is also important for creativity and achieving Group Genius.
12. Ability to bring more experience at one place: Every project and any project brings several or a series of challenges/problems. It is always easier to solve these problems when a group of intelligent brain working together.
13. Efficient learning: Gives an excellent idea how to start a work in real world. This gives an opportunity to see how experienced scientists work. This a good opportunity to learn. Papers, books, tend to tell you how to do something, but don't give you a sense of what it is to actually do that something.
14. Caution: Don't fall into the trap of thinking that your non-expert question will annoy the experts. Quite to the contrary such questions are the highest form of flattery.
15. Access to wider range of techniques: Within any give lab group, department, institution, or company there are only so many techniques available to answer the scientific questions that interest you. Collaboration makes all techniques available.
16. Deeper research: In a collaboration you are forced to do more that clip the top of trees. A concern that is often raised is that other will steal your ideas. If your ideas are easily stolen, face it, they are not deep enough.

If someone does steal your shallow ideas you should be happy. Then you can move on the deeper more interesting aspects.

17. Funding: Funding agencies believe and understand in the power of collaboration.
18. Increased number of publications: The deeper the research the more the publications.
19. Students and post docs: There is no better way to find good staff than networking. There are no better and more concrete networks than the networks that are built through collaborations.
20. Higher likelihood of having a spinoff: Similar to the above, its unlikely that working on your own you will know enough or have the ability to create a spinoff company.
21. Fun: Success brings fun.
22. Knowledge of what others are doing: You can read papers or look at patent filings, yet there is no better way to know what others are doing than talking to them. In industry and in research it is always best to be where everyone else is.
23. Less risk: Risk moderation is much easier when you have a whole group to draw upon.
24. Liveliness: When you are working in a collaborative network and you come across an unexpected finding, it is far more likely that you can exploit that finding in the setting of a collaboration.
25. Early adopters: You collaboration partners are almost by definition your early adopters for your novel approach, new technology, or new hypothesis. It all begins with a dedicated group of core believers.
26. Impressing investors: That what you are doing is accepted by a group of leaders in the field is no better argument for convincing investors. This is also true for funding agencies.

Potential Problems with Collaborative Research

Different working style of different collaborators. Collaborators with different attitudes have different working styles, e.g. a collaborator with laid-back attitude may be happy to finalise a collaborative deal over a cup of coffee but at the same time the other side by be very particular about the paper work. In any case, shared grants, data, and materials require more formal written agreements involving grants-and-contracts offices at their respective universities.

Difference in Nature of Work

Nature of work differ from one field to another e.g. biomedical laboratories work 24 hours a day whereas but other disciplines may have 8 to 10 hours of routine. Statisticians working on analysing data may move faster than the social-science researchers surveying hundreds of people in a population for data.

Difference in Language

Researchers speaking different languages may cause problems. The crucial point is to presume nothing and to put everything on the table for discussion as early in the relationship as possible. Differences between academic & industrial research with respect to sharing of data and results: So many times industries are not willing to share their know how and data whereas universities are willing to publish.Any area can be a potential area for collaborative research. It depends upon the researcher to find out the collaborator and an appropriate research problem.

Potential Areas for Collaborative Research

- Materials including:
- ODS (Oxide dispersion strengthened alloys)
- Carbon (including graphite, carbon waste materials, SiC).
- Materials performance, Corrosion.
- Non-destructive evaluation.
- Failure mechanisms including creep.
- Reactor Physics (codes, design).
- Waste forms and management (including glass, ceramic and composite)
- Few funding agencies:

EPSRC (Engineering and Physical Sciences Research Council)

UKIERI (UK India Education and Research Initiative)

British Council

ERASMUS PLUS

The INDIGO funding programme, officially referred to as the New Indigo Partnership Programme (NPP) until 2014 and INNO INDIGO Partnership Programme (IPP) since 2014 - supports Indian-European multilateral research and networking projects.

- Few funding agencies:

Indo-US Public-Private Joint Networked Centre

Indo-US Science and Technology Forum

Rajiv Gandhi Technical University, MP

Faculty Recharge Program (FRP)

Scientific Writing

- Research: Meaning, Purpose, Types of Research,

Steps in Research, Identification,

- Selection and Formulation of Research Problem,
- Internet as a source in identifying gap areas from literature reviews and emerging trends.
- Data VALIDATION STATISTICAL SIGNIFICANCE
- Lit. survey
- Scientific Communication, reporting scientific info.in report, magazine or news paper
- JOURNALS -choice of journals,

Thesis, dissertation

- What do want to communicate
- Do you have enough data?
- Where do you want to communicate? Read few papers in the journal.
- Understand the format.
- Read the Instructions to authors Editor gets first his/her first impression from the general get
- Abstract, should give the summary of work,
- Keywords
- Clarity, short sentences singular, plural sufficient data.
- Careful about plagiarism.
- Introduction- relevance, background.
- Summarize what is already known, what is discussed in the paper,
- Material and methods- should give sufficient details so that the work can be repeated.

Material and Methods

Sources, quality of materials,

How were the experiments conducted? Give sufficient details.

Reproducibility.

Results

Discussions-what did you achieve?

Implication of the work

- Conclusions, outcome of the work.
- Future prospective.
- References and notes how to give references

- Supplementary information
- Relevance of the journal
- Online submission
- Format
- Always use polite language even when you contradict others, no slang, use minimum words
- Pay attention to tense.
- Statistics, units, abbreviation, ethics
- Spell check, grammar
- Acknowledgements: funding agencies, facility providers, mentors, peers. IPR ISSUES (fig. 2.10 & 2.11).

Fig. 2.10: Onion peel

(Source: Based on review of literature, 2018)

Fig. 2.10: Peel of onion

(Source: Based on review of literature, 2018)

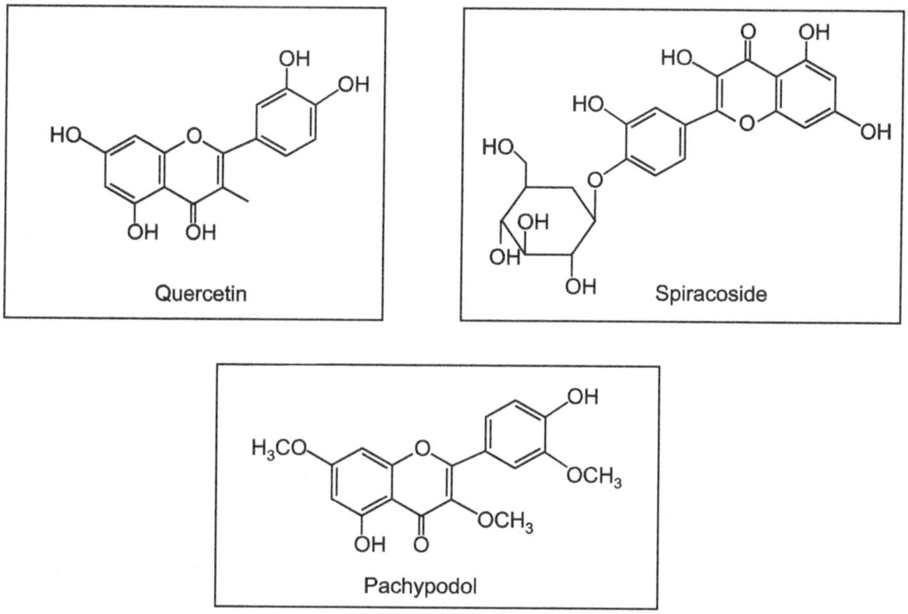

Fig. 2.11: Phytochemical based on onion peel
(Source: Based on review of literature, 2018)

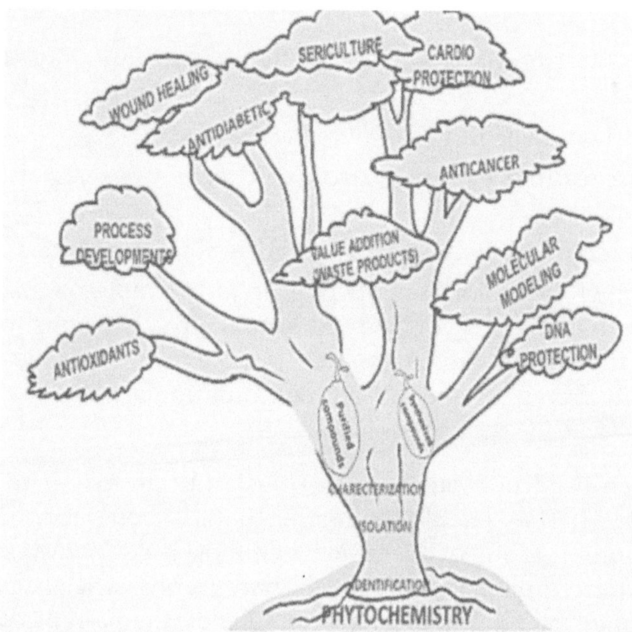

Fig. 2.12: Branches of photochemistry
(Source: Based on review of literature, 2018)

DATA INTERPRETATION

Data Interpretation is one of the easy sections of one day competitive Examinations. It is an extension of Mathematical skill and accuracy. Data interpretation is nothing but drawing conclusions and inferences from a comprehensive data presented numerically in tabular form by means of an illustration, viz. Graphs, Pie Chart etc. Thus the act of organising and interpreting data to get meaningful information is Data Interpretation. Data Interpretation questions are based on information given in tables and graphs. These questions test your ability to interpret the information presented and to select the appropriate data for answering a question.

1. Get a general picture of the information before reading the question. Read the given titles carefully and try to understand its nature.

2. Avoid lengthy calculations generally, data interpretation questions do not require to do extensive calculations and computations. Most questions simply require reading the data correctly and carefully and putting them to use directly with common sense.

3. Breakdown lengthy questions into smaller parts and eliminate impossible choices.

4. Use only the information given and your knowledge of everyday facts, such as the number of hours in a day, to answer the questions based on tables and graphs.

5. Answer the questions asked and not what you think the questions should be.

6. Be careful while dealing with units.

7. To make reading easier and to avoid errors observe graphs keeping them straight.

8. Be prepared to apply basic mathematical rules, principles and formulae.

9. Since one of the major benefits of graphs and tables is that they present data in a form that enables you to readily make comparisons, use this visual attribute of graphs and tables to help you answer the questions. Where possible, use your eyes instead of your computational skills.

Tables

Tables are often used in reports, magazines and newspaper to present a set of numerical facts. They enable the reader to make comparisons and to draw quick conclusions. It is one of the easiest and most accurate ways of presenting data. They require much closer reading than graphs of charts and hence are difficult and time consuming to interpret. One of the main purposes of tables is to make complicated information easier to understand. The advantage of presenting data in a table is that one can see the information at a glance. While answering questions based on tables, carefully read the table title and the column headings. The title of the table gives you a general idea of the type and often the purpose of the information presented. The column headings tell you the specific kind of information given in that column. Both the table title and the column headings are usually very straight forward.

Graphs

There may be four types of graphs:

1. *Circle Graphs:* Circle graphs are used to show how various sectors are in the whole. Circle graphs are sometimes called Pie Charts. Circle graphs usually give the percent that each sector receives In such representation the total quantity in question is distributed over a total angle of 360°. While using circle graphs to find ratios of various sectors, don't find the amounts each sector received and then the ratio of the amounts. Find the ratio of the percents, which is much quicker.
2. *Line Graphs:* Line graphs are used to show how a quantity changes continuously. If the line goes up, the quantity is increasing; if the line goes down, the quantity is decreasing; if the line is horizontal, the quantity is not changing.
3. *Bar Graphs:* Given quantities can be compared by the height or length of a bar graph. A bar graph can have either vertical or horizontal bars. You can compare different quantities or the same quantity at different times. In bar graph the data is discrete. Presentation of data in this form makes evaluation of parameters comparatively very easy.
4. *Cumulative Graphs:* You can compare several categories by a graph of the cumulative type. These are usually bar or line graphs where the height of the bar or line is divided up proportionally among different quantities.

I. Directions (Qs. 1-5) study the following table and answer the questions given below it.

Production of sugar by six major production units of India in Million Tonnes

Month/Product ion Unit	A	B	C	D	E	F
April	310	180	169	137	140	120
May	318	179	177	162	140	122
June	320	160	188	173	135	130
July	326	167	187	180	146	130
August	327	150	185	178	145	128

Fig. 2.13: Production of sugar by six major production units of India (in Million Tonnes)
(Source: Based on review of literature, 2018)

Plagiarism

- Comes from the Latin word meaning "to kidnap"
- Examples of plagiarism:

- o Copying someone else's words without proper citation
- o Stealing someone else's ideas
- o Stealing someone else's intellectual property

Bottom Line: Cite sources properly and minimize quotations in research reports

What is plagiarism?

- Presenting another's original thoughts or ideas as your own
- Using another's exact words without proper citation

Fig. 2.14: Plagiarism of a paper

(Source: Based on review of literature, 2018)

Why is Plagiarism Wrong?

If you plagiarize, you are cheating yourself. You don't learn to write out your thoughts in your own words, and you don't get specific feedback geared to your individual needs and skills. Plagiarism is dishonest because it misrepresents the work of another as your own.

*Unintentional plagiarism is still cheating.

Is it Really Such a Big Problem?

According to the website Plagiarism.org" Recent studies indicate that approximately 30 percent of all students may be plagiarizing on every written assignment they complete".

- Plagiarism is an extensive problem.
- Many universities now have honor codes and students can be failed or even expelled if they are found guilty of plagiarism.
- Plagiarism damages the reputation as a sign of a lack of integrity, of laziness, and maybe an indication that the individual is not as smart as they would like everyone to believe.

Catching the Plagiarist

The internet has made plagiarism easier with access to term paper mills, search engines, encyclopedias, etc. In response, websites have been developed which help teachers analyze papers and develop strategies to prevent plagiarism.

Some sites are:

http://plagiarism-detector.com/

http://www.turnitin.com/

http://www.millikin.edu/wcenter/plagiarism3.html

These websites will allow to upload full papers or portions of the paper and will search all internet resources to determine if the information is original or has been plagiarizedPlagiarism-Detector Pro (software).

Strategies to Avoid the Plagiarism

- Maximum 20% similarity index is allowed for a research article.
- Isolate the reasons why plagiarism occurs.
- Identify the different types of plagiarism.
- Integrate plagiarism prevention.

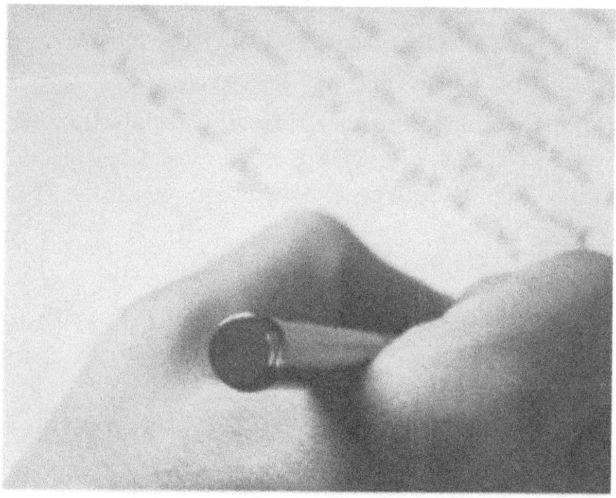

Fig. 2.15: Strategies to avoid the plagiarism
(Source: Based on review of literature, 2018)

Guidelines for Avoiding Plagiarism

- Use your own words and ideas.
- Give credit for copied, adapted, or paraphrased material.
- Avoid using others' work with minor "cosmetic" changes.
- There are no "freebies." (nothing is free of charge).
- Beware of "common knowledge."

Use your Own Words and Ideas

- This is a skill that improves with practice.
- It requires an understanding of the topic.
- It requires that you give yourself credit for your own abilities.

Give credit for copied, adapted or paraphrased material.

- If you repeat another's exact words, you MUST use quotation marks and cite the source.
- If you adapt a chart or paraphrase a sentence, you must still cite.
- Paraphrase means that you restate the author's ideas, meaning, and information in your own words.

Avoid using others' work with minor "cosmetic" changes.

- Examples: using "less" for "fewer," reversing the order of a sentence, changing terms in a computer code, or altering a spread sheet layout. If the work is essentially the same, give credit.

There are no "freebies.

ALWAYS cite words, information, and ideas you use if they are new to you (learned in your research). No matter where you find it – even in an encyclopedia or on the Internet – you cite it.

Beware of "common knowledge.

You don't have to cite "common knowledgebut the fact must really be commonly known. That GeorgeWashington was the first U.S. president is common knowledge. That George Washington was an expert dancer is not common knowledge.

Unintentional Plagiarism

- Paraphrasing poorly: changing a few words without changing the sentence structure of the original, or changing the sentence structure but not the words.
- Quoting poorly: putting quotation marks around part of a quotation but not around all of it, or putting quotation marks around a passage that is partly paraphrased and partly quoted.
- Citing poorly: omitting an occasional citation or citing inaccurately.

Intentional Plagiarism

- Passing off as one's own pre-written papers from the Internet or other sources.
- Copying an essay or article from the Internet, on-line source, or electronic database without quoting or giving credit.
- Cutting and pasting from more than one source to create a paper without quoting or giving credit.

- Borrowing words or ideas from other students or sources without giving credit.

Plagiarism Prevention: Be authentic

- Develop a topic based on previously written material but write something new and original
- Rely on opinions of experts on a topic but improve upon those opinions
- Give credit to researchers while making your own contribution
- Follow a standard documentation method such as MLA or APA format

Plagiarism of Words

– The use of another's exact words without citing the author

– Incorrect

- Plagiarism is the reproduction of someone else's words, ideas or findings and presenting them as one's own without proper acknowledgement.

– Correct

- Plagiarism is the "reproduction of someone else's words, ideas or findings and presenting them as one's own without proper acknowledgement" (Undergraduate Course Handbook: 2008, p.24)

Plagiarism of Structure

- Paraphrasing another's words by changing sentence construction or word choice with citation
- Paraphrasing while maintaining original sentence construction with acknowledging the source

Fig. 2.16: Plagiarism of authorship

(Source: Based on review of literature, 2018)

- Plagiarism of Ideas
- Presenting another's ideas as your own without giving the person credit
- Submitting a paper without citing or incorrectly citing
- another's ideas
- Plagiarism of Authorship
- Turning in a replication of another's work
- Submitting a paper that you got off the internet or from a friend and presenting it as your own

Plagiarism of Self

- The use of previous work for a separate assignment
- Although these were you original words and thoughts, receiving credit for a previous assignment is considered cheating

The Penalties of Plagiarism

Although plagiarism can be intentional or unintentional, both have consequences.

- Receiving zero on the assignment
- Failing the course
- Suspension
- Expulsion

How to Cite the Sources?

If you wish to avoid accusations of plagiarism, you must cite your sources properly. Several websites exist which can help you. Sort your sources alphabetically by Author's last name. Articles without authors are organized alphabetically, numbers go before A

Citation

Research concept acknowledging the use of another's ideas. More precisely, a citation is an abbreviated alphanumeric expression (e.g. [Newell84]) embedded in the body of an intellectual work that denotes an entry in the bibliographic references section of the work for the purpose of acknowledging the relevance of the works. Citation content can vary depending on the type of source and may include: *Book:* author(s), book title, publisher, date of publication, and page number(s) if appropriate. *Journal:* author(s), article title, journal title, date of publication, and page number(s).Patent: author(s), title, patent office, patent application no., year eg: Wang, J. and McVean, C. A. 17-β-4-acetamide-4-azasteroids as androgen receptor modulators. In patent WO099707, 2005. *Newspaper:* author(s), article title, name of newspaper, section title and page number(s) if desired, date of publication.*Web site:* author(s), article and publication title where appropriate, as well as a URL, and a date when the site was accessed. *Interview:* name of interviewer, interview descriptor (ex. personal interview) and date of interview.

Conclusions

But when you present a work for a grade:

- It must be entirely your own work, written by you in your own words, and containing your own interpretations, ideas, approaches etc.
- It must state clearly where you got other people's words or major ideas.
- It must state clearly where you got your charts, diagrams, photos, graphics, and media (including sound, video and digital images.

REFERENCES

Hayat, Tsahi; Lyons, Kelly (2017). "A Typology of Collaborative Research Networks". Online Information Review. 41 (2): 155–170. doi:10.1108/OIR-11-2015-0368.

Lowry, Paul Benjamin; Curtis, Aaron; Lowry, Michelle René (2004). "Building a Taxonomy and Nomenclature of Collaborative Writing to Improve Interdisciplinary Research and Practice" (PDF). Journal of Business Communication. 41: 66. doi:10.1177/0021943603259363.

Onrubia, Javier; Engle, Anna (2009). "Strategies for Collaborative Writing and Phases of Knowledge Construction in CSCL Environments". Computers & Education. 53 (4): 1256–1265. doi:10.1016/j.compedu.2009.06.008.

Ritchie, Stephen M.; Rigano, Donna L. (2007). "Writing Together Metaphorically and Bodily Side-by-side: An Inquiry into Collaborative Academic Writing" (PDF). Reflective Practice. 8 (1): 123–135. doi:10.1080/14623940601139087.

Ede, L.; Lunsford, A. (1990). Singular Text/Plural Authors: Perspectives on Collaborative Authoring. Carbondale: Southern Illinois University Press.

Button, Kathryn; Johnson, M.J.; Furgerson, P. (1996). "Interactive Writing in a Primary Classroom" (PDF). The Reading Teacher. 49 (6): 446–454.

Lassig, Carly J.; *et al.* (2009). "Writing Together, Learning Together: The Value and Effectiveness of a Research Writing Group for Doctoral Students" (PDF). Australian Association for Research in Education 2009 International Research Conference.

Tomlinson, Bill; *et al.* (2012). "Massively Distributed Authorship of Academic Papers"(pdf). In Joseph A. Konstan. CHI '12 Extended Abstracts on Human Factors in Computing Systems. Alt.Chi at the 30th ACM Conference on Human factors in Computing Systems (CHI 2012), Austin, TX, USA. New York, NY, USA: ACM. pp. 11–20. doi:10.1145/2212776.2212779. ISBN 978-1-4503-1016-1. Retrieved 1 May 2018.

Matarese, Valerie (2013). "Collaborative Research Writing: Developmental Editing with an Underlying Educational Vein". In Matarese, V. Supporting Research Writing: Roles and Challenges in Multilingual Settings. Oxford: Chandos. pp. 221–235. ISBN 1843346664.

King, Carla (1 April 2014). "6 Great Self-Publishing Tools for Small Press and Author Co-Ops". PBS.org. Retrieved 10 May 2015.

Lomas, Natasha (2014-09-22). "Authorea Nabs $610k For Its Bid To Become A 'Google Docs For Scientists'". TechCrunch.

"Getting Started with Atlas". Retrieved 10 May 2015.

"GitLab About - Built with GitLab". Retrieved 10 May 2015.

Scientific Research Methodology : *Concepts and Quality*
Edited by: and Dr. Pawan Kumar 'Bharti' and Dr. Prasann Kumar
ISBN: 978-93-86841-95-7
Edition: 2019
Published by: Discovery Publishing House Pvt. Ltd., New Delhi (India)

3

Writing for Quality of Research

[1]Prasann Kumar and [2]Shweta Pathak

ABSTARCT

Research that involves human subjects or participants raises unique and complex ethical, legal, social and political issues. Research ethics are specifically interested in the analysis of ethical issues that are raised when people are involved as participants in research. There are three objectives in research ethics. The first and broadest objective is to protect human participants. The second objective is to ensure that research is conducted in a way that serves the interests of individuals, groups and/or society as a whole. Finally, the third objective is to examine specific research activities and projects for their ethical soundness, looking at issues such as the management of risk, protection of confidentiality and the process of informed consent.

Keywords: Agriculture, Biotic, Crop, Density, Energy, Forage

Introduction

- Qualitative studies are being used in policy formulation, implementation and evaluation.
- Mixed methods research.
- Options for disseminating study results include journals, books, newsletters, conference presentations, and others.
- A journal that publishes papers only after they have been reviewed by experts in the field.
- Reviews are either single or double blinded.
- Acceptance, Minor/Major Revision, Rejection.

Academy of Management Journal

- The articles published in the Academy of Management Journal must make strong theoretical contributions.

[1] Department of Agronomy, School of Agriculture, Lovely Professional University, Jalandhar, Punjab, 144411, India

[2] Department of Plant Physiology, I.Ag. Sci., BHU., Varanasi, 221005, U.P., India

- All articles published in the Academy of Management Journal must also be relevant to practice.
- All articles published in the Academy of Management Journal must be accessible to the Academy's wide-ranging readership.
- Manuscripts will be evaluated by the action editor in terms of their contribution-to-length ratio. Typically, papers should be no longer than 40 double-spaced pages (using one-inch margins and Times New Roman 12-point font), inclusive of references, tables, figures and appendixes.

Things to Think When Choosing A Journal

- What journals publish papers on topics similar to yours?
- What audience will your paper appeal to?
- What journal will provide a good opportunity to disseminate your study results to a wide audience?
- Is the journal indexed so that people will find your paper easily?
- What is the journal's "impact" score?
- Read widely on topics of interest to you. Where are the papers published?
- Visit websites of various journals to learn more.

Frequently Asked Questions

- Can I submit a paper to more than one journal at a time?
- Can I publish something after presenting it at a conference?
- Can I present something at a conference that I've already published?
- How do I prepare my paper for submission?
- What happens after I submit my paper?
- What happens after my paper has been accepted for publication?
- What happens if my paper is rejected?

Getting It Done: Some General Tips

- Read a lot of papers! Good writers are avid readers.
- Don't wait until you have all of your thoughts clearly formulated before you start to write. Thinking and writing happen together.
- Make a 2 to 3 hour writing session a regular part of your schedule (daily or weekly).

What Characterizes Successful Writing?

- Good writing is clear and concise.
- Get to the point and avoid jargon.
- Limit the scope of your paper. Focus on a few key points.

- Your objective is to communicate to your reader (not to prove your expertise).
- Be honest.

Parts of the Qualitative Research Report

- Introduction
- Description of aims
- Sampling and recruitment
- Data collection
- Topics/ questions that were covered
- Data processing (transcribe, translate, etc.)
- Data analysis approach
- Statement about ethical review and informed consent

Introduction

- Define the problem, why is it important?
- Review what is currently known about the problem.
- Indicate how your data can fill the gaps and make us more informed about the problem.
- Include abundant references to published literature
- Description of data collection and analytical techniques
- Report of the interpretation and analyses
- Implications of findings
- Future research

Guidelines for Reviewing Literature

- If you quote a reference, quote precisely. Use quotation marks.
- Record complete bibliographic information for each reference source.
- Focus on the literature that relates to your paper topic most closely, is most significant, and is up up-to to-date.
- Make sure you include "landmark" studies.
- Take notes on the sources you read, summarize them for yourself and note the key points. This will help you build arguments for your introduction and conclusion.
- Include literature that represents conflicting sides of a contentious issue in order to be fair.

Writing the Methodology

- Description of aims

- Sampling and recruitment
- Data collection
- Topics/ questions that were covered
- Data processing (transcribes, translate, etc.)
- Data analysis approach
- Statement about ethical review and informed consent

Writing the Results Section

- Give the readers information on the sample so they can understand from where the data are coming.
- If you are drawing on multiple sources of data (in-depth interviews and FGD) then describe the samples separately.
- Typically a description of the sample is provided at the beginning of the Results section.

Should you Include a Table with Demographic Data on the Sample?

- This is a technique borrowed from quantitative papers
- It may make sense for qualitative datasets with relatively large sample sizes (i.e over 50, 100). But for small datasets (under 30) may not make sense to use a table to describe the sample.
- No rules on how to present qualitative findings.
- You need to think about how to organize the presentation of findings to help the reader get these takeaway messages.
- Present themes with supportive quotes
- Use a theoretical framework to organize the presentation of results
- Organize findings, according to chronology
- Organize findings, according to sub-groups interviewed
- Use case studies to illustrate the themes
- Use diagrams to display relationships of themes

To Count or not to Count when Presenting Qualitative Findings ?

- Anytime we take raw data and put it into categories, it implies a numbered nature of these patterns.
- However, we need to be cautious about how we represent quantification of qualitative findings.
- 3 of the 12 informants said ....
- More than 50% of informants mentioned that........
- A problem arises when using percentages to describe small samples; when people read percentages, they immediately infer the meaning of this for a larger population.

- In qualitative research, the text (words of our informants) is our data, and thus we usually end up presenting some direct quotations.
- Readers lose sight of the main point, when there are too many quotes.

Writing the Discussion

- The discussion section *argues* a point in the context of other published literature.
- What are the implications of my study for stakeholders?
- What are the limitations of my study?

Conclusion

- Paragraphs (no more than 2) that pull the whole paper together
- Hit your main points again

Finishing the Report

- Title
  - Eliminate "A Qualitative Study of . . ."
- Title page
- Abstract
  - Overall objective of research
  - Brief explanation of research method
  - Brief summary of results

Using the APA/ Harvard Style Manual

- Citing others' work
- Creating the reference list
- Complete alphabetical list by authors' last names
- Includes all literature cited in the report
- Accuracy

Authorship

- The person who has made the greatest contribution to the paper is to be listed first with remaining authors listed in order of their contribution.

Comments from Reviewers

- In fact, case study is just the right technique. It would be good to elaborate the time taken for the interviews, the type of questions asked, more details on the interviewees etc. More elaborated method section.
- This criticism regards the description of the data. While the paper does provide some quantitative information about the dataset, more information about the "thickness" of the data (Geertz, 1973) is required.

- In terms of discussion, I gather that the qualitative data is interpreted to provide strength to the argument developed. However, I am not able to find the argument arising from the data leading to the four groups presented later.

Teamwork

- Qualitative research is time-consuming and involves a high degree of skills and expertise. Undertake qualitative research as part of a team. Discuss early versions of your work with people who are able to provide constructive and developmental feedback.

Journal and Contribution

- Select a journal at the start of the research project.
- Study a few very good related qualitative research papers.

Writing

- Start writing, right from the start. Writing is thinking.
- Develop your writing style. Be to the point, well structured, focused.
- Tell a story to the reader that develops from a motivation and a question to a conclusion in a logical way.
- Remove unnecessary parts, which distract the reader from main line (baby-killing).

Method

- The research method section is important and not straightforward. Tell the readers what you did, but also why. Be as transparent as possible.

Results

- Present the data analysis/results in a structured fashion, close to the research questions.
- Reviewers dislike the messy presentation of results of many qualitative research papers (figure 3.1 & 3.2).

Fig. 3.1: Understanding qualitative research

(Source: Based on a Review of Literature, 2018)

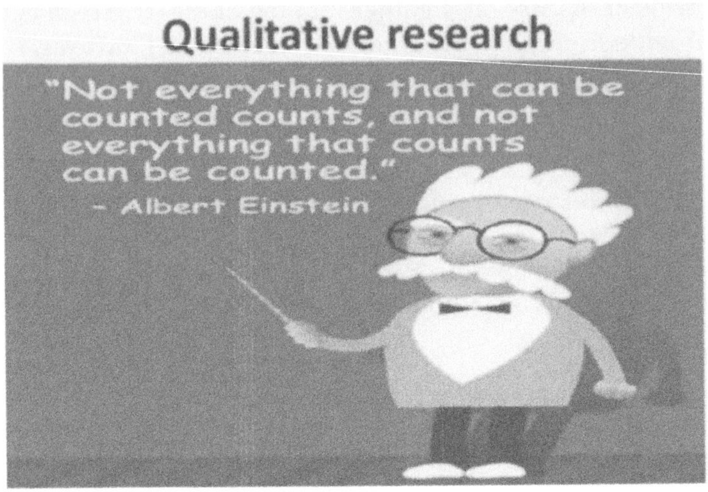

Fig. 3.2: Quality research

(Source: Based on a Review of Literature, 2018)

Qualitative Versus Quantitative Research

In the words of psychology professor Wayne Weiten, "No single research method is ideal for all purposes and situations. Much of the ingenuity in research involves selecting and tailoring the method to the question at hand" (Psychology: Themes and Variations, 2014).

Two Big Questions?

- Subjectivity or Bias?
- Generalisability?

Qualitative and Quantitative:

- Quantitative research only answers the question "how many" or "how often" and qualitative research, answers the questions "how", "why" (Maxwell, 2005) and "what" (Lee *et al.*, 1999).
- Qualitative research studies are generally used for exploring phenomena and not testing hypothesis (Wilson, 1998).
- Analogy of two children (Cecil Helman)
- Explaining illogical behavior/deviations

Which is better?

- Qualitative research is usually used for exploration of issues in depth and detail.
- The purpose of qualitative research is not generalisation. Complementary to each other.

"Objective reality can never be captured. We know a thing only through its representations....a qualitative researcher is like a quilt maker or a jazz improviser." -Denzin and Lincoln (1994). Qualitative research is a situated activity that locates the observer in the world. It consists of a set of interpretive, material practices that turn the world into a series of representations, including field notes, interviews, conversations, photographs, recordings, and memos to the self. ... This means that qualitative researchers study things in their natural settings, attempting to make sense of or to interpret, phenomena in terms of the meanings people bring to them (Denzin and Lincoln, 2005). Qualitative research is inquiry that is grounded in the assumption that individuals construct social reality in the form of meanings and interpretations, and that these constructions tend to be transitory and situational. The dominant methodology is to discover meanings and interpretations by studying cases intensively in natural settings and subjecting the resulting data to analytical induction."-Borg and Gall (1996).

Keywords in QRM

- Research Question or Hypothesis
- Natural Context (In-Situ)
- Through the eyes of others
- Open-ended questions
- Flexible and Emergent Research Design
- Researcher- the most important instrument (Interpretation)
- Reflexivity
- Purpose?

Distinctive Qualities of Qualitative Research

- Importance of context
- Researcher-as-instrument
- Participant-researcher relationship
- Skill set of the researcher
- Flexibility of the research design
- Messy analysis and inductive approach

* Adapted from Applied Qualitative Research Design: A Total Quality Framework Approach (Roller, M. R. & Lavrakas, P. J., 2015)(Figure 3.3).

- Are you feeling better today?
- Will you please do me a favor?
- Is that your final answer?
- Would you like to go to a movie tonight?
- Is math your favorite subject?

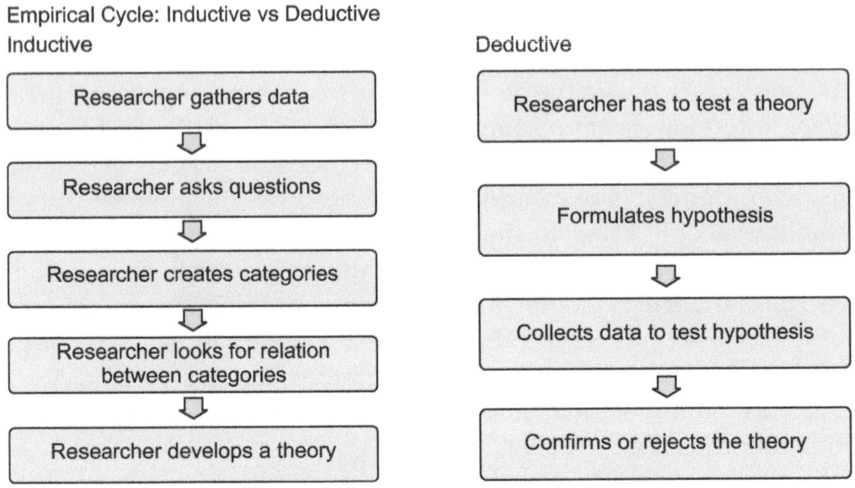

Fig. 3.3: Empirical cycle: Inductive vs Deductive

(Source: Based on review of literature, 2018)

Flow of Qualitative Research

- Start: Unprocessed and Open Problem
- Instrument(s) for Data Collection
- Transcription of Data
- Preliminary classification of data
- Narrowing down (Convergence and Divergence)
- Further analysis (possibly with new data)
- Reporting and writing

Characteristics

- Natural Setting
- Collecting data in the field at the site
- Researcher as key instrument
- Researchers collect data themselves
- Multiple sources of data
- Interviews, observations, documents
- Inductive data analysis
- Identifying set of themes from data (general to specific)
- Participant's meeting
- Through the eyes of participants
- Emergent design
- Flexible Research Design

- Contextual lens
- Cultural/Social/Political/Historical Context
- Interpretive Inquiry
- Interpretation of data
- Holistic Inquiry
- Sketching a larger picture

When to Use Qualitative Research?

- Why & How?
- Hearing silenced voices
- Complex detailed understanding of phenomena
- Empowering respondents and de-emphasizing power relationships
- Writing in a literary style to convey stories
- Understanding context or settings
- Developing theories
- Explaining linkages in theories and models

Commitment of Researcher

- Extensive time in the field
- Complex data analysis
- Writing effectively
- Constantly evolving process

Limitations

- Lack of theoretical framework to begin
- Character of Qualitative Data
- Researcher's Bias
- Reliability/Generalisation
- Sample Size
- Open Question: Uncertainty

Features of a Good Study

- Beginning with a single focus
- Unusual angles
- Ethical
- Writing persuasively
- Background of the researcher
- Rigorous Data Collection
- Explicit Assumptions

- Using a standard method: Ethnography, Narrative Inquiry, Grounded theory, Case-study and Phenomenology

Types

- Ethnography
- Phenomenology
- Grounded Theory
- Narrative Research
- Case Study

Data Collection

- Data Collection Circle
- Locating site/ individuals
- Gaining access and making rapport
- Purposeful sampling
- Collecting data
- Recording information
- Resolving field issues
- Storing data

Sampling Technique

Sampling

- According to Frenkel and Devers (2000), purposive or judgmental sampling is "in sync with the goal and logic of qualitative research"
- It is the deliberate selection of a sample based upon "knowledge of the population, its elements, and nature of the research goal" (Babbie, 1990)
- Researcher establishes criteria and rationale for selection
- Goal is not generalization of findings but *rich descriptions* by respondents
- Despite the limitation of researcher's judgment, it enables data collection from "... whom one can learn a great deal about issues of central importance to research" (Patton, 1990).
- Sampling is "informant-driven" rather than "theory-driven" (Lee, 1999).
- Besides, the sample size in qualitative research is usually small (Crouch and Mckenzie, 2006) and probability sampling would lead to a large sampling error.

Purposive Sampling (Patton, 1990)

- Extreme or deviant case sampling
- Intensity sampling
- Maximum variation sampling

- Homogenous sampling
- Stratified purposeful sampling
- Snowball sampling
- Criterion sampling
- Theory based sampling
- Confirming and disconfirming cases
- Opportunistic sampling
- Sampling politically important cases
- Convenience sampling

Sample Size

Because your goal in qualitative research is to describe and interpret rather than to generalize, there are no hard rules about how many you should study. Lichtman (2006)

- Lichtman (2006): 10 or even smaller
- Mason (2010): 31
- Charmaz (2006): 25
- Ritchie *et al.* (2003): Under 50
- Crouch and Mckenzie (2006): Less than 20
- The logic of small sample size in qualitative research is that small sample sizes, less than 20, allow the researcher to associate closely, thereby, enhancing the validity of findings.
- Crouch and Mckenzie (2006)
- Sample size is determined by the aim of the study.
- -Charmaz (2006)
- Ending data collection is closely connected to the research problem and the depth and richness of the data collected
- -McMillan and Schumacher (2001)
- There are no rules for sample size in qualitative inquiry; it depends on what you want to know, the purpose of inquiry, what's at stake, what will be useful, what will have credibility, and what can be done with available time and resources.
- -Patton (1990)
- Sample size is chosen iteratively as the study progresses, new categories, themes or explanations stop emerging from the data or in other words data saturates -(Marshall, 1996)
- The point of redundancy- Lincoln and Guba (1985).

It is difficult to determine data saturation because new themes can always emerge. The researcher must stop data collection and analysis when new information starts becoming counterproductive because there is an excess of information for the researcher to manage; sometimes the researcher has no choice and must settle for a theoretical scheme that is less developed than desired.- Strauss and Corbin (1990). Time and cost constraints also play a role in sample size determination- (Patton, 1990; Baker and Edwards, 2012).

To sum up:

- The onus of determining the sample size lies with the researcher.
- Sample size is decided during the course of study.
- There is no minimum or maximum sample size in qualitative research; the researcher must be able to justify whatever sample size is used.

Data Collection Methods

- Interviews
- Focus Group Discussions
- Participant/ Non-Participant Observation

Interview

- An Interview is an oral communication between the researcher and the respondent. -Gall *et al.* (2007).
- It is the most familiar method for collecting data in qualitative research. -Dicicco-bloom and Crabtree (2006).
- It is used when the researcher wants to obtain more detailed information on a topic than might be gleaned from a questionnaire. -(Adams and Cox, 2008).
- Qualitative interviews are "loosely structured" and "open" to what the interviewers want to express. -Alvesson (2003).
- Interviews involve a deeper expression of the "interviewer's self" (Gubrium and Holstein, 2001) and help to understand "the complete picture" of what has happened and what should be done (Boyce and Neale, 2006) by providing in-depth insights.

Classification

- Informal conversational interview
- Guided interview
- Standardized open-ended interview

Examples

- An email was sent to each expert with an explanation of the research and a request to participate. Following the email, the person was contacted via telephone to set up an interview. Some of the participants declined citing time constraints. Over a period of eight months, from February, 2013 to September, 2013, 50 individual interviews were completed. The high response rate of 83.34 percent is attributable to the use of personal contacts and personalized method of contacting.

- The effective sample consisted of 30 academicians and 20 professionals from the industry. The interviews were conducted in the following cities: Delhi, Mumbai, Bangalore, Ahmedabad, Lucknow and Haridwar. Details of the sample, including respondent profiles, have been elaborated in the next chapter. The list of respondents, along with date and place of the interview, has been included in the appendix.
- The interviews were conducted in the office or residence of the interviewees. A schedule (see Figure 4.1, 4.4) was prepared for the guidance of the interviewer and the typical duration of each interview was two to three hours. Field notes were prepared during the interview to support data analysis (Morrow and Smith, 2000).

Focus Group Discussions

- Groups of eight to twelve target consumers, usually (but not always) a relatively homogeneous group . . . brought together to discuss a specific set of issues under the guidance of a leader trained to stimulate and focus the discussion (Kotler, 1987).
- Focus group discussions were first mentioned as a market research technique in the 1920s (Kitzinger, 1924).
- They differ from other group interviews or activities as they are highly structured and focused (Linton, 2005).
- The basic purpose is data collection by exploring pre-identified issues presented to the group (Ibid.).

Examples

A total of ten focus group discussions was conducted with a convenience sample of 84 students, who completed or would complete Management programs between 2009 and 2014, in ten different institutes including an IIM, two IITs, three university departments and four private business schools across the country. The discussions were conducted in the premises of the institutes with prior permission. An email was sent to the Director or Head of the Department of fifty different institutes with an explanation of the background of research and a request for permission. Following the email, the person was contacted via telephone. Many institutes declined citing confidentiality and time constraints. Over a period of three months, from August, 2013 to October, 2013, ten focus group discussions were completed in ten different institutes. The duration of the discussions varied from 45 minutes to 60 minutes. The researcher played the role of a moderator to conduct the session. Field notes were prepared during the discussion by a research assistant to support data analysis (Morrow and Smith, 2000). The details of the questions discussed have been elaborated in the following chapter.

Observations

- Certain kinds of research questions can best be answered by observing how people act or how things look.
- There are different roles with regard to observation: Naturalistic (Non participant) Observer Participant Observer.

Challenges

- Observer Effect
- Observer Bias

Qualitative Research: Reliability and Validity

Fig. 3.4: Qualittive Research and their realiability and valifdity
(Source: Based on review of Literature, 2018)

Reliability and Validity

Reliability: the degree to which a measurement procedure produces similar outcomes when it is repeated.

Validity: tests for determining whether a measure is measuring the concept that the researcher thinks is being measured.

Qualitative Research: Reliability and Validity

The standards for quantitative research like objectivity, reliability and no bias are problematic for qualitative research but "rationality, rigor, and fairness can still be sought" Smith (1994). Most of the researchers have preferred to use terms other than reliability and validity while dealing in qualitative research Shenton (2004).

Reliability and Validity

- Different terminology is used because "the details of qualitative research" are different from qualitative research. Agar (1986)

- One such widely used term is trustworthiness proposed by Lincoln and Guba (1985).

Validation Strategies

- Prolonged engagement & persistent observation
- Triangulation
- Peer review or debriefing
- Clarifying researcher bias
- Member checking
- Rich description
- External audit

Triangulation

- Methods triangulation
- Data source triangulation

Member Checking

For this validation strategy, I convene a focus group composed of participants in my study and ask them to reflect on the accuracy of the account. I do not take back to participants my transcripts or the raw data, but take them my preliminary analyses consisting of description or themes. I am interested in their views of these written analyses as well as what was missing-Creswell (2007).

Recommendations

- Engage in at least two of them in any given study
- Triangulation, writing with detailed and thick description, and member checking are the most popular and cost-effective procedures
- Peer audits and external audits are more time consuming and may involve substantial costs to the researcher
- After coding, say, three to four transcripts, we then met and examined the codes, their names, and the text segments that we coded.
- We took a realistic stance and sought to establish an 80% agreement of coding on these passages (Miles and Huberman, 1994).
- Substantive contribution
- Aesthetic merit
- Reflexivity
- Impact
- The trustworthiness in this study was ensured by methods propounded by different researchers as explained in Krefting (1990), Shenton (2004),

Alvesson and Skoldberg (2000), Morrow and Smith (2000) and Lietz *et al.* (2006) like intensive involvement with research, identification of data rich sources, triangulation by using different methods of data collection and interviewing different stakeholders, frequent debriefing sessions, peer scrutiny, respondent validation, detailed description of data collection and explanation of the contextual factors, family background of respondents, researcher and reflexivity.

ABSTRACT TYPES

Brand Love in Emerging Market: A Qualitative Investigation

Purpose: The purpose of this paper is to explore the nature of brand love, the antecedents and consequences of brand love and the obstacles to brand love in the context of Asian market. Brand love is an emerging concept in the domain of consumer psychology. It has been regarded as the motivating force behind contemporary hedonic consumption. Yet little qualitative exploration has been done to understand brand love especially in the context of emerging Asian market.

Design/methodology/approach: This article is grounded in consumers' everyday experiences of loving particular brands. Semi-structured depth interviews have been conducted.

Findings: Based on the findings of the depth interviews, a conceptual framework has been developed showing the antecedents and consequences of brand love. This study also throws light on the specific psychological phenomenon of the emerging market consumers. The findings form the basis for a discussion of the theoretical and practical implications of brand love in the context of emerging economy.

Originality/value: Value of this article lies in developing a grounded theory of brand love in the context of emerging Asian market.

Keywords: Brand love, Sustainable marketing, Brand nostalgia, Brand surrealism

Inside the Boardroom: Exploring Board Member Interactions

Purpose: This study aims to open up the black box of the boardroom by directly observing directors' interactions during meetings to better understand board processes.

Design/methodology/approach: We analyze videotaped observations of board meetings at two Australian companies to develop insights into what directors do in meetings and how they participate in decision-making processes. The direct observations are triangulated with semi-structured interviews, mini-surveys and document reviews.

Findings: Our analyses lead to two key findings: while board meetings appear similar at a surface level, boardroom interactions vary significantly at a deeper level (i.e. board members participate differently during different stages of discussions), and factors at multiple levels of analysis explain differences in interaction patterns, revealing the complex and nested nature of boardroom discussions.

Originality/value: This study complements existing research on boardroom dynamics and provides a systematic account of director interactions during board meetings.

Keywords: Board of directors, Board meetings, Boardroom dynamics, Board observations

What is Sustainable Fashion?

Purpose: The purpose of this paper is to examine what the term sustainable fashion means from the perspective of organisations, experts, and consumers.

Design/methodology/approach: This research is qualitative in nature, utilising a multi-methods case study approach (semi-structured interviews, semiotics, questionnaires).

Findings: Findings indicate that interpretation of sustainable fashion is context and person dependent. A matrix of key criteria provides the opportunity to find common elements.

Research limitations/implications: Due to the nature of this research the sample size is limited and may not be generalised.

Practical implications: An important implication is that defining sustainable fashion is vital in order to avoid challenges, such as greenwashing, which were faced in other industries that have a longer history in sustainable practices.

Originality/value: The paper proposes a matrix that allows organisations to clearly identify their collections as sustainable.

Keywords: UK, Sustainability, Fashion, Sustainable fashion, organisation, Sustainable fashion criteria

Interact with Me on my Terms: A Four Segment Facebook Engagement Framework for Marketers

Facebook is used by over 1 billion highly heterogeneous users each month. However, there exists little guidance for marketers when it comes to actionable consumer engagement strategies for this social media platform. The purpose of this article is to profile key segments of Facebook users and build an implementable marketing strategy framework that can help marketers better target their Facebook consumers, and better craft their marketing mix and Facebook campaigns. Based on focus group interviews and a qualitative survey, four distinct types of Facebook users are identified and profiled: attention seekers, devotees, connection seekers and entertainment chasers. Correspondingly, a four-segment marketing strategy framework is proposed to guide content creation and engage consumers in thriving Facebook brand communities.

Keywords: Facebook, engagement, word-of mouth, branding, qualitative

Communication Management on Social Networking Sites: Stakeholder Motives and Usage Types of Corporate Facebook, Twitter and YouTube Pages

Purpose: Over the last years, many corporations have started to maintain profile pages on social networking sites (SNS), but research on how and why organizational stakeholders use these profile pages has not kept pace. The paper aims to discuss these issues.

Design/methodology/approach: The study applies a perspective of uses-and-gratifications (U & G) to investigate the reasons why politicians and digital natives consume and interact with corporations on SNS. In total, 65 semi-structured interviews were conducted and analyzed using qualitative content analysis.

Findings: Results suggest that the two stakeholder groups differ in their motivations, as well as behavior to use corporate profile pages. Digital natives seem to prefer Facebook to interact with companies, politicians prefer Twitter. Corporate YouTube pages are almost not important to any of the groups.

Research limitations/implications: The qualitative nature of the study does not allow for generalizations of the findings to larger populations. Suggestions for further research are addressed in the discussion section.

Originality/value: This is the first study in the field of communication management, which applies a micro-level approach to interviewing users of corporate communication; in order to reveal the reasons why and how they use corporate social networking profile pages.

Keywords: Social networking sites, Communication management, Stakeholder analysis, Social media,Public relations, Corporate communications

CEOs' Views on Reputation Management

This paper summarises the findings arising from a series of extended qualitative interviews with 14 CEOs and chairmen from leading UK corporations and international organisations. The purpose of the interviews was to try to establish the value that CEOs attach to public relations, and to get a sense of how they would assess its value and contribution to overall business and organisational performance. The study also tried to determine the role CEOs play in reputation management. The findings conclude that CEOs do not expect or look for a simple return on investment (ROI) for public relations expenditure; that public relations is used regularly to enhance and protect reputation; that public relations has become mission critical for businesses and the management of reputation; that CEOs themselves take overall responsibility for the management of corporate reputation; that the CEO's personal reputation is closely linked to that of the corporation; that CEOs' profiles and the media demands made of them have never been higher; that public relations can influence organisational strategy; and that high calibre people working in public relations are highly sought after and valued by CEOs. There are many lessons and implications for public relations practitioners.

Competitive Priorities and Supply Chain Strategy in the Fashion Industry

Purpose: The purpose of this paper is to explore how high-performing companies in the fashion industry align their supply chain strategy with their competitive priorities.

Design/methodology/approach: In order to answer the research question, case study research on four fashion companies most competitive in the global market. The primary sources of information for the case studies were interview data.

Findings: Based on in-depth interviews with top managers at the companies, propositions are reached: the competitive priorities are closely linked with the firm's choice of target market, which in turn determines its supply chain strategy, including both sourcing and channel strategy.

Research limitations/implications: This paper shows how in-depth case studies based on Interview data about best practices in the fashion industry can contribute to the literature by linking firm's competitive priorities with its supply chain strategy.

Originality/value: The research framework is unique in that it combines important concepts and theories in business strategy, outsourcing, and SCM literature. Implications from the in-depth case studies on best practices in the fashion industry can help managers make a decision on supply chain strategy more effectively.

Keywords: Supply chain management, Outsourcing, Channel strategy, Coordination, Fashion industry, Case studies, Interviews

Sustainable Development: A Qualitative Inquiry into the Current State of the UK Construction Industry

Purpose: Despite the surge of interest in construction sustainability and the many Government initiatives encouraging reform in the UK construction industry (CI), the prevalence of sustainable development (SD) in the industry is still largely lagging behind that of other industries. Given the amount of focus and activity identified nationally in this area, the purpose of this paper is to investigate the reasons why this is not being translated into action and to seek counsel from industry professionals as to how they believe change can be achieved with a particular focus on how they believe higher education institutions (HEIs) can contribute.

Design/methodology/approach: An explorative, qualitative study using three focus groups was of construction professionals.

Findings: Despite a lack of action, many in industry support sustainability and actively attempt to engage in sustainable practices but a number of barriers preclude successful implementation. Government initiatives are having a positive impact, with participants believing that both Government and HEIs are imperative in driving the sustainability agenda forward.

Originality/value: Previous research in this area has generally adopted a quantitative approach. Adopting a qualitative approach provides a more in depth view as to why the status quo remains with regards to SD in the CI.

Factors Influencing International Retailers' Market Entry Mode Strategy: Qualitative Evidence from the UK Fashion Sector

Research on the internationalisation of retail firms has focused on many diverse themes such as the motivations for internationalisation, individual company experiences and the direction and extent of international retail activity. One particular aspect of the retailer internationalisation process that has remained relatively under researched is entry mode choice. Furthermore, while research on fashion retailing is increasing, the internationalisation of the sector has been largely neglected in the literature. The aim of the current work is to provide an initial attempt at redressing this research gap. The paper reports findings from an in-depth study into the entry mode choice decision process of seven major UK international fashion retailers. It is found that entry mode strategy emerges over time as a result of a combination of historical, experiential, financial, opportunistic, strategic and company-specific factors.

Market Segmentation in Managerial Practice: A Qualitative Examination

This paper offers an examination of the ways in which managers implement market segmentation. Market segmentation practices are examined in the context of the UK apparel retail sector. A qualitative research framework, which draws on Weick's (1995a) sensemaking approach, is adopted. Managerial insights are evidenced through a key-informant interviewing method within 10 case-organisations. The results indicate a number of plausible, managerial reasons for not pursuing sophisticated segmentation solutions. An underlying issue is a widely held belief in the adequacy and manageability of gross-level, descriptive segmentation approaches. Market segmentation was also seen as a managerial concept from which to inform decision-making but not for determining it or supplanting it. Segmentation thus represents an important sense making tool, often for communicative purposes. According to evidence revealed in this inquiry, contemporary applications and uses of market segmentation no longer provide synergy with the methodological and conceptual foundations of the concept.

Keywords: Market segmentation, consumer lifestyle, fragmentation, fashion retailing

The Role and Need of Offering Workshops and Courses on Workplace Spirituality

Purpose: The purpose of this paper is to present the experiences and findings of a course in workplace spirituality in a time and stage where corporate greed and organizational instability run rampant.

Design/methodology/approach: The authors analyzed workshop dialogues and reviews of participants' as well as their changed perceptions.

Findings: There are some interesting common factors in corporations that perform according to spiritual guidelines and a highly interactive program on organizational analysis contributes tremendously to the levels of responsibility and awareness of participants.

Research limitations/implications: Limitations to the research are: the population used for data was limited, as it consisted of business and management students at the MBA level; and the findings were only gathered from one cohort, and might provide increased themes when extended over multiple courses in multiple semesters. Future research could apply this study on other populations for a greater foundation in findings.

Practical implications: Organizations that adhere to the spiritual mindset are more successful, have happier employees, and are more aware of their environmental responsibilities.

b– The paper shows that in these times when corporate greed, dishonesty, and environmental neglect have been exposed so dramatically, courses on workplace spirituality are of high importance and lead to valuable insights for immediate and nonimmediate stakeholders.

Keywords: Workplace, Spirituality, Courses, Employees, Values, Spiritual audits, Performance, Universities, Curricula, Business ethics.

Green Management: The State of Practice, Research, Teaching, Training and Consultancy in Indian Business Schools

Purpose: The purpose of this research paper is to study the green management practices and research, teaching, training and consulting in green management in Indian business schools as management education, particularly business schools are among one of the fastest growing industry of Indian economy on one hand and also they have a responsibility to train managers and future managers; provide guidance in terms of consultancy and create new knowledge i.e. research in green management.

Design/methodology/approach: A questionnaire was developed based on literature review which was first tested and discussed with experts and then used for the survey of 500 top business schools in India which were at least five years old out of the 950 business schools in India.

Findings: The study shows not so good state of research, teaching, training and consultancy on one hand and below average performance in practice of green management within business schools in India. The findings are not encouraging and Indian business schools need to give more attention to the subject of green management both in theory and practice.

Originality/value: This study has made an attempt to study and document the current state of Indian business schools on green management.

Keywords: India, Environment, Emerging markets, Economic sustainability.

Conclusion

For the most part, research ethics has traditionally focused on issues in biomedical research. The application of research ethics to examine and evaluate biomedical research has been well developed over the last century and has influenced much of the existing statutes and guidelines for the ethical conduct of research. However in humanities and social science research, different kinds of ethical issues arise. New and emerging methods of conducting research, such as auto-ethnography and participatory action research raise important but markedly different ethical issues and obligations for researchers. Research involving vulnerable persons, which may include children, persons with developmental or cognitive disabilities, persons who are institutionalized, the homeless or those without legal status, also raises unique issues in any research context. Research ethicists everywhere today are challenged by issues that reflect global concerns in other domains, such as the conduct of research in developing countries, the limits of research involving genetic material and the protection of privacy in light of advances in technology and Internet capabilities. In Canada, current debates and challenges in research ethics include the changing notions of what constitutes research and therefore requires formal ethics review, the oversight and monitoring of the work of Research Ethics Boards (known as Institutional Review Boards, in the U.S.) at federal and provincial levels, the jurisdiction of Research Ethics Boards in academic, clinical and corporate settings, the increasing multidisciplinarity of research collaborations and pursuits and challenges created by rigorous federal and provincial privacy legislation. This is by no means an exhaustive list of the kinds of live issues there are in research ethics today. Aside from the epistemological and philosophical issues in this dynamic field, research ethicists also face anecdotal issues at the level of individual research ethics reviews, systemic issues related to the institutions in which research ethics reviews are carried out and social, legal and political issues related to governance and oversight of research ethics activities.

REFERENCES

Allen, C. (1996) What's Wrong with the 'Golden Rule'? Conundrums of Conducting Ethical Research in Cyberspace, *The Information Society*, **12**, 2, 175-187.

Boehlefeld, S.P. (1996) Doing the Right Thing: Ethical Cyberspace Research, *The Information Society*,**12**, 2, 141-152.

Kock, N.F. (1999) A Case of Academic Plagiarism, *Communications of the ACM*, **42**, 7, 96-104.

Martin, B. (1994) Plagiarism: A Misplaced Emphasis, *Journal of Information Ethics*, **3**, 2, 36-47.

Martin, B. (1999) Suppressing Research Data: Methods, Context, Accountability and Responses, *Accountability in Research*, **6**, 333-372.

Onken, M., Garrison, S., Dotterweich, S. (1999) Research Ethics Among AACSB Faculty and Deans: Why Isn't There More Whistleblowing?, *Journal of Information Ethics*, **8**, 1, 10-19.

Thomas, J. (1996) Introduction: A Debate about the Ethics of Fair Practices for Collecting Social Science Data in Cyberspace, *The Information Society*, **12**, 2, 107-117.

Thomas, J. (1996) When Cyberresearch Goes Awry: The Ethics of the Rimm 'Cyberporn' Study, *The Information Society*, **12**, 2, 189-198.

Waskul, D. and Douglass, M. (1996) Considering the Electronic Participant: Some Polemical Observations on the Ethics of On-Line Research, *The Information Society*, **12**, 2, 129-139.

Internet

Bashinski, J., Balke, B., Williams, J.M., Holmes, N., Bosley, J.J., Rosenwald, J., Prince, C.G. Choi, B. and Denton, T. (2000) The Ethics of Personalization, *Communications of the ACM*, **43**, 11, 11-15.

Clarke, R. (1999) Ethics and the Internet: The Cyberspace Behaviour of People, Communities and Organisations, *Business & Professional Ethics Journal*, **18**, 3-4, 153-167.

Kelly, E.P. and Rowland, H.C. (2000) Ethical and Online Privacy Issues in Electronic Commerce, *Business Horizons*, **43**, 3, 3.

King, S.A. (1996) Researching Internet Communities: Proposed Ethical Guidelines for the Reporting of Results, *The Information Society*, **12**, 2, 119-127.

Kronenberg, V. (1999) Beware of Geeks Bearing Gifts: Ethical Implications of Current Market Models of the Internet, *Business & Professional Ethics Journal*, **18**, 3-4, 125-152.

Langford, D. (1996) Ethics and the Internet: Appropriate Behaviour in Electronic Communication, *Ethics and Behavior*, **6**, 2, 91-106.

Reid, E. (1996) Informed Consent in the Study of On-Line Communities: A Reflection on the Effects of Computer-Mediated Social Research, *The Information Society*, **12**, 2, 169-174.

Scheibal, W.J. and Gladstone, J.A. (2000) Privacy on the Net: Europe Changes the Rules, *Business Horizons*, **43**, 3, 13.

Spinello, R.A. and Tavani, H.T. (2001) The Internet, Ethical Values, and Conceptual Frameworks: An Introduction to CyberEthics, *Computer and Society*, **31**, 2, 5-7.

Scientific Research Methodology : *Concepts and Quality*
Edited by: and Dr. Pawan Kumar 'Bharti' and Dr. Prasann Kumar
ISBN: 978-93-86841-95-7
Edition: 2019
Published by: Discovery Publishing House Pvt. Ltd., New Delhi (India)

4

Ethics in Research

Calling Citizen for Sustainable Research

[1]Prasann Kumar and [2]Shweta Pathak

GRAPHICAL ABSTRACT

Keywords: Agriculture, Biotic, Crop, Ethics, Research, Science

Introduction

- Society norms adopted by a group
- A conception of conduct that is right or wrong
- Deal with fundamental human relationships

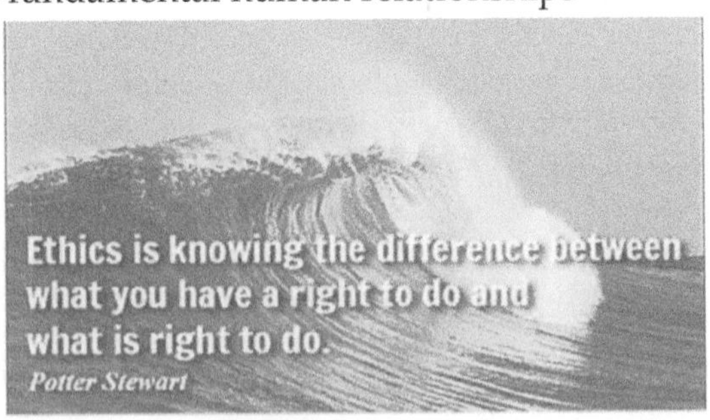

Fig. 4.1: What is ethics?

(Source: Based on review of literature, 2018)

[1] Department of Agronomy, School of Agriculture, Lovely Professional University, Jalandhar, Punjab, 144411, India

[2] Department of Plant Physiology, I.Ag. Sci., BHU., Varanasi, 221005, U.P., India

Reasons for Ethical Behavior

- Every researcher must receive precise, appropriate credit.
- Prevent harming others
- Improve relations
- Improve productivity
- Protect idea from others
- Stop possible ill or bad uses of research
- Promote personal morality

Ethical Principles

1. Autonomy
2. Beneficence
3. Non-malfeasance
4. Justice
5. Fidelity
6. Confidentiality

Autonomy

- Respect for Persons
- Treat individuals as autonomous agents
- Do not use people as a means to an end
- Allow people to make choices for themselves
- Provide extra protection to those with limited autonomy
    - o *Voluntary Participation*
    - o *Informed Consent*
    - o *Protection of Privacy & Confidentiality*
    - o *Right to Withdraw without Penalty*

Beneficence

- Action that is done for the benefit of others
- Acts of kindness or charity that go beyond duty
- Obligations derived from beneficence
    - o Do no harm
    - o Prevent harm
    - o Prevent evil
    - o Promote good

- *Risks are justified by the benefits*
- *Risks are minimized*
- *Conflicts of interest are managed to avoid bias*

Non-malfeasance

Moral principle that one should refrain from harming others ("first, do no harm"). Physicians must refrain from providing ineffective treatments or acting with malice toward patients. This principle, however, offers little useful guidance to physicians since many beneficial therapies also have serious risks. The pertinent ethical issue is whether the benefits outweigh the burdens.

Justice

- Treat people fairly
- Fair sharing of burdens and benefits of research
    - o *Vulnerable subjects are not targeted for convenience*
    - o *People are not selected as subjects because of their ease of availability or compromised position*
    - o *People who are likely to benefit are not excluded*

Fidelity

The principle that one should keep one's promises.

Fidelity may be defined as the extent to which delivery of an intervention adheres to the protocol or program model originally developed.

Fidelity measurement has increasing significance for evaluation, treatment effectiveness research, and service administration.

Confidentiality

Must maintain the confidentiality of medical information. Confidentiality respects patient autonomy and encourages patients to present for care and be candid. Study codes may be used on data collection instruments in place of identifying information to protect participants' responses / data when data documents are stored or out in the open (Figure 4.2).

Fig. 4.2: Research ethics

(Source: Based on review of literature, 2018)

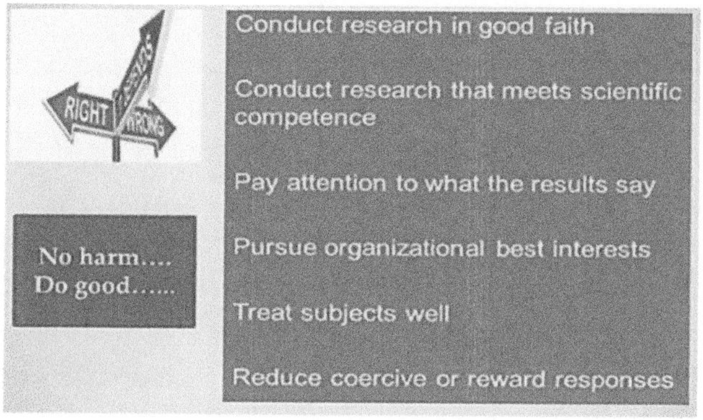

Fig. 4.3: No harm do good
(Source: Based on review of literature, 2018)

Integrity

"Strict adherence to a moral code, reflect in transparent honesty and complete harmony in what one thinks, says and does."

Honesty

1. Good and truthful: not lying, stealing or cheating
2. Not hiding the truth about someone or something: not meant to deceive someone
3. Showing or suggesting a good and truthful character

Objectivity

"Striving (as far as possible or practicable) to reduce or eliminate biases, prejudices by relying on variable data"

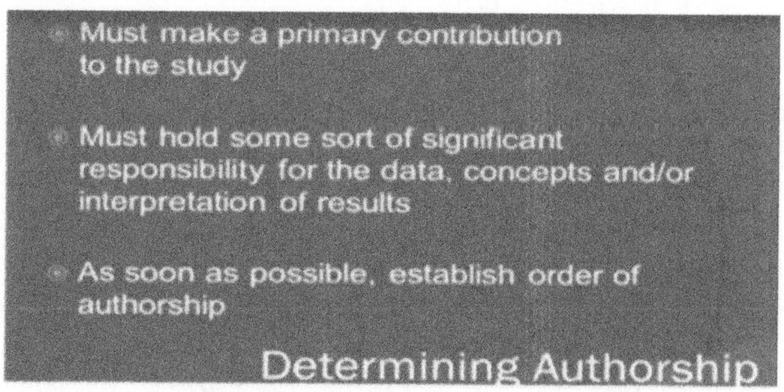

Fig. 4.3a: Determination of Authorship
(Source: based on review of literature, 2018)

Responsible Conduct of an Ethical Researcher

What if another student fabricates data- and you know it?

What should you do?

Are you obligated to do anything?

History of Unethical Research

- Tuskegee Experiment (1932-1972)-American researchers purposely withheld treatment for 399 African-American people with syphilis for the sole purpose of studying the long term effects of the disease.
- Willowbrook Study (1963-1966)-Children with developmental disabilities were deliberately infected with Hepatitis (some were even fed fecal matter). Purpose of the study was to examine the course of the disease and to test a potential immunization.
- Human radiation experiments by the US Department of Defense & Atomic Energy Commission.
- Milgram's Obedience Study-Researchers asked participants to "Pseudo-shocking" confederates in order to examine obedience.
- Zimbardo's Stanford Prison Experiment (1971). Study had to be ended prematurely because of abusive behaviors generated participants who where assigned as guards over those subjects that were assigned as prisoners.

Ethical Codes

- Nazis.

  The need for regulation and codes of behavior emerged from revelations of the research atrocities committed by the Nazis.
- Nuremberg Code.

  This 1947 code for biomedical research was the first to focus on the importance of informed consent.
- Helsinki Declaration.

  This 1964 declaration provided guidance in such areas as the use of animals for research purposes.
- The American Sociological Association (ASA) adopted a formal code of ethics in 1969.
- American Psychological Association (1982).

The Ethical Principles in the Conduct of Human Research with Human Participants

- The National Research Act (1974)

  Passed by Congress for the purpose of protecting human subjects participating in experiments.Of course, while it's essential to have codes, the responsibility for ethical research ultimately lies with the individual researcher.

The Belmont Report

- The National Commission for the Protection of Human Subjects of Biomedical and Behavioral Research - April 18, 1979
    1. Boundaries Between Practice and Research
    2. Basic Ethical Principles
    3. Applications (of Principles)
- The Belmont Report (1979) is the major ethical statement guiding human research in the United States.

Institutional Review Board

- To provide standards of conducting ethical research, and to protect human an animal subjects, the National Research Act (law in 1974) established the Institutional Review Board
- Any research project that receives federal money must demonstrate that its methods are ethical
- http://irb.ufl.edu/

HIPAA

- The Health Insurance Portability and Accountability Act (HIPAA) … 1996.
- A comprehensive federal protection plan that ensures continuity of healthcare coverage for individuals changing jobs; includes a provision that impacts on the management of health information; seeks to simplify the administration of health insurance; and aims to combat waste, fraud, and abuse in health insurance and health care.

International Conference on Harmonization (ICH)

- ICH was created in 1990 (Brussels).
- The ICH "process" was 1st drawn up at a Steering Committee meeting in Washington, March 1992 and amended in Tokyo, September 1992.
- Agreement between the EU, Japan and the USA to harmonize different regional requirements for registration of pharmaceutical drug products.
- Unique because joint effort by regulators and associated pharmaceutical industry trade associations.

Benefits of Harmonisation

- Improved quality of medicines
- Elimination of duplicative effort
- Optimising utilisation of resources

- Strengthening of individual regulatory agencies
- Standardisation of regulatory requirements
- Effective medicine regulation

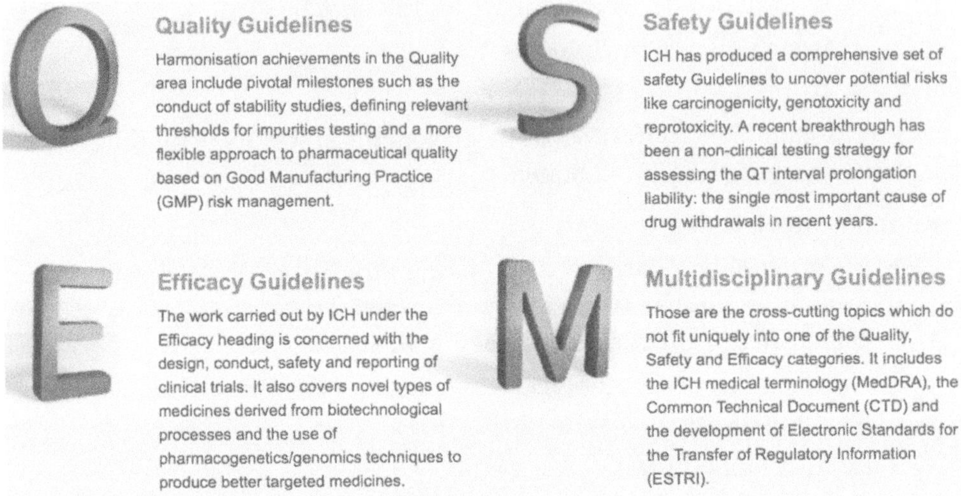

Fig. 4.4: ICH Guidelines

(Source: Based on review of literature, 2018)

ETHICS IN PRECLINICAL STUDIES

Ethical Principles Related to Animal Experiments

These Principles and Guidelines are based on the recognition that in their need to resolve their problems, human beings cannot dispense with experimentation on live animals, on the one hand, while the ethical principles of "respect for life" and respect for the "dignity of creation" demand that they protect animals, on the other.These Ethical Principles and Guidelines for Experiments on Animals were formulated jointly by the Swiss Academy of Medical Sciences (SAMS) and the Swiss Academy of Sciences (SCNAT) in 1983.

Ethical Principles Related to Animal Experiments

Committee for the Purpose of Control and Supervision of Experiments on Animals (CPCSEA)

- Responsible conduct of an animal experiment
- Respect for life
- Maximum gain in knowledge is achieved using the minimum possible number of laboratory animals
- If the suffering of individual animals can be reduced significantly through the use of a larger number of animals, the reduction of individual suffering shall take priority

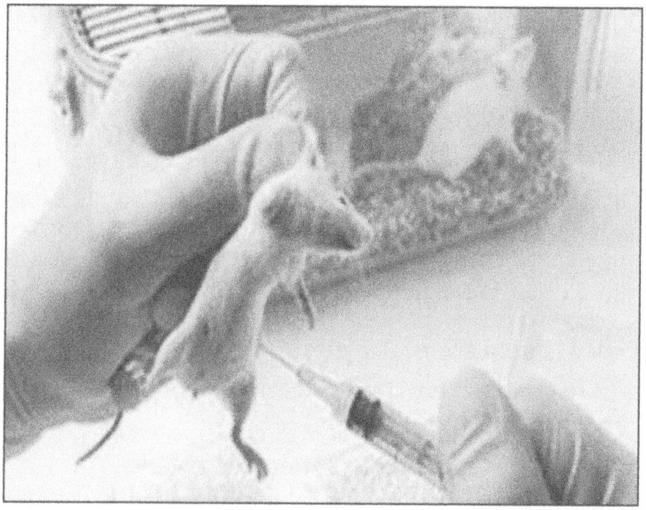

Fig. 4.5: Ethical Principles related to animal experiments
(Source: Based on review of literature, 2018)

- If pain, suffering or stress are inevitable concomitants of an experiment, their duration and intensity must be limited to the minimum
- Experiments on animals shall be carried out in accordance with the latest developments. Known prophylactic, diagnostic and therapeutic processes
- **Ethics in clinical studies**

Fig. 4.6: Ethics in clinical research
(Source: based on review of literature, 2018)

Clinical Evaluation of Drugs/Devices/Diagnostics/Vaccins /Herbal Remedies

Human studies designed to evaluate the safety, effectiveness, or usefulness of an intervention includes research on therapeutics, diagnostic procedures and preventive measures including vaccines

As per the revised Schedule 'Y' of the Drugs & Cosmetic Act (2005), "a clinical trial is a systematic study of new drug(s) in human subject to generate data for discovering and/or verifying the clinical, pharmacological (including pharmacodynamics, and pharmacokinetics), and/or adverse effects with the objective of determining the safety and/or efficacy of the new drugs"

The Clinical Trials Usually are of 3 Types

(*i*) studies where intervention is clearly "demarcated research" such as phase I trial of a new compound

(*ii*) studies with a mix of standard medical practices and specific research elements, *e.g. trials of two competing antinausea drugs following standard* chemotherapy;

(*iii*) studies involving research on therapeutic practices, such as the trial of two already approved anti-diabetic drugs

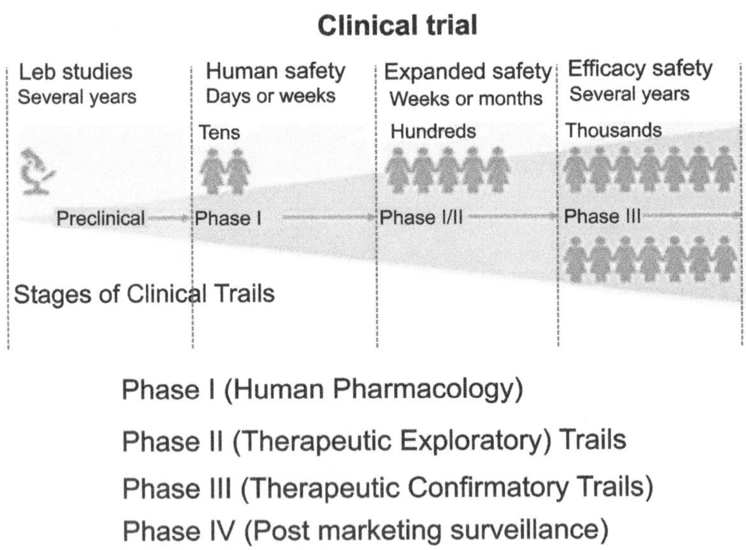

Fig. 4.7: Clinical trial

(Source: Based on review of literature, 2018)

Guideline for Drug Evaluation

- Protocol using placebo requires careful consideration before approval.
- Denial of the available treatment to control (placebo) group of patients is unethical.

- Trials of drugs without the approval of the Indian Regulatory Authority and appropriate agencies should be dealt with according to the law of the land.
- The criteria for termination of a trial must be defined *a priori in the proposal* of the trial and plan of interim analysis must be clearly presented.

Good Clinical Practices (GCP)

The guideline was developed with consideration of the current good clinical practices of the European Union, Japan, and the United States, as well as those of Australia, Canada, the Nordic countries and the World Health Organization (WHO). Clinical trials should be conducted in accordance with the ethical principles (Declaration of Helsinki, and GCP) .A trial should be initiated and continued only if the anticipated benefits justify the risks. The rights, safety, and well-being of the trial subjects are the most important considerations and should prevail over interests of science and society.

Ethics for Human Genetics and Genomics Research

Clinical research in the area of human genetics and human genome, including gene therapy, is subject to general ethical considerations of protection from harm and voluntariness of participation.

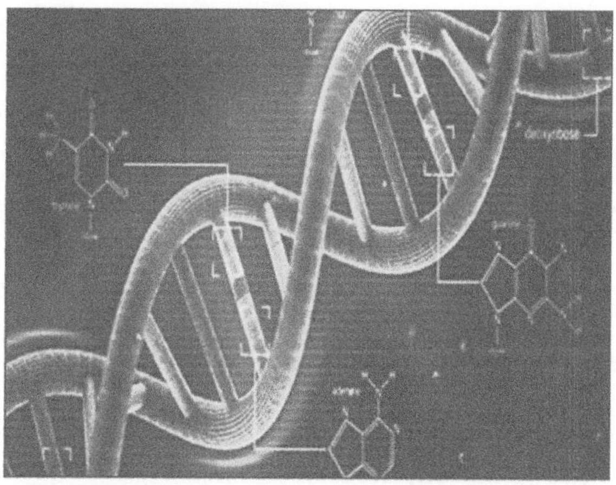

Fig. 4.8: Ethics for human genetics and genomics research
(Source: Based on review of literature, 2018)

The Institutional Ethical Committees reviewing research proposals related to research on human genetics should have necessary expertise, e.g. Central Ethical Committee (ICMR) and / or National Bioethics Committee (DBT) to organize national debates on such issues to evolve consensus on them.

Concerned with the misuse of genetic tests, particularly for the pre-selection of sex, the Government of India has enacted a law known as "The Prenatal Diagnostic Techniques (Regulation & Prevention of Misuse) Act 1994".

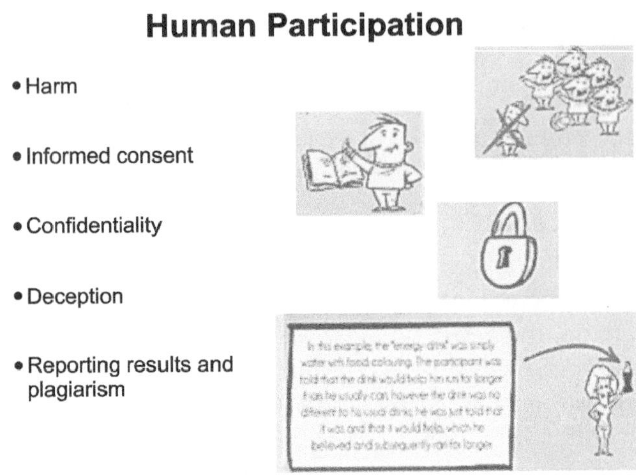

Fig. 4.9: Human participation

(Source: Based on review of literature, 2018)

Reporting Research Results

- Results of research studies should be reported in a honest, accurate manner
  - o Researchers cannot "massage" data to fit their hypotheses
  - o Researchers cannot make up or report false results
  - o Researcher must report what they find, even if the data does not support their initial hypotheses
  - o Researchers should ensure that data is being collected consistently (do checks of research assistants)
  - o Researchers should give the proper credit (authorship) to those who have earned it

Plagiarism

- Comes from the Latin word meaning "to kidnap"
- Examples of plagiarism:
  - o Copying someone else's words without proper citation
  - o Stealing someone else's ideas
  - o Stealing someone else's intellectual property

Bottom Line: Cite sources properly and minimize quotations in research reports

What is Plagiarism?

- Presenting another's original thoughts or ideas as your own
- Using another's exact words without proper citation

Why is Plagiarism Wrong?

- If you plagiarize, you are cheating yourself. You don't learn to write out your thoughts in your own words, and you don't get specific feedback geared to your individual needs and skills. Plagiarism is dishonest because it misrepresents the work of another as your own.
- Unintentional plagiarism is still cheating.
- Plagiarism is an extensive problem.
- Many universities now have honor codes and students can be failed or even expelled if they are found guilty of plagiarism.
- Plagiarism damages the reputation as a sign of a lack of integrity, of laziness, and maybe an indication that the individual is not as smart as they would like everyone to believe.

Catching the Plagiarist

The internet has made plagiarism easier with access to term paper mills, search engines, encyclopedias, etc. In response, websites have been developed which help teachers analyze papers and develop strategies to prevent plagiarism. These websites will allow to upload full papers or portions of the paper and will search all internet resources to determine if the information is original or has been plagiarized Plagiarism-Detector Pro (software)

Strategies to Avoid Plagiarism

- Maximum 20% similarity index is allowed for a research article
- Isolate the reasons why plagiarism occurs
- Identify the different types of plagiarism
- Integrate plagiarism prevention

Guidelines for Avoiding Plagiarism

v Use your own words and ideas.

v Give credit for copied, adapted, or paraphrased material.

v Avoid using others' work with minor "cosmetic" changes.

v There are no "freebies." (nothing is free of charge)

v Beware of "common knowledge."

Use Your Own Words and Ideas

- This is a skill that improves with practice.
- It requires an understanding of the topic
- It requires that you give yourself credit for your own abilities.

Give Credit for Copied, Adapted, or Paraphrased Material.

- If you repeat another's exact words, you MUST use quotation marks and cite the source.

- If you adapt a chart or paraphrase a sentence, you must still cite.
- Paraphrase means that you restate the author's ideas, meaning, and information in your own words

Avoid Using Others' Work with Minor "Cosmetic" Changes

Examples: using "less" for "fewer," reversing the order of a sentence, changing terms in a computer code, or altering a spread sheet layout. If the work is essentially the same, give credit.

There are no "Freebies"

ALWAYS cite words, information, and ideas you use if they are new to you (learned in your research). No matter where you find it – even in an encyclopedia or on the Internet – you cite it.

Beware of "Common Knowledge."

You don't have to cite "common knowledge," BUT the fact must really be commonly known. That George Washington was the first U.S. president is common knowledge; That George Washington was an expert dancer is not common knowledge

Unintentional Plagiarism

- Paraphrasing poorly: changing a few words without changing the sentence structure of the original, or changing the sentence structure but not the words.
- Quoting poorly: putting quotation marks around part of a quotation but not around all of it, or putting quotation marks around a passage that is partly paraphrased and partly quoted.
- Citing poorly: omitting an occasional citation or citing inaccurately.

Intentional Plagiarism

- Passing off as one's own pre-written papers from the Internet or other sources.
- Copying an essay or article from the Internet, on-line source, or electronic database without quoting or giving credit.
- Cutting and pasting from more than one source to create a paper without quoting or giving credit.
- Borrowing words or ideas from other students or sources without giving credit.

Plagiarism Prevention: Be authentic

- Develop a topic based on previously written material but write something new and original

- Rely on opinions of experts on a topic but improve upon those opinions
- Give credit to researchers while making your own contribution
- Follow a standard documentation method such as MLA or APA format

First Type of Plagiarism

- **Plagiarism of Words**

  – The use of another's exact words without citing the author

  – Incorrect

- Plagiarism is the reproduction of someone else's words, ideas or findings and presenting them as one's own without proper acknowledgement.

  – Correct

- Plagiarism is the "reproduction of someone else's words, ideas or findings and presenting them as one's own without proper acknowledgement" (Undergraduate Course Handbook: 2008, p.24)

Second Type of plagiarism

Plagiarism of Structure

- Paraphrasing another's words by changing sentence construction or word choice with citation
- Paraphrasing while maintaining original sentence construction with acknowledging the source

Third Type of Plagiarism

Plagiarism of Ideas

Presenting another's ideas as your own without giving the person credit

Submitting a paper without citing or incorrectly citinganother's ideas

Fig. 4.10: Plagiarism type

(Source: Based on review of literature, 2018)

Fourth Type of Plagiarism

Plagiarism of Authorship

Turning in a replication of another's work

Submitting a paper that you got off the internet or from a friend and presenting it as your own

Fig. 4.11: Fourth type of plagiarism

(Source: Based on review of literature, 2018)

The Fifth Type of Plagiarism

Plagiarism of Self

- The use of previous work for a separate assignment
- Although these were you original words and thoughts, receiving credit for a previous assignment is considered cheating

Fig. 4.12: Fifth type of plagiarism

(Source: Based on review of literature, 2018)

The Penalties of Plagiarism

Although plagiarism can be intentional or unintentional, both have consequences.

- Receiving zero on the assignment
- Failing the course
- Suspension
- Expulsion

How to Cite the Sources?

If you wish to avoid accusations of plagiarism, you must cite your sources properly. Several websites exist which can help you. Sort your sources Alphabetically by Author's last name. Articles without authors are organized alphabetically, numbers go before A.

Citation

More precisely, a citation is an abbreviated alphanumeric expression (e.g. [Newell84]) embedded in the body of an intellectual work that denotes an entry in the bibliographic references section of the work for the purpose of acknowledging the relevance of the works.

Citation content can vary depending on the type of source and may include:

Book: author(s), book title, publisher, date of publication, and page number(s) if appropriate.

Journal: author(s), article title, journal title, date of publication, and page number(s).

Patent: author(s), title, patent office, patent application no., year eg: Wang, J. and McVean, C. A. 17-β-4-acetamide-4-azasteroids as androgen receptor modulators. In patent WO099707, 2005

Newspaper: author(s), article title, name of newspaper, section title and page number(s) if desired, date of publication.

Web site: author(s), article and publication title where appropriate, as well as a URL, and a date when the site was accessed.

Interview: name of interviewer, interview descriptor (ex. personal interview) and date of interview.

Organization of Reference Material/Bibliography

A bibliography may be arranged by author, topic, or some other scheme. The organized listing of books (enumerative bibliography) and the systematic, description of books as physical objects (descriptive bibliography).Citation styles vary. An entry for a book in a bibliography usually contains the following elements:creator(s), title, publisher and place of publication, date of publication. An entry for a journal or periodical article usually contains:Creator, article title, journal title, volume, pages, date of publication.

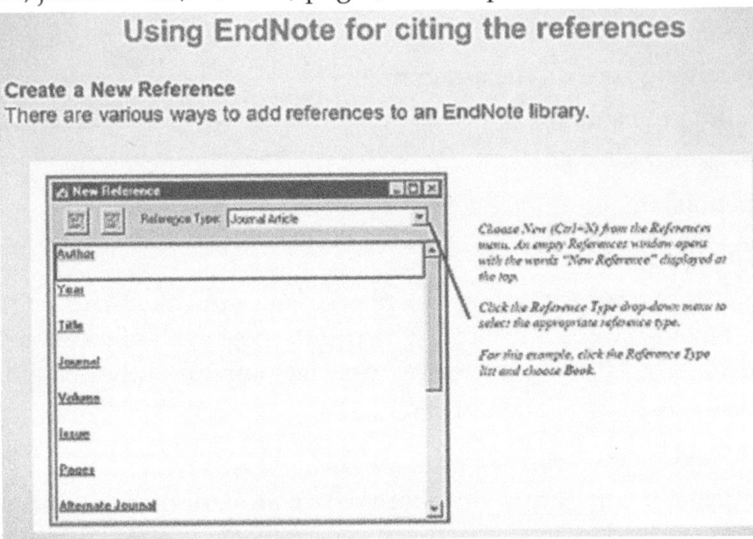

Fig. 4.13: Using endnote for citing the reference

(Source: based on review of literature, 2018)

Enter the reference information beginning with the author names. Author names can be entered two ways: either "First Middle Last" such as "Carol Margaret Jacobson" or "Last, First Middle" such as "Jacobson, CarolMargaret." Individual author names must be entered one per line. *Close the Reference window choosing* ***Close Reference (Ctrl+W or Cmd+W) from the File menu.*** All information is automatically saved when you close a window

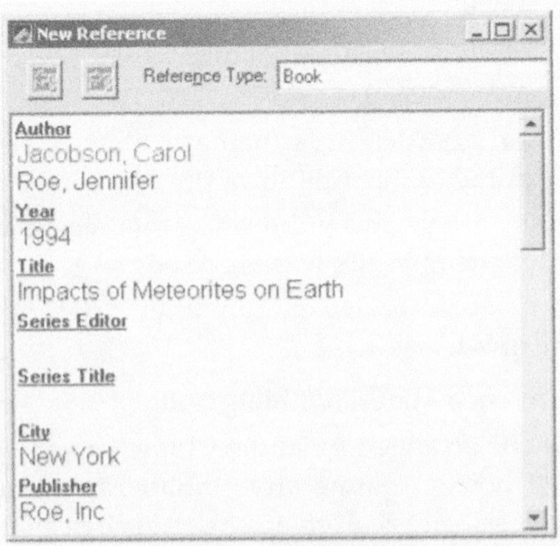

Fig. 4.14: New reference addition

(Source: based on review of literature)

1. Run a simple search in PubMed e.g. for "swine flu"
2. Select a few results using the tick boxes
3. Click Send to button, and choose File
4. Choose MEDLINE format
5. Click Create File and save it e.g. to desktop
6. Open your EndNote Library
7. Click the Collect tab then Import References
8. Use Browse to locate the saved text file (e.g. on your desktop)

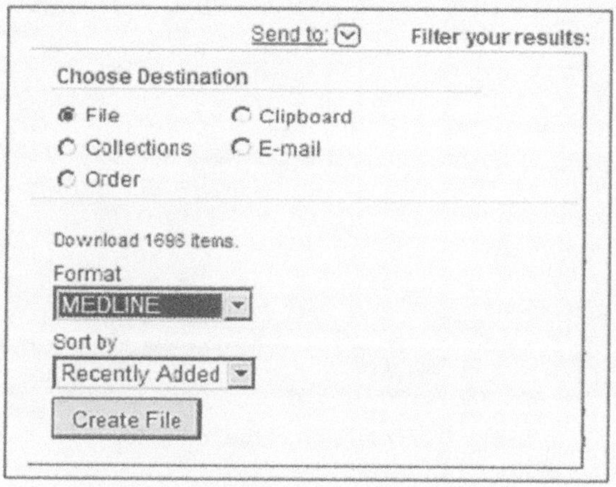

Fig. 4.15: Import the reference

(Source: based on review of literature, 2018)

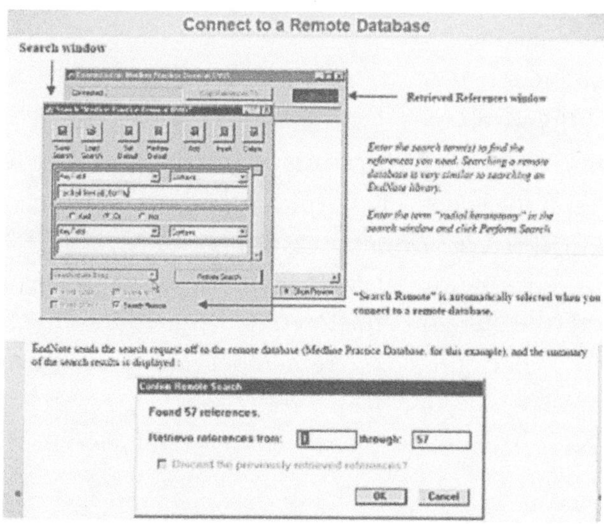

Fig. 4.16: Connect to a remote database

(Source: Based on review of literature, 2018)

Save the References

At this point you can peruse the retrieved references to see which ones you would like to keep. Save the references you want by transferring them into one of your own End Note libraries.

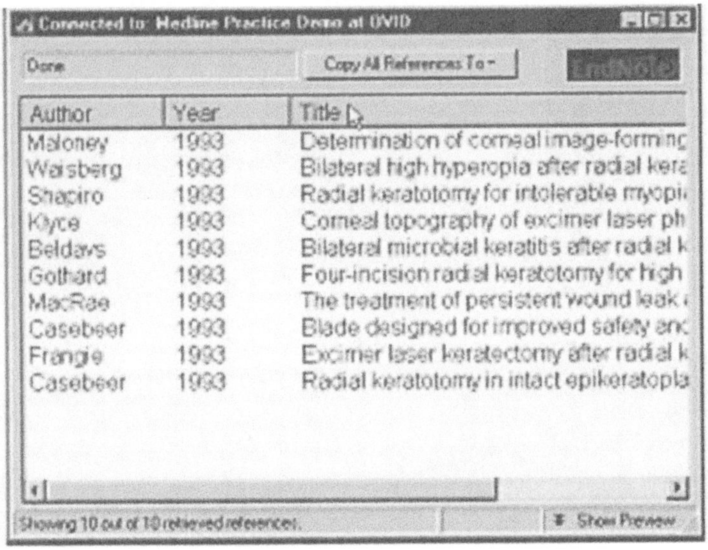

Fig. 4.17: Addition of the reference

(Source: based on review of literature, 2018)

Display the EndNote X3 toolbar

1. Open Word
2. Click the View tab
3. Click Toolbars
4. *Click EndNote X3
5. Click the CWYW preferences button on the EndNote X3 toolbar
6. In the Preferences box, click Application
7. Select EndNote Web from the drop-list
8. Enter your EndNote Web/Web of Knowledge account email and password (the one you registered and signed into the service with)
9. You should check the box to remember your preferences i.e. username and password
10. Click OK

Conclusion

- It must be entirely your own work, written by you in your own words, and containing your own interpretations, ideas, approaches etc.

- It must state clearly where you got other people's words or major ideas.
- It must state clearly where you got your charts, diagrams, photos, graphics, and media (including sound, video and digital images.

REFERENCES

Ethical Guidelines to Publication of Chemical Research (ACS Pubs. Div.) http://pubs.acs.org/userimages/Content Editor/1218054468605/ethics.pdf.

"On Being a Scientist: Responsible Conduct in Research"; National Academy Press, Wash. D.C, 2009 (http://www.nap.edu/catalog/12192.html.

IEEE Policy Statement on Self-Plagiarism (http://www.comsoc.org/pubs/jrnal/transcom/Self_Plagiarism.pdf).

Managing Allegations of Scientific Misconduct: A Guidance Document for Editors, January 2000, Office of Research Integrity, Office of Public Health and Science, U.S. Dept. of Health and Human Services http://ori.dhhs.gov.

Scientific Research Methodology : *Concepts and Quality*
Edited by: and Dr. Pawan Kumar 'Bharti' and Dr. Prasann Kumar
ISBN: 978-93-86841-95-7
Edition: 2019
Published by: Discovery Publishing House Pvt. Ltd., New Delhi (India)

5

Collaborative Research with Positive Mind

[1]Prasann Kumar and [2]Shweta Pathak

GRAPHICAL ABSTARCT

Introduction

Top Ten problems of Humanity for next 50 years (Source: **Richard E. Smalley**)

1. Energy; 2. Water; 3. Food; 4. Environment; 5. Poverty; 6. Terrorism &War; 7. Disease, 8. Education; 9. Democracy;10. Population

Characteristics

Complex• Challenging• Global• Beyond silos• Interconnected

Meeting these challenges requires

- A high dose of innovation
- Nimbleness
- Multiple Perspectives
- Team work

1 Department of Agronomy, School of Agriculture, Lovely Professional University, Jalandhar, Punjab, 144411, India

2 Department of Plant Physiology, I.Ag. Sci., BHU., Varanasi, 221005, U.P., India

Fig. 5.1: Team work and final product
(Source: based on review of literatre, 2018)

Recent research suggests that the most successful innovation occurs at the boundaries/ Interfaces

It allows people

- to come up with new/different viewpoints on a subject
- to break down and restructure our knowledge about the subject in order to gain new insights into its nature
- to use their imagination and create/invent new things

What is Collaborative Research?

Over the past 50 years, research collaborations have increased across all disciplines. The term collaboration initially referred to researchers working together within the same discipline, within an institution or in different institutions.

Collaborations can be as simple as one researcher sharing reagents or techniques within the same lab or they can be as complex as multi-centered clinical trials that involve academic research centers, private hospitals, and for-profit companies studying thousands of patients in different states or countries.

"Interdisciplinary research can be one of the most productive and inspiring of human pursuits".

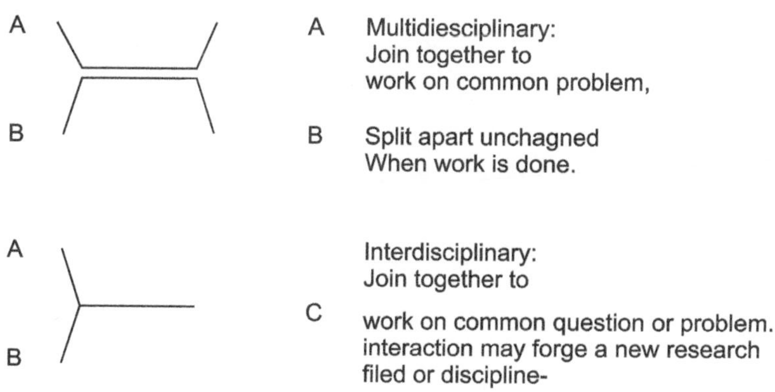

Fig. 5.2: Multidisciplinary research
(Source: based on review of literature, 20180

"Interdisciplinary research is a mode of research by teams or individuals that integrates information, data, techniques, tools, perspectives, concepts, and/ or theories from two or more disciplines or bodies of specialized knowledge to advance fundamental understanding or to solve problems whose solutions are beyond the scope of a single discipline or area of research practice."

In multi-disciplinarity, researchers from two or more disciplines work together on a common problem, but without altering their disciplinary approaches or developing a common conceptual framework.

True inter-disciplinarity occurs when researchers from two or more disciplines pool their approaches and modify them so that they are better suited to the problem at hand.

Interdisciplinary Research

We define interdisciplinary research as occurring where the contributions of the various disciplines are integrated to provide holistic or systemic outcomes.

Interdisciplinary research can be sub-divided into:

- Research which aims to further the expertise and competence of academic disciplines themselves, e.g. through developments in methodology which enable new issues to be addressed or new disciplines or sub-disciplines to be formed.
- Research which is problem focused and addresses issues of social, technical and/or policy relevance with less emphasis on discipline-related academic outcomes.

Interdisciplinary

Interdisciplinarity is a type of academic collaboration in which specialists drawn from two or more academic disciplines work together in pursuit of common goals.

Fig. 5.3: Inter-disciplinarity

(Source: based on review of literature, 2018)

Interdisciplinary programs arise from a conviction that the traditional disciplines are unable or unwilling to address an important problem.

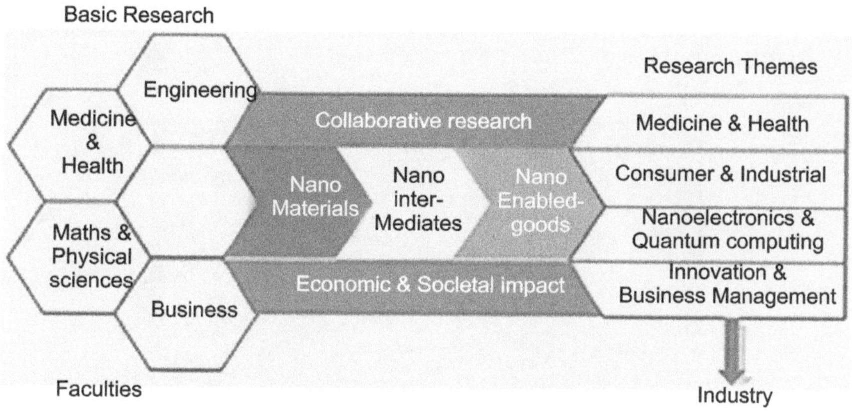

Fig. 5.4: Interdisciplinary programs
(Source: based on review of literature, 2018)

- Interdisciplinary programs arise from new research developments, such as nanotechnology, which cannot be addressed without combining the approaches of two or more disciplines.
- Quantum information processing, which amalgamates elements of quantum physics and computer science.
- Bioinformatics, which combines molecular biology with computer science.
- Imaging science, amalgamates elements of engineering, physics, mathematics, *visual perception, color science,* and chemistry.
- Materials Science, amgamating physics, chemistry and engineering.

Interdisciplinary thinking is rapidly becoming an integral feature of research as a result of four powerful drivers:

- *the inherent complexity of nature and society*
- *the desire to explore problems and questions that are not confined to a single discipline,*
- *the need to solve societal problems,*
- *the power of new technologies*

Challenges to Interdisciplinary Research

- The current system of academic advancement favors the independent investigator
- Most institutions house scientists in discrete departments
- Interdisciplinary science requires interdisciplinary peer-review

- Interdisciplinary research teams take time to assemble and require unique resources
- Language and communication issues
- Institutional structures and procedures
- Divergences in worldviews across disciplines

Fig. 5.5: Challenges to Interdisciplinary Research

(Source: based on review of literature, 2018)

- Disciplines have distinct analytic tools concepts and methods.
- Disciplines have distinct languages and representations (terminology and notation – e.g., math vs music).
- Disciplines have distinct mechanisms for demonstrating knowledge (proof, score, demo, product, paper).
- Disciplines have distinct mechanisms for proprietariness (authorship, patents, copywrites, open source, etc.)
- Students - eager, but untrained.
- Faculty - untrained, tenure-scared, time limited, peer-inhibited, but natural curious.
- Fields - tend to be conservative - "that's not physics!""that's not economics!".
- Administration - designed to support school & departmental structure, discipline-centric.
- Structure - Office space, teaching areas, research labs, all arranged by discipline.
- Granting Agencies - designed to support disciplines.

Due to ... the barriers, interdisciplinary research areas are strongly motivated to become disciplines themselves. If they succeed, they can establish their own research funding programs and make their own tenure and promotion decisions. In so doing, they lower the risk of entry"

Examples of former interdisciplinary research areas that have become disciplines include neuroscience, biochemistry, materials science, and biomedical engineering.

Fig. 5.6: Multidisciplinary

(Source: based on review of literature, 2018)

- Communicate........ and then communicate again
  — Don't assume anything.
- Define expectations of who will do what
- Discuss authorship in advance
  — Different disciplines have different standards for determining authors
- Discuss data and material management
  — Don't assume everyone knows who will be doing what
- Discuss intellectual property
  — Is there any background IP? Is IP likely?
- Discuss accountability
  —Find out in advance if there are any conflicts of interest

What Motivates Inter-disciplinary Research?

Motivations for setting up interdisciplinary research programmes might include:

- the nature of the subject is interdisciplinary (e.g. transport, environment)
- researchers are transferring information from the laboratory to the real world

  the research is user driven (not necessarily commercial)
- the research is particularly relevant to policy making in complex areas
- single discipline research has encountered a bottle-neck and more than one discipline is needed to make a breakthrough

For individuals engaging in interdisciplinary research motivations might include a desire to:

- engage with 'real world' problems
- tackle socially relevant issues
- contribute to the advancement of academic disciplines

Skills Needed by Interdisciplinary Researchers

In interdisciplinary research, personality and attitudes of researchers are at least as important for success as discipline base and specialization. Useful characteristics are:

- flexibility, adaptability, creativity
- curiosity about, and willingness to learn from, other disciplines

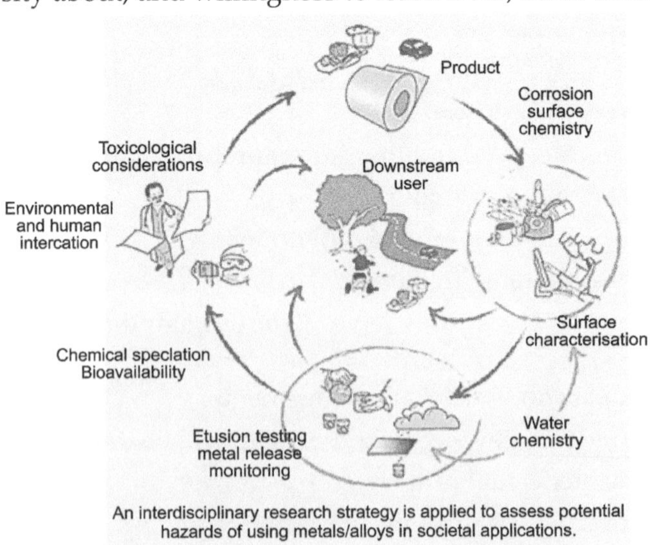

Fig. 5.7: Skills for interdisciplinary research

(Source: based on review of literature, 2018)

- an open mind to ideas coming from other disciplines and experiences
- good communication and listening skills
- an ability to bridge the gap between theory and practice
- a good team worker

Research collaborations allow researchers to answer questions they wouldn't be able to if they worked alone. The challenges for the investigators engaged in collaboration is a need to understand what the project's main goal is, and what role each collaborator must play in order to achieve that goal.

While collaborators may work independently from each other at certain stages of the research, they should always be cognizant of the project's larger picture. They can increase the likelihood of a positive outcome by clearly delineating roles and responsibilities, developing management plans and fostering cooperation and a sense of fairness and accountability.

Fig. 5.8: How do we change the world
(Source: based on review of literature, 2018)

How to do Good Research with Positive Mind

When we think about how people work, the naive intuition we have is that people are like rats in a maze — that all people care about is money, and the moment we give them money, we can direct them to work one way, we can direct them to work another way. This is why we give bonuses to bankers and pay in all kinds of ways. And we really have this incredibly simplistic view of why people work, and what the labor market looks like.

At the same time, if you think about it, there's all kinds of strange behaviors in the world around us. Think about something like mountaineering and mountain climbing. If you read books of people who climb mountains, difficult mountains, do you think that those books are full of moments of joy and happiness? No, they are full of misery. In fact, it's all about having difficulty walking, and difficulty breathing — cold, challenging circumstances. And if people were just trying to be happy, the moment they would get to the top, they would say, **"This was a terrible mistake. I'll never do it again."**

Fig. 5.9: How to do research with positive mind

(Source: based on review of literature, 2018)

Fig. 5.10: Challenging circumstances

(Source: based on review of literature, 2018)

Instead, enjoying movies or cola people go down, and after they recover, they go up again. And if you think about mountain climbing as an example, it suggests all kinds of things. It suggests that we care about reaching the end, a peak. It suggests that we care about the fight, about the challenge. It suggests that there's all kinds of other things that motivate us to work or behave in all kinds of ways.

Fig. 5.11: Challenging circumstances
(Source: based on review of literature, 2018)

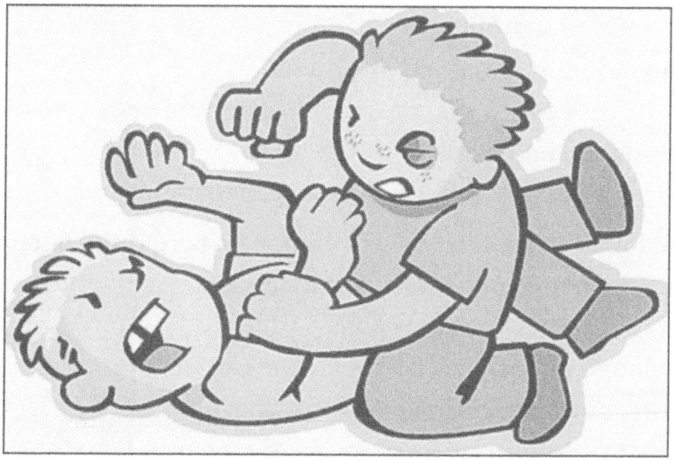

Fig. 5.12: Cola people
(Source: based on review of literature, 2018)

Motivation: Why should I do Research?

- Internal drive
- Research interest (sense of achievement/fulfillment, curiosity)
- Strong ambition (self-expectation)
- External drive

- Degree and diploma
- Parents, teachers, friends
- Peer pressure (sense of honor and responsibility)
- Small success

Enjoyment

- Research has to be something you like to do
- Don't do it for some other reason (money, recognition, fame, jobs, etc.)
- If you enjoy it, more chances that the results will be interesting, and all the other things will come
- Just relax and have fun
- Think carefully if this is what you like
- If you can imagine a better life, you should go and take that life

Research Problem Selection

- Good research largely depends on the selected problem
- 90% of a research job is done when you find a good problem.
- A good problem is difficult to find
- Not too easy or too difficult
- How to select a problem?
- Is it an old problem or a new problem?
- Usually, new problems have more opportunities
- Is it a significant problem?
- Practically important yet technically challenging

The Key Ingredients of Research: Contribution (Where is the beef?)

- One major contribution is better than many small ones
- What is the contribution type?
- Knowledge discovery, invention, integration, application
- Identify, describe, and demonstrate the big idea
- Asking the right problem, then asking the problem right
- Innovation! Innovation! Innovation!

The Right Problem and the Right Way to Ask Problem

- Asking the problem right can lead to asking the right problem
- Can we predict reliability?
- Can we predict reliability with models?
- Can I predict reliability with user experience?

- The problem of the problem: How to identify a good research problem?
- Where are you standing? The importance of review of literature
- Do you have a theory?
- Methodology: Do it in a rigid scientific way
- Writing is a critical thinking: How to make your research paper published in top journals

What is Research Study?

A research study must:

- Ask a research question
- Identify a research group or population
- Describe a research method
- Test or measure something
- Summarize the results

Three Basic Research Activity

- Describing some phenomena that we perceive in the world,
- Articulating a theory to account for the phenomena, and
- Testing how well the theory accounts for the phenomena.

The Problem of Identifying a Good Research Problem

- The objective of a research is to find out an answer to an interesting, valuable, but unanswered question.
- To make people interested in your research, you must ask them a question that they have not thought of but anxious to know the answer.
- In academic, too much emphasis is put on the rigorous of research methodology rather than the importance of research question.

How to Select a Good Research Problem?

- Be sensitive to new trends: to be at the frontier.
- Do not limit yourself to traditional way of thinking.
- Do not repeat what people have already done: the importance of review of literature.
- Do not provide solution without identifying a problem: first is why then is how.

How to Select a Good Research Problem?

- To be original. Discover a research problem from real world rather than mimic other people in an academic world.

- Work with people with different discipline. Do not limit your research in your discipline only.
- Broaden your view (knowing the context) first, narrow down to be focused, then broaden again for future research.
- "To wrestle with unexpected and arrive at new understanding that challenges old way of thinking is the crux of good research".

Writing Papers is a Skill

- Many papers are badly written
- Good writing is a skill you can learn
- It's a skill that is worth learning
- You will get more brownie points (more papers accepted etc.)
- Your ideas will have more impact
- You will have better ideas

Fig. 5.13: The purpose of your paper

(Source": based on review of literature, 2018)

Papers communicate ideas

- Your goal: to infect the mind of your reader with **your idea**, like a virus
- Papers are far more durable than programs (think Mozart)

Fig. 5.14: Paper communication idea
(Source: based on review of literature, 2018)

The Idea

- Figure out what your idea is
- Make certain that the reader is in no doubt what the idea is. Be 100% explicit:
- "The main idea of this paper is...."
- "In this section we present the main contributions of the paper."
- Many papers contain good ideas, but do not distil what they are.

Fig. 5.15: The importance of review of literature
(Source: based on review of literature, 2018)

- Do not reinvent the wheels
- To be knowledgeable in the research field
- To be accepted by the research community

- Reviewer wants to know where the paper fits with others on the same topic as well as how it differs from them
- An effective review create a strong foundation for advance knowledge
- An review should identify critical knowledge gaps and thus identify research directions
- Avoid grocery list of papers without comment
- Do not limit your thinking to existing literature.

How to Identify Relevant Literature

- Searching leading journal first
- Search based on topics or authors (Research gate)
- Go backward and forward through citation
- Take advantages of electronic resources and searching tools
  (*a*) Proquest ABI/ Inform
  (*b*) ISI Web of Science
  (*c*) Scholar.google.com

Do you have Theory?

- What is theory? An explanation of a class of phenomena
  A. theories are more general
  B. theories explain why things are related; whereas hypothesis just say that they are related theories generate hypothesis
- The number 1 reason papers are rejected from journal is for lack of theory
- Use other's work to support your theory, not as your own theory

Fig. 5.16: what is theory

(Source: based on review of literature, 2018)

Most people say not that much. And this is because our kids are so valuable, not just because of who they are, but because of us, because they are so connected to us, and because of the time and connection.By the way, these are my kids, which, of course, are wonderful and so on. Which comes to tell you one more thing, which is, much like our builders, when they look at the creature of their creation, we don't see that other people don't see things our way.

Conduct Research in a Rigid Scientific Way

Keep your mind open and keep yourself up with the new information and techniques.

- Methods are tools- the instruments, techniques and procedures-by which a science gathers and analyzes information.
- All research methods should be regarded as bounded opportunities to gain knowledge and limitation to that knowledge.
- Multiple methods may be used to reduce the individual method's weakness.

Fig. 5.17: Keep your mind open
(Source: based on review of literature, 2018)

Research Methods

- Select an appropriate method and do it well.
- Never try to prove your hypothesis, just try to test your hypothesis. Let your data show you the way.
- Make good analysis and explanations- Statistically Sound.
- Admit the limitation and weakness of your study.

The Decision on Journal Selection

- Study the profile of target journal: Will my paper fit into the community of the journal readers?
- Cost/benefit analysis: the value of top journal is high but what are the chances of success and how long can I afford to wait?
- Aim high with high quality of work

Selling Your Paper to the Editors

- Read the authors guidelines
- Make sure your paper follows the journal's formatting guidelines
- Introduction: Why should I read your paper? Grab the reviewer's attention from the very beginning
- Literature review: Positioning your paper in big picture
- Research originality: Do not repeat what other had done, extend it. Clarity- Define the concept clearly before using them. Use table and figures to highlight key points.
- Methodology: Provide sufficient detail
- Analysis: Offer theoretical explanation for expected and unexpected results
- Conclusion: Emphasize your contributions but also admit your limitations
- Revision: Accept that criticism improve quality. Acknowledge that reviewer have a point
- Our goal is to produce good research results, to make advancements in science and technology
- NOT to get a job, or to make more money, ...
- If we do good research, these things will come, but they are not the goal, they are a side effect
- If we go for the wrong goal, good research will probably not come, and not even the goal
- Intellectual curiosity
- How does it work? What if you change this? Why did you do this? ...
- Ask questions to everybody (and to yourself) and in all circumstances
- Look at what others do
- Can be very helpful in learning how to recognize the interesting questions

Fig. 5.18: Curiosity
(Source: based on review of literature, 2018)

- Good research needs time
- Don't expect great results immediately
- Theorems may be hard to prove
- Coding may take more time that initially thought to be bug-free
- Experiments need to be tuned to show interesting results and lessons
- Allow ample time to do either theoretical or empirical research

Fig. 5.19: Patience for research
(Source: based on review of literature, 2018)

- Research has to be something you like to do
- Don't do it for some other reason (money, recognition, fame, jobs, etc.)
- If you enjoy it, more chances that the results will be interesting, and all the other things will come
- Just relax and have fun
- Think carefully if this is what you like
- If you can imagine a better life, you should go and take that life

Fig. 5.20: Problem formulation

(Source: based on review of literature, 2018)

- Working only on the details of your latest propagator or theorem can be useful for the next paper
- But devote some time also to think about the larger picture
- What are the important problems in my field?
- Read what others work on
- Discuss with other students, your supervisor, anybody you meet at the conferences

Fig. 5.21: Find the suitable problem

(Source: based on review of literature, 2018)

- Being able to find and evaluate previous work
- Look for what others have done **before** starting your research project
- It helps defining and tuning your problem
- May give you ideas on how to solve it
- Avoids reinventing the wheel and wasting time
- Find suitable tools to answer a question or to solve a well-posed problem
- Be able to **adapt** yourself to the context
- Turn a problematic situation into an interesting research problem
- Read, read, read
- Don't get discouraged, a solution can always be found

Fig. 5.22: Find the suitable problem

- If you are too sure of your research results, you will never notice the flaws
- If you are too unsure, you will never start
- Flaws should be considered and noted, they may be useful later to modify the theory to make space for them
- This can be a source of great results
- Have your work read by others and listen to the comments and suggestions
- Humbleness: there is always something you can learn from others
- A system or a tool may be a useful object, and experiments may be good, but what is most important is the general lesson learnt by developing it

- Others (or yourself) can use this lesson to build different tools or to define other experiments
- Same also for a theorem, but less crucial since a theorem is already a way to abstract and generalize what has been seen in a specific case
- Learn also from failures (or from rejected papers)
- Work locally, think globally
- Work hard on your specific propagator, but think about the general consequences of your results
- Independent thoughts
- Not just following others' ideas
- Courage to pursue your ideas
- Self-confidence
- Also courage to know when to stop
- Don't worry to state your ideas and to be criticised
- Better to be criticised than to be ignored
- No need for people who follow others

Fig. 5.23: Self courage

(Source: based on review of literature, 2018)

Communicating Your Results

- A paper
- A talk
- A Ph.D. thesis
- General advice:

- The idea and motivation is important, not just the technical details
- The simpler your way to present your idea, the more chances people will pay attention

Finally, believe that possibility is always ready to come true.

The Power of Positive Thinking

Positive thinking sounds useful on the surface. (Most of us would prefer to be positive rather than negative.) But "positive thinking" is also a soft and fluffy term that is easy to dismiss. In the real world, it rarely carries the same weight as words like "work ethic" or "persistence."Research is beginning to reveal that positive thinking is about much more than just being happy or displaying an upbeat attitude. Positive thoughts can actually create real value in your life and help you build skills that last much longer than a smile. The impact of positive thinking on your work, your health, and your life is being studied by people who are much smarter than me. One of these people is Barbara Fredrickson. Fredrickson is a positive psychology researcher at the University of North Carolina, and she published a landmark paper that provides surprising insights about positive thinking and its impact on your skills. Her work is among the most referenced and cited in her field, and it is surprisingly useful in everyday life. Researchers have long known that negative emotions program your brain to do a specific action. When that tiger crosses your path, for example, you run. The rest of the world doesn't matter. You are focused entirely on the tiger, the fear it creates, and how you can get away from it. In other words, negative emotions narrow your mind and focus your thoughts. At that same moment, you might have the option to climb a tree, pick up a leaf, or grab a stick — but your brain ignores all of those options because they seem irrelevant when a tiger is standing in front of you. This is a useful instinct if you're trying to save life and limb, but in our modern society we don't have to worry about stumbling across tigers in the wilderness.

Conclusion

The problem is that your brain is still programmed to respond to negative emotions in the same way — by shutting off the outside world and limiting the options you see around you. For example, when you're in a fight with someone, your anger and emotion might consume you to the point where you can't think about anything else. Or, when you are stressed out about everything you have to get done today, you may find it hard to actual start anything because you're paralyzed by how long your to-do list has become. Or, if you feel bad about not exercising or not eating healthy, all you think about is how little willpower you have, how you're lazy, and how you don't have any motivation. In each case, your brain closes off from the outside world and focuses on the negative emotions of fear, anger, and stress — just like it did with the tiger. Negative emotions prevent your brain from seeing the other options and choices that surround you. It's your survival instinct. Now, let's compare this to what positive emotions do to your brain. This is where Barbara Fredrickson returns to the story.

REFERENCES

Alexander, Ron. "CHRONICLE". Retrieved 2018-04-17.

A., Cosby, James. Devil's Music, Holy Rollers and Hillbillies: How America Gave Birth to Rock and Roll. Jefferson, North Carolina. p. 26. ISBN 9781476662299. OCLC 934885191.

Barnes, Bart (1993-12-26). "The Rev. Norman Vincent Peale, 'Positive Thinking' Author, Dies". Washington Post. ISSN 0190-8286. Retrieved 2018-04-17.

Bonventre, Peter (October 1977). "The Hypnotic Hitter". Newsweek.

Chandler, Russell (1993-12-26). "Norman Vincent Peale, 'Minister to Millions,' Dies: Religion: Mixing Faith and Psychology, author of 'The Power of Positive Thinking' Spread Inspiration Worldwide". Los Angeles Times. ISSN 0458-3035. Retrieved 2018-04-17.

Ellis, Albert, (1985). Overcoming Resistance: Rational-emotive Therapy with Difficult Clients. New York: Springer Pub. Co. p. 147. ISBN 9780826149107. OCLC 11814057.

Fuller, Edmund. "Pitchmen in the Pulpit". The Saturday Review: 28–29.

"How Norman Vincent Peale Taught Donald Trump to Worship Himself". POLITICO Magazine. Retrieved 2018-04-17.

Krumm, John M. (1961). Modern Heresies. Seabury Press. p. 35.

Murphy, R. C. "Reverend Peale's Panacea". Nation. **180**: 398–400 – via EBSCO.1913-2007.,

Meyer, Donald. "The Confidence Man". New Republic. **133**: 8–10 – via EBSCO.

Meyer, Donald (1980). The Positive Thinkers: Religion as Pop Psychology, from Mary Baker Eddy to Oral Roberts (1st Pantheon ed.). New York: Pantheon Books. p. 261. ISBN 9780307828231. OCLC 569523574.

"Norman Vincent Peale Books - Biography and List of Works - Author of 'A Guide To Confident Living'". www.biblio.com. Retrieved 2018-04-17.

Staff, From Times; Reports, Wire (2008-02-08). "Pastor's Wife Co-founded Guideposts". Los Angeles Times. ISSN 0458-3035. Retrieved 2018-04-17.

The Power of Positive Thinking. 2003-03-12. ISBN 9780743234801.

"Trump Crowd Size Estimate May Involve 'The Power of Positive Thinking'". NPR.org. Retrieved 2018-04-17.

Seligman, Martin E. Authentic Happiness: Using the New Positive Psychology to Realize Your Potential for Lasting Fulfillment (First Free Press trade paperback ed.). New York. p. 96. ISBN 9780743247887. OCLC 893679602.

Scientific Research Methodology : *Concepts and Quality*
***Edited by:* and Dr. Pawan Kumar 'Bharti' and Dr. Prasann Kumar**
ISBN: 978-93-86841-95-7
***Edition:* 2019**
***Published by:* Discovery Publishing House Pvt. Ltd., New Delhi (India)**

6 Lab Practices in Environmental Engineering

[1]Prasann Kumar and [2]Shweta Pathak

ABSTARCT

Environmental engineering system is the branch of engineering concerned with the application of scientific and engineering principles for protection of human populations from the effects of adverse environmental factors; protection of environments, both local and global, from potentially deleterious effects of natural and human activities; and improvement of environmental quality. Environmental engineering system can also be described as a branch of applied science and technology that addresses the issues of energy preservation, protection of assets and control of waste from human and animal activities. Furthermore, it is concerned with finding plausible solutions in the field of public health, such as waterborne diseases, implementing laws which promote adequate sanitation in urban, rural and recreational areas. It involves waste water management, air pollution control, recycling, waste disposal, radiation protection, industrial hygiene, animal agriculture, environmental sustainability, public health and environmental engineering law. It also includes studies on the environmental impact of proposed construction projects.

Keywords: Agriculture, Branch, Cadmium, Environment, Forage, Gap.

Introduction

- **Definition**: GLP embodies a set of principles that provides a framework within which laboratory studies are planned performed, monitored, reported and archived.
- GLP is sometimes confused with the standards of laboratory safety like wearing safety goggles and lab coats.

Need for Global Practices

- In the early 70's FDA became aware of cases of poor laboratory practice all over the United States (figure 6.1).

[1] Department of Agronomy, School of Agriculture, Lovely Professional University, Jalandhar, Punjab, 144411, India

[2] Department of Plant Physiology, I.Ag. Sci., BHU., Varanasi, 221005, U.P., India

- FDA decided to do an in-depth investigation on 40 toxicology labs.
- They discovered a lot fraudulent activities and a lot of poor lab practices.
- Examples of some of these poor lab practices found were
  1. Equipment not been calibrated to standard form, therefore giving wrong measurements.
  2. Incorrect/inaccurate accounts of the actual lab study
  3. Inadequate test systems

Fig. 6.1: Global Practices in Lab
(Source: Based on review of literature, 2018)

- One of the labs that went under such an investigation made headline news.
- The name of the Lab was Industrial Bio Test. This was a big lab that ran tests for big companies such as Procter and Gamble.

Fig. 6.2: Examples related to experiments
(Source: Based on review of literature, 2018)

- It was discovered that mice that they had used to test cosmetics such as lotion and deodorants had developed cancer and died.
- Industrial Bio Test lab threw the dead mice and covered results deeming the products good for human consumption.
- Those involved in production, distribution and sales for the lab eventually served jail time.

Standard Operating Procedures (SOP)

- Written procedures for a laboratories program
- They define how to carry out protocol-specified activities
- Most often written in a chronological listing of action steps
- They are written to explain how the procedures are suppose to work
- Routine inspection, cleaning, maintenance, testing and calibration
- Actions to be taken in response to equipment failure.
- Analytical methods
- Definition of raw data
- Keeping records, reporting, storage, mixing, and retrieval of data

Important Questions to be Answered for Any Analytical Instrument

- What is the equipment being used for (Figure 6.3)?
- Is the instrument within specification and is the documentation to prove this available?
- If the instrument is not within specifications, how much does it deviate by?
- If the instrument is not within specifications what action has been taken to overcome the defect?
- Can the standards used to test and calibrate the instrument be traced back to national standards?

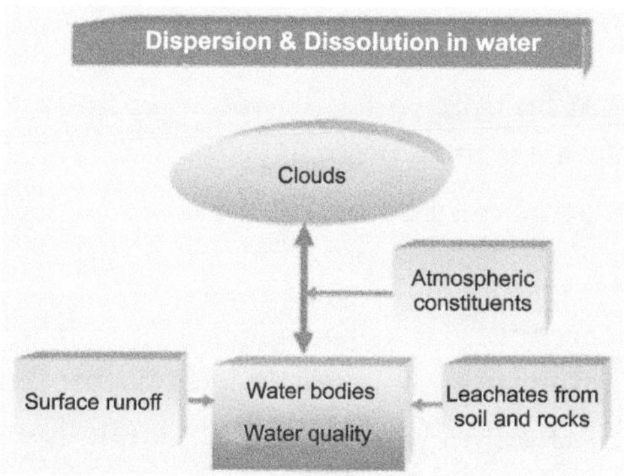

Fig. 6.3: Dispersion & Dissolution in water

(Source: Based on review of literature, 2018)

VARIOUS TECHNIQUES

Titrimetric Methods of Analysis

Volumetric analysis refers to a collection of methods in which the volume of a solution of accurately known concentration, the standard solution, required to react quantitatively with the analyte is determined. The process is known as titration. Standard solution is generally added from the burette (but not always).

- The solution in the burette is termed the titrant.
- Equivalence point is the point at which the analyte is totally consumed.
- Endpoint is where there is an observable change in the system such as colour change of an indicator. This point should be very close to the equivalence point.
- As a general rule the volume of titrant should be within 15-30 ml. Less than this volume introduces considerable relative errors and more than this volume is time and chemical consuming.

Advantages and Disadvantages of Titrimetric Analysis

Time

- Requires a standardisation step to obtain the exactly known concentration of the standard solution.
- Individual titration is generally rapid and should be completed within 10 minutes, excluding sample preparation.

Sensitivity

- Requires fairly concentrated samples to be successful. Generally limited to a lower level of 0.001M and an upper level of 0.5M.

Accuracy

- Is dependent on the accuracy of the standard solution.
- Also dependent on the availability of an endpoint determination close to the equivalence point.
- Can obtain accuracies of better than 1%.

Specificity

- NaOH will react with all acidic species..... it is unable to differentiate between a combination of acidic species within the one sample.
- Removal of most interferents is well documented.
- Specificity can be increased by altering the method ......EDTA can be made specific for calcium and magnesium by adjusting the pH.

Cost

- Relatively cost effective in terms of equipment for general titration with indicator endpoints.
- Costs are increased if an electrical means of endpoint detection is required.

GRAVEMETRIC ANALYSIS

Definition

Gravimetric analysis describes a set of methods in analytical chemistry for the quantitative determination of an analyte based on the mass of a solid. For instance, the measurement of solids suspended in a water sample: A known volume of water is filtered, and the collected solids are weighed.

Principle

The principle behind the gravimetric analysis is that the mass of an ion in a pure compound and can be determined. Later, used to find the mass percent of the same ion in a known quantity of an impure compound.

Types of Gravimetric Analysis

There are 4 fundamental types of gravimetric analysis. Of which, there are 2 common types of gravimetric analysis involving changes in the phase of the analyte to separate it from the rest of a mixture, resulting in a change in mass.

Volatilization Gravimetry

Volatilization Gravimetry involves separating components of our mixture by heating or chemically decomposing the sample.

Precipitation Gravimetry

Precipitation Gravimetry uses a precipitation reaction to separate one or more parts of a solution by incorporating it into a solid.

Electrogravimetry

Electrogravimetry is a method used to separate and quantify ions of a substance, usually a metal.

Thermogravimetric

Thermogravimetric is a method of thermal analysis in which changes in physical and chemical properties of materials are measured as a function of increasing temperature or as a function of time.

Steps Followed in Gravimetric Analysis

- Preparation of a solution containing a known weight of the sample.
- Separation of the desired constituent.
- Weighing the isolated constituent.

- Computation of the amount of the particular constituent in the sample from the observed weight of the isolated substance.

Advantages of Gravimetric Analysis

If methods of gravimetric analysis are followed carefully, it provides exceedingly precise analysis. The gravimetric analysis is used to determine the atomic masses of many elements to six-figure accuracy. It provides a little room for instrumental error and does not require a series of standards for calculation of an unknown.

Disadvantages of Gravimetric Analysis

Gravimetric analysis usually provides only for the analysis of a single element, or a limited group of elements, at a time. Comparing modern dynamic flash combustion coupled with gas chromatography with traditional combustion analysis.

VARIOUS INSTRUMENTS AND THEIR WORKING PRINCIPLE

The pH electrode used in the pH measurement is a combined glass electrode. It consists of sensing half cell and reference half cell, together form an electrode system. The sensing half cell is a thin pH sensitive semi permeable membrane, separating two solutions, viz., the outer solution, the sample to be analyzed and the internal solution, enclosed inside the glass membrane and has a known pH value. An electrical potential is developed inside and another electrical potential is developed outside, the difference in the potential is measured and is given as the pH of the sample.

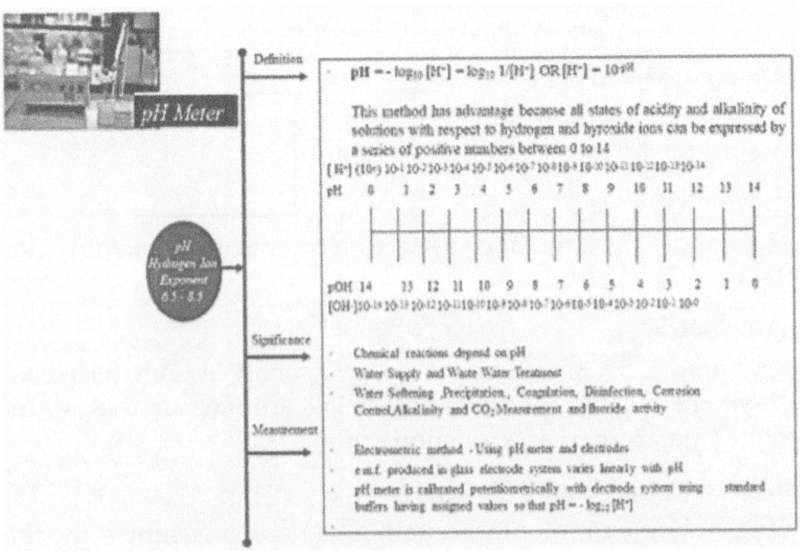

Fig. 6.4: pH meter and their use for measurement

(Source: Based on Review of Literature, 2018)

Conductivity is measured with a probe and a meter. A voltage is applied between the two electrodes in the probe immersed in the sample water. The drop in voltage caused by the resistance of the water is used to calculate the conductivity per centimeter.

Conductivity (G), the inverse of resistivity (R) is determined from the voltage and current values according to Ohm's law. i.e. R=V/I then, g=1/R=I/V.

The meter converts the proble measurement to micro mhos per centimeter and displays the result for the user.

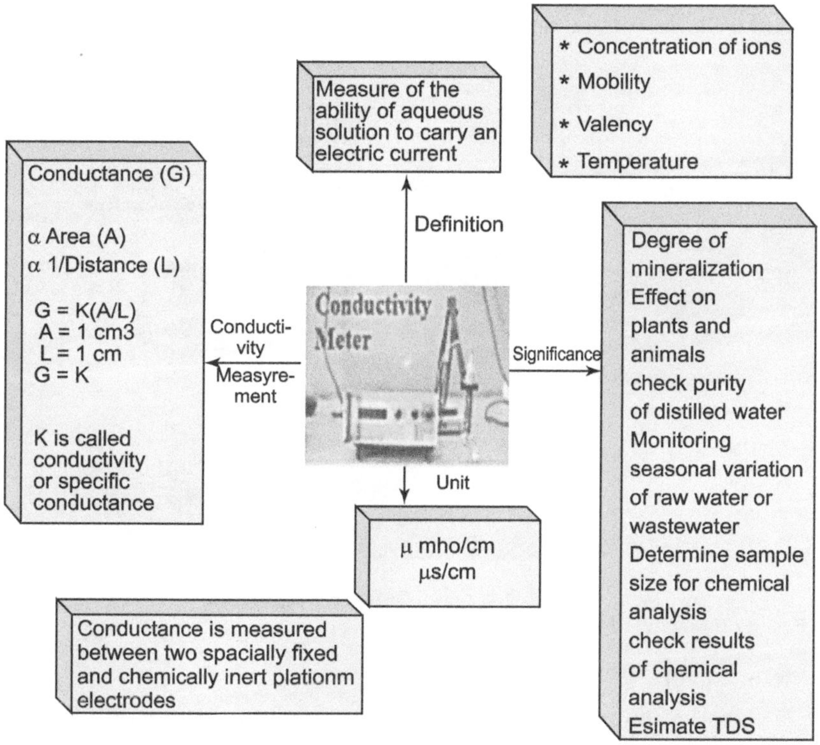

Fig. 6.4a: Conductivity meters

(Source: Based on review of literature, 2018)

NEPHLOTURBIDITY METER

- Nephelometry and Turbidimetry are used for continuous monitoring of air and water pollution. In water, turbidity is monitored whereas in air, smoke and dust are monitored.
- In nephelometry, light is passed through the sample solution (suspended particles) directly and the amount of scattered radiation is measured generally at 90°C.

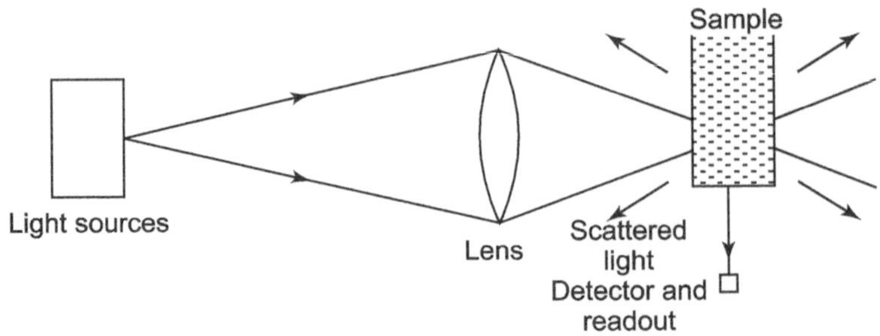

Fig. 6.5: Mechanism of Nephelometry

(Source: Based on Review of Literature, 2018)

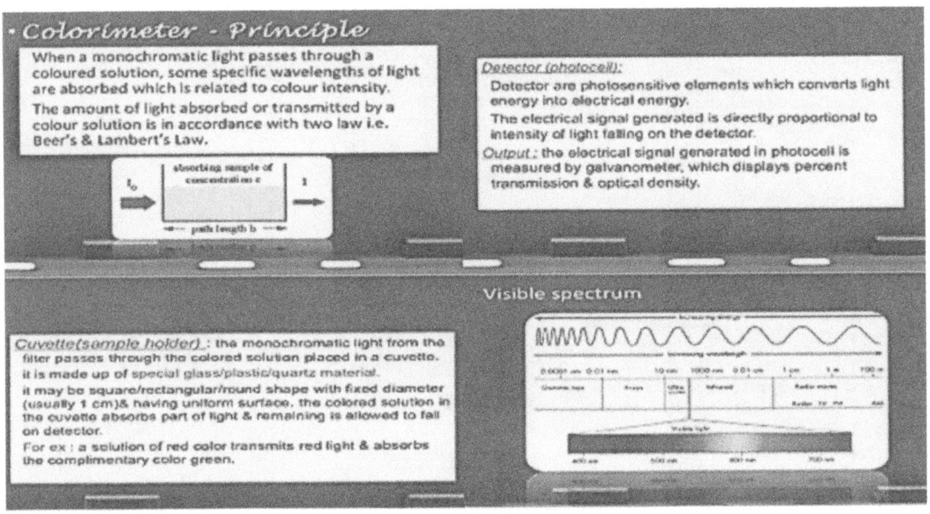

Fig. 6.6: Calorimetry principle

(Source: Based on Review of Literature, 2018)

Sound Meter Level

- A sound level meter is an instrument designed to respond to sound in approximately by the same way as the human ear and to give objective, reproducible measurements of sound pressure level. There are many different sound measuring systems available. Although different in detail, each system consists of a microphone, a processing section and a read-out unit.
- The read-out unit displays the sound level in dB, or some other derived unit such as dB(A) (which means that the measured sound level has been A-weighted). The signal may also be available at output sockets, in either AC or DC form, for connection to external instruments such as level or tape recorders to provide a record and/or for further processing.

- Sound level meters should be calibrated in order to provide precise and accurate results. This is best done by placing a portable acoustic calibrator, such as a sound level calibrator or a Piston Phone, directly over the microphone.

Fig. 6.7: Sound meter level
(Source: Based on Review of Literature, 2018)

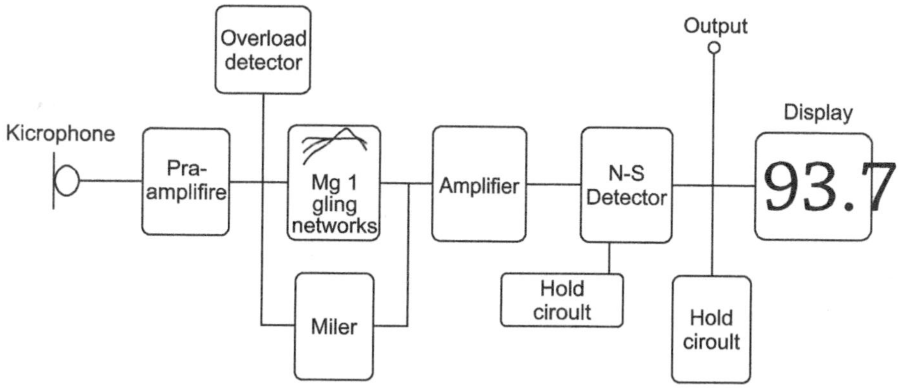

Fig. 6.8: Schematic diagram of Sound Level Meter
(Source: Based on Revie of literature, 2018)

High Volume Sampler

- High volume air samplers typically sample more than 1500 cubic metres (m^3) of air over a 24-hour period.

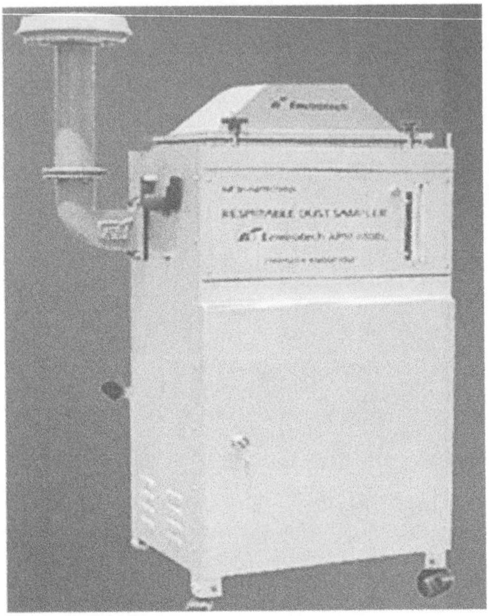

Fig. 6.9: High volume sampler
(Source: Based on review of Literature, 2018)

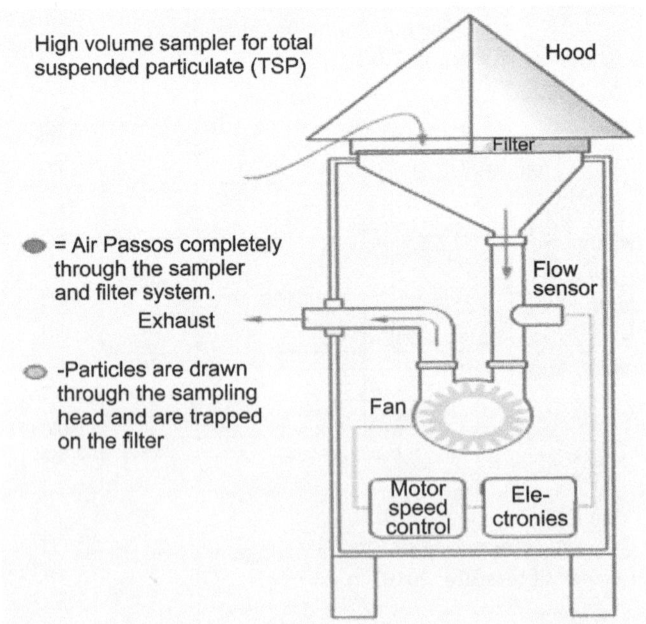

Fig. 6.10: High volume sampler for total suspended particulates
(Source: Based on review of Literature, 2018)

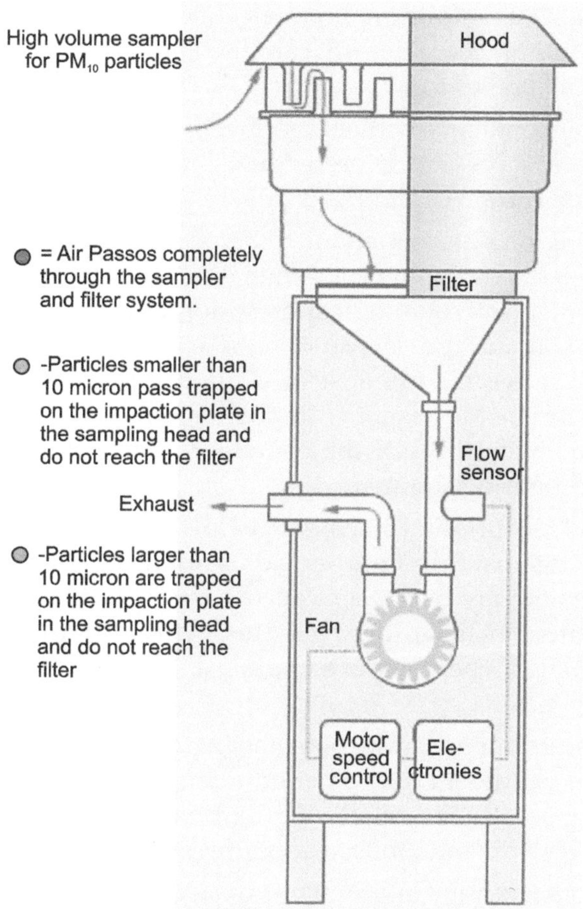

Fig. 6.11: High volume sampler for PM_{10} Particles
(Source: Based on Review of Literature, 2018)

Collection & Preservation of Samples

The objective of sampling is to collect representative sample. Representative sample by means a sample in which relative proportions or concentration of all pertinent components will be the same as in the material being sampled. Moreover, the same sample will be handled in such a way that no significant changes in composition occur before the tests are made. The sample volume shall optimally be small enough that it can be transported and large enough for analytical purposes.

General Requirements

- Obtain a sample that meets the requirements of the sampling program and handle it so that it does not deteriorate or become contaminated before it is analyzed.

- Ensure that all sampling equipment is clean and quality-assured before use. Use sample containers that are clean and free of contaminants. Bake at 450°C all bottles to be used for organic analysis sampling.
- Fill sample containers without prerinsing with sample; prerinsing results in loss of any pre-added preservative and sometimes can bias results high when certain components adhere to the sides of the container.
- Depending on determinations to be performed, fill the container full (most organic compound determinations) or leave space for aeration, mixing, etc. (microbiological and inorganic analyses). If the bottle already contains preservative, take care not to overfill the bottle, as preservative may be lost or diluted. Except when sampling for analysis of volatile organic compounds, leave an air space equivalent to approximately 1% of the container volume to allow for thermal expansion during shipment.
- Special precautions (discussed below) are necessary for samples containing organic compounds and trace metals. Since many constituents may be present at low concentrations (micro-grams or nanograms per liter), they may be totally or partially lost or easily contaminated when proper sampling and preservation procedures are not followed.
- Composite samples can be obtained by collecting over a period of time, or at many different over a period of time, depth, or at many different sampling points. The details of collection vary with local conditions, so specific recommendations are not universally applicable.
- Sometimes it is more informative to analyze numerous separate samples instead of one composite so that variability, maxima and minima can be determined.
- Because of the inherent instability of certain properties and compounds, composite sampling for some analytes is not recommended where quantitative values are desired (examples in-residual, iodine, hexavalent chromium, nitrate, volatile organic compounds, radon-222, dissolved oxygen, ozone, temperature, and pH). In certain cases, such as for BOD, composite samples are routinely by regulatory agencies. Refrigerate composite samples for BOD and nitrite.
- Important factors affecting results are the presence of suspended matter or turbidity, the method chosen for removing a sample from its container, and the physical and chemical brought about by storage or aeration. Detailed procedures are essential when processing (blending, sieving, filtering) samples to be analyzed for trace constituents, especially metals and organic compounds.

- For metals it often is appropriate to collect both a filtered and an unfiltered sample to differentiate between total and dissolved metals present in the matrix. Be aware that some metals may partially sorb to filters. Beforehand, determine the acid requirements to bring the pH to <2 on a separate sample. Add the same relative amount of acid to all samples; use ultrapure acid preservative to prevent contamination. When filtered samples are to be collected, filter them, if possible, in the field, or at the point of collection before preservation with acid. Filter samples in a laboratory-controlled environment if field conditions could cause error or contamination; in this case filter as soon as possible.

Record of Sample

- General information

  Sample identification number, Location, Sample collector

  Date and hour

  Sample type (Grab or composite)
- Specific information

  Water temperature, Weather, Stream blow, Water level

  Any other information
- The information may be attached tag, labeling or writing on container with water proof ink.

  Description of sampling points, by map using landmarks

Use Global Positioning System

- When samples are collected from a river or stream, observed results may vary with depth, stream flow and distance from each shore.
- Selection of the number and distribution of sites at which samples should be collected depends on study objectives, stream characteristics, available equipment and other factors.
- If equipment is available, take an integrated sample form top to bottom in the middle of the main channel of the steam or from side to side at mid-depth. If only grab or catch samples can be collected, preferably take them at various points of equal distance across the steam; if only one sample can be collected, take it in the middle of the main channel of the stream and at mid-depth.
- Rivers, streams, lakes, and reservoirs are subject to considerable variations from normal causes such as seasonal stratification, diurnal variations, rainfall, runoff and wind.
- Choose location, depth and frequency of sampling depending on local conditions and the purpose of the investigation.
- Avoid areas of excessive turbulence because of potential loss of volatile constituents and of potential presence of denser-than-air-toxic vapors.

Water Quality Measurement

To measure concentration of the constituents in quantity for characterisation of water for different uses:

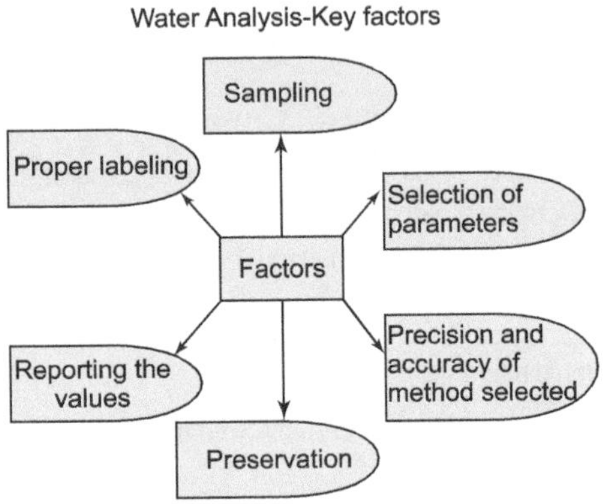

Fig. 6.12: Water analysis- key factors

(Source: Based on review of literature, 2018)

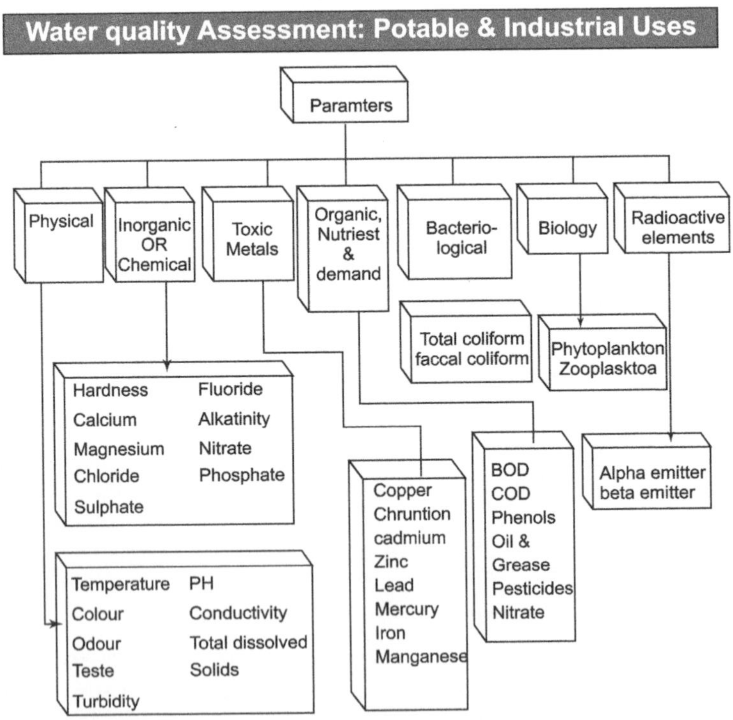

Fig. 6.13: Water quality Assessment: Potable & Industrial uses

(Source: Based on review of literature, 2018)

- Of the various parameters in potable water few are objectionable even when present in very small quantity.

- Others if only present in unusual quantities as to relegate the water from the potable to the unusable class.
- The analyst familiar with water quality characterisation will often select parameters to be measured based on experience and intuition.

Water quality consideration

- Irrigation
  - ➢ pH
  - ➢ Conductivity
  - ➢ Sodium &Potassium
  - ➢ Nutrients
  - ➢ Specific compounds
- Industries
  - ➢ As per specific requirement
  - ➢ Domestic Consumption
  - ➢ As per BIS Standards
  - ➢ Water Bodies
  - ➢ As per CPCB guidelines

Table 6.1: Classification of Inland Surface Water

S. No.	Characteristics	A'	B'	C'	D'	E'
1.	Dissolved Oxygen, mg/L, Min	6	5	4	4	-
2.	Biochemical Oxygen Demand, mg/L, Max	2	3	3	-	-
3.	Total Coliform Organisms*, MPN/100 mL, Max	50	500	5000	-	-
4.	Total Dissolved Solids, mg/L, Max	500	-	1500	-	2100
5.	Chlorides (as Cl), mg/L, Max	250	-	600	-	600
6.	Colour, Hazen Units, Max	10	300	300	-	-
7.	Sodium Absorption Ratio, Max	-	-	-	-	26
8.	Boron (as B), mg/L, Max	-	-	-	-	2
9.	Sulphates (as SO_4), mg/L, Max	400	-	400	-	1000
10.	Nitrates (as NO_3), mg/L, Max	20	-	50	-	-
11.	Free Ammonia (as N), mg/L, Max	-	-	-	1.2	-
12.	Conductivity at 25°C, micromhos/cm, Max	-	-	-	1000	2250
13.	pH value	6.5-8.5	6.5-8.5	6.5-8.5	6.5-8.5	6.5-8.5
14.	Arsenic (as As), mg/L, Max	0.05	0.2	0.2	-	-
15.	Iron (as Fe) , mg/L, Max	0.3	-	50	-	-
16.	Fluorides (as F), mg/L, Max	1.5	1.5	1.5	-	-
17.	Lead (as Pb), mg/L, Max	0.1	-	0.1	-	-
18.	Copper (as Cu), mg/L, Max	1.5	-	1.5	-	-
19.	Zinc (as Zn), mg/L, Max	15	-	15	-	-

(**Source:** Based on review of Literature, 2018)

DISSOLVED OXYGEN

- Dissolved oxygen is important in precipitation and dissolution of inorganic substances in water

Need

- To assess quality of raw water
- To check on pollution
- Determination of biological changes by aerobic or anaerobic organisms
- D.O. is the basis of BOD test to evaluate pollution potential of wastes
- All aerobic biological wastewater treatment processes
- Important factor in corrosion.

Principle

- Oxygen present in sample oxidizes the divalent manganous to its higher valency which precipitates as a brown hydrates oxide after addition of NaOH and KI.
- Upon acidification, manganese revert to divalent state and liberates Iodine from KI equivalent to D.O. content in the sample.
- The liberated Iodine is titrated against standard (N/40) solution of Sodium thio sulphate using starch as an indicator.

Procedure

- Collect sample in BOD bottle
- 2 ml $MnSO_4$+ 2.ml Alkali iodide-azide + closes topper
- Mix well + allow the ppt to settle
- Add 2 ml concentrated H_2SO_4 + mix well till ppt dissolves
- Take 203 ml (Correspond to 200 ml) sample in a conical flask + titrate against Sodium thiosulphate (0.025 N) till pale yellow colour + starch + titrate till blue to colourless

Calculation

- 1 ml of 0.025N $Na_2S_2O_3$ = 0.2 mg of O_2
- D.O. in mg/l = (0.2 × 1000) × ml of thiosulphate 200

  Results : D.O. mg/l

Interferences

- Ferrous ion
- Ferricion
- Nitrite
- Microbialmass
- High suspended solids

Principle

- The BOD test is based upon determinations of dissolved oxygen
- It can be measured directly
- In general, a dilution procedure is applied.

Procedure

Preparation of dilution water

- Aerate the required volume of D.W. by bubbling compressed air for 1-2 days to attain D.O. saturation
- Add 1 ml eachper litre of dilution water Phosphate buffer

Magnesium sulphate

Calcium chloride Ferric chloride

- Mixwell
- In case, waste not expected sufficient bacterial population, add seed (2 ml settle sewage / litre of dilution water)

Determination of D.O.

(*i*) Samples and ii) Blank, on initial and after 5 days

- 2ml $MnSO_4$ + 2 ml Alkali-iodide-azide + stopper immediately
- Mix well + allow the ppt. tosettle
- Add 2 ml concentrated H_2SO_4 + mix well till ppt. dissolve
- Take 203 ml (correspond to 200 ml) sample in a conical flask
- Titrate against sodium thiosulphate (0.025 N) till pale yellow colour + starch solution + blue colour + titrate till colourless

Observations

D_0 = D.O. in sample on 0th day D_1= D.O. in sample on 5th day C_0 = D.O. in Blank on 0th day C_1 = D.O. in Blank on 5th day

$C_0 - C_1$ = D.O. depletion in dilution water alone

$D_0 - D_1$ = D.O. depletion in sample + dilution water $(D_0 - D_1) - (C_0 - C_1)$ = D.O. depletion due to microbes

1 ml of 0.025 N sodium thiosulphate = 0.2 mg of Oxygen

D.O. in mg/l = (0.2 × 1000) × ml of thiosulphate 200

B.O.D. in mg/l $(D_0 - D_1) - (C_0 - C_1)$ mg × Decimal fraction of sample used

Results

B.O.D. 5 days at 20° C = mg/l

Interferences

- Ferrous ion

- Ferricion
- Nitrate
- Microbial mass
- High suspended solids
  - ➢ Lack of nutrients in dilution water
  - ➢ Lack of acclimated seed organisms
  - ➢ Presence of heavy metals
  - ➢ Presence of toxic materials

Bacteria

Single cell microscopic organisms lacking chlorophyll Coliform group

Contamination

- Insanitary condition of surrounding area
- Unhygienic practices
- Discharge/seepage of sewage and domestic waste water

Need

- Impact on water quality
- Potability for human consumption
- To prevent water-borne diseases
- To assess the quality of raw and treated water
- Specially to detect Faecal Contamination

Bacteriological analysis: mainly includes estimation of

- Totalc oliforms
- Faecal coliforms

Approved techniques generally used as per "Standard Methods for the examination of water and wastewater"

- Membrane Filter (MF)
- Multiple Tube Dilution (MTD)

MF-technique Principle

Biochemical reactions are used to detect the various groups of micro-organisms.

MF-technique - Merits

- Results in 24 hours (MTD - 48 to 96 hours)
- Larger volume of samples can be tested (MTD - less volume)

- Results with greater precision (MTD - MPN)
- Require less laboratory space (MTD – More space)
- Easy processing (MTD –Tedious)
- Useful during normal and emergencies (MTD – Difficult in emergencies)

Limitations: Samples with More Turbidity

Coloured water is not acceptable for drinking (Aesthetic as well as toxicity reasons).

Industrial wastewater require colour removal before discharge into water courses.

Definition

- The term colour means true colour that is the colour of water from which turbidity has been removed. True colour of water is due to dissolved material.
- Apparent colour is due to suspended matter as well as due to substances on solution removed by filtration.

Unit for Measurement of Colour

- Unit for colour measurement is based on platinum cobalt scale

Methods for Colour Measurement Visual Comparison Method

- Colour of the sample is determined by visual comparison with known concentration of coloured colutions prepared by diluting stock platinum cobalt solution
- OR properly calibrated glass coloured disk is used for comparison
- This method is useful for potable water and water in which colour is due to naturally occuring materials
- This method is not applicable to most highly coloured industrial waste water

Spectrophotometric Method

- This method is applicable to potable and waste both domestic and industrial.
- In this method light absorbed or transmitted is measured at dominant wavelength of a particular hue of sample.
- Spectrophotometer should have an effective operating range from 400 to 700 nm before measurement remove turbidity either by filtration or by centrifuging Colour hues for dominant wavelengths ranges are.

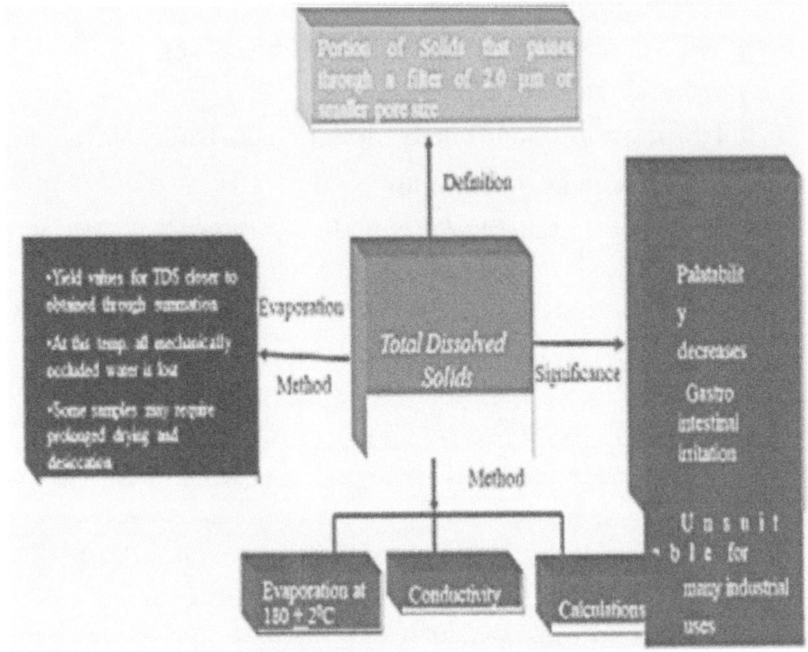

Fig. 6.14: Total dissolved solid

(Source: Based on review of Literature, 2018)

AIR

Sampling Locations

Sampling locations are in general governed by factors like objectives, method of sampling and resources available. If the objective is to study health hazards and material damages, then locations should be kept close to the objects where the effects are being studied and should be kept at breathing level in the population centres, hospitals, schools, etc. For vegetation, it should be at foliage level. For background concentration, sampling location should be away from the sources of pollution. It can also be done by gridding the entire area to get statistically recommended values.

The number of locations however depends upon the variability of concentration over the area under survey. A spot checking may be done to decide the location besides considering practical factors.

Period of Sampling, Frequency and Duration

Period, frequency and duration of sampling should be appropriate to the objectives of the study. It should be such that the measurable quantities are trapped in the sample at the end of the sampling. It is preferable to observe sampling period consistent with the averaging times for which air quality standards of the given pollutants are specified.

NOISE

Site Selection Criteria

Site of an area shall be selected such that it meets the land use pattern as prescribed in the standard e.g. Industrial, Commercial, Residential & Silence Zone.

(A) General: 1. The station should be located at the ambient level i.e. away from the direct source, away from any vibration and any obstruction.

2. Categorize the area with land use pattern.

(B) Specific: Always use tripod stand at above the ground level of 1 to 1.5 m for areas. Hand held monitoring should be avoided.

(C) Case Specific Locations: DG Sets up to 800 kW at about 1 m distances from all sides. DG Sets more than 800 kW at about 1 m distance of acoustic enclosure.

Petrol and Kerosene Gensets Sound power level is measured in anechoic room so as to have segregated noise level.

Fire crackers 4 m from the bursting point, there shouldn't be reflecting surface around 15m radius.

Vehicle 0.5m from the exhaust point.

(D) Positioning of the instrument: Microphone must be placed 1.2 -1.5m above the ground level.

In dry conditions with a wind speed of less than 5 m/s.

Isolate the instrument from strong vibration and shock.

Calibration

- Make sure that the instrument is properly calibrated. Measurements should be accepted as valid only if the calibration level from before and after the noise measurement agrees to within 1.0 dB. The sound level meter and calibrator will hold a current calibration certificate traceable to national standards.
- Start the calibrator and put on 1 KHz frequency calibration on two values 94 dB and 114 dB. If instrument is shows more than ± 0.3 dB differences adjust the calibration. Calibration is done O.K. now instrument is ready for monitoring.

Monitoring time: The monitoring should be carried out minimum 75% of the prescribed Day time (06.00 am to 22.00 pm) and Night time (22.00 pm to 06.00 am).The exercise has to be carried out for 6 to 8 hrs. in the said time frame of day & night. It is always preferable to have large number of data sets thus 1sec sampling frequency is recommended.

Monitoring Parameters: Leq, L10, L90, L50, Lmax, Lmin, (with 1 sec sampling period at all locations).

Monitoring Protocol: The following criteria will be observed when undertaking the noise monitoring:

- During ambient noise monitoring sound comes from more than one direction, it is important to choose a microphone and mounting which gives the best possible Omni directional characteristics;
- The noise measurement equipment will be supervised continuously during the monitoring period and notes will be made of the date, time and prevailing weather conditions;
- Immediately prior to and following each noise measurement session the accuracy of the noise level meter shall be checked using an acoustic calibrator generating a known sound pressure level at a known frequency;
- Noise measurements should not be made in fog and rain;
- A wind shield will be used at all times to prevent interference of reflecting noise;
- As far as is practicable, the pause facility on the noise measurement equipment will be used to exclude extraneous noise (e.g. low flying aircraft and road traffic passing in front of the microphone) so that the results recorded are representative of the site noise. If possible for extraneous noise/other source background noise can be eliminated from final reading by using the following formula:

Lpressure = 10.log [10(Lp/10) – 10(LpBackground/10)]

Monitoring Records

(*i*) The date, time, location and duration of the measurement;

(*ii*) All predominant noise sources will be noted, which may include extraneous noise such as road traffic, aero-planes and other activity;

(*iii*) Weather conditions will be recorded including wind speed and approximate direction, cloud cover, rain and ground frost;

Monitoring Data Submission

The particulars of the measurements recorded by the noise level meter shall be furnished in the monitoring data sheet. A typical flow chart may be adopted for uniformity in the monitoring.

Monitoring Inferences

The monitoring inferences should be drawn on the basis of final data sheet viz. compliance to the specified standard, violation of standard, average Leq, noise intensity L50, L90 etc. and suggest corrective action.

Conclusion

Ever since people first recognized that their health is related to the quality of their environment, they have applied principles to attempt to improve the quality of their environment. The ancient Indian Harappan civilization utilized early sewers in some cities more than 5000 years ago. More specifically, the Indus Valley Civilization (also called the Harappan civilization) had advanced control over the water in their society. The public work structures found at various sites in the area include wells, public baths, storage tanks, a drinking water system, and a city-wide sewage collection system. They also had an early version of a canal irrigation system that was needed for their large scale agriculture. The Romans constructed aqueducts to prevent drought and to create a clean, healthful water supply for the metropolis of Rome. In the 15th century, Bavaria created laws restricting the development and degradation of alpine country that constituted the region's water supply.

REFERENCES

"Architecture and Engineering Occupations: Occupational Outlook Handbook U.S. Bureau of Labor Statistics". Bls.gov. 2012-03-29.

Beychok, Milton R. (1967). Aqueous Wastes from Petroleum and Petrochemical Plants (1st ed.). John Wiley & Sons. LCCN 67019834.

Beychok, M.R. (2005). Fundamentals of Stack Gas Dispersion (4th ed.). Author-published. ISBN 0-9644588-0-2.

Career Information Center. Agribusiness, Environment and Natural Resources (9th ed.). Macmillan Reference. 2007.

Tchobanoglous, G.; Burton, F.L. & Stensel, H.D. (2003). Wastewater Engineering (Treatment Disposal Reuse) / Metcalf & Eddy, Inc (4th ed.). McGraw-Hill Book Company. ISBN 0-07-041878-0.

Turner, D.B. (1994). Workbook of Atmospheric Dispersion Estimates: An Introduction to Dispersion Modeling (2nd ed.). CRC Press. ISBN 1-56670-023-X.

Scientific Research Methodology : *Concepts and Quality*
Edited by: and Dr. Pawan Kumar 'Bharti' and Dr. Prasann Kumar
ISBN: 978-93-86841-95-7
Edition: 2019
Published by: Discovery Publishing House Pvt. Ltd., New Delhi (India)

7

Correlation, Regression and Factor Analysis

Three Dimensional Approach For Statistical Research

[1]Prasann Kumar and [2]Shweta Pathak

GRAPHICAL ABSTRACT

Degree of Correlation (r)

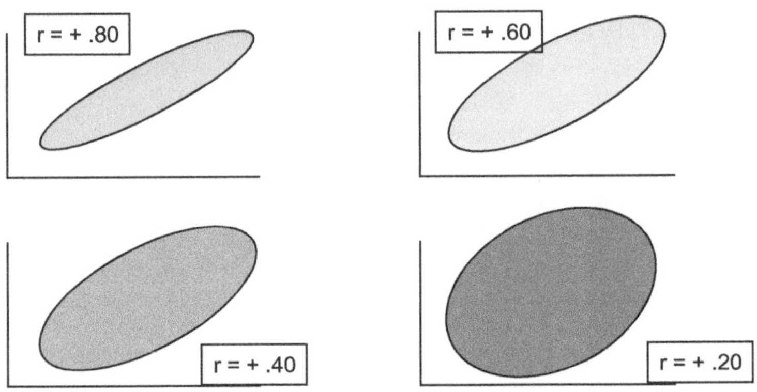

Keywords: Analysis, Correlation, Difference, Factor, Regression

Introduction

Types of correlation

Methods of studying correlation

(*a*) Scatter diagram

(*b*) Karl pearson's coefficient of correlation

(*c*) Spearman's Rank correlation coefficient

(*d*) Method of least squares

- Correlation: The degree of relationship between the variables under consideration is measure through the correlation analysis.

[1] Department of Agronomy, School of Agriculture, Lovely Professional University, Jalandhar, Punjab, 144411, India

[2] Department of Plant Physiology, I.Ag. Sci., BHU., Varanasi, 221005, U.P., India

- The measure of correlation called the correlation coefficient.
- The degree of relationship is expressed by coefficient which range from correlation (–1 d″ r e″ +1)
- The direction of change is indicated by a sign.
- The correlation analysis enable us to have an idea about the degree & direction of the relationship between the two variables under study.
- Correlation is a statistical tool that helps to measure and analyze the degree of relationship between two variables.
- Correlation analysis deals with the association between two or more variables.

Types of Correlation
Type I

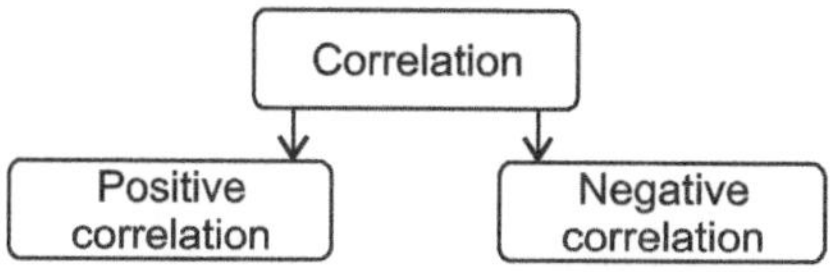

Fig. 7.1: Types of correlation

(Source: based on review of literature, 2018)

Types of Correlation Type I

- **Positive Correlation:** The correlation is said to be positive correlation if the values of two variables changing with same direction.

  Ex. Pub. Exp. & sales, Height & weight.

- **Negative Correlation:** The correlation is said to be negative correlation when the values of variables change with opposite direction.

  Ex. Price & qty. demanded.

Direction of the Correlation

- **Positive relationship** – Variables change in the same direction.
- As X is increasing, Y is increasing
- As X is decreasing, Y is decreasing
- E.g., As height increases, so does weight.
- **Negative relationship** – Variables change in opposite directions.
- As X is increasing, Y is decreasing
- As X is decreasing, Y is increasing
- E.g., As TV time increases, grades decrease

More Examples

- **Positive relationships**
- water consumption and temperature.

- study time and grades.
- **Negative relationships:**
- alcohol consumption and driving ability.
- Price & quantity demanded

Types of Correlation
Type II

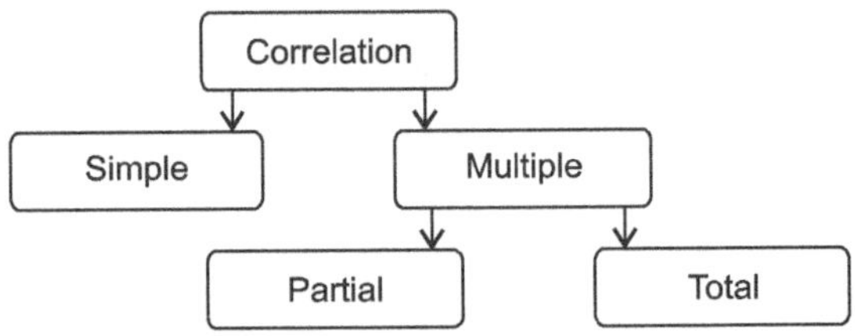

Fig. 7.2: Type of correlation type II

(Source: based on review of literature, 2018)

Types of Correlation Type II

- **Simple correlation:** Under simple correlation problem there are only two variables are studied.
- **Multiple Correlation:** Under Multiple Correlation three or more than three variables are studied. Ex. $Q_d = f(P, P_C, P_S, t, y)$
- **Partial correlation:** analysis recognizes more than two variables but considers only two variables keeping the other constant.
- **Total correlation:** is based on all the relevant variables.

Types of Correlation
Type III

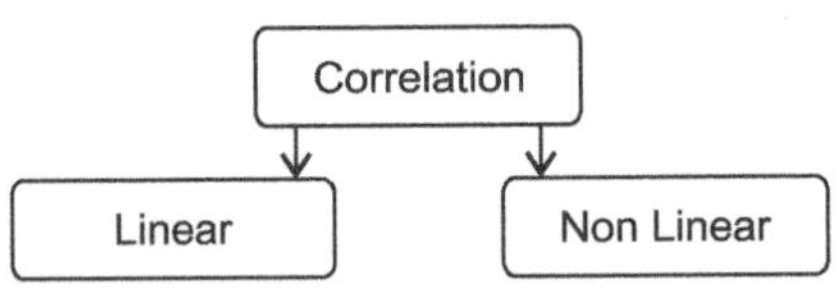

Fig. 7.3: Type of correlation type III

(Source: based on review of literature, 2018)

- **Linear correlation:** Correlation is said to be linear when the amount of change in one variable tends to bear a constant ratio to the amount of change in the other. The graph of the variables having a linear relationship will form a straight line.

  Ex X = 1, 2, 3, 4, 5, 6, 7, 8,

  Y = 5, 7, 9, 11, 13, 15, 17, 19,

  Y = 3 + 2x

- **Non Linear correlation:** The correlation would be non linear if the amount of change in one variable does not bear a constant ratio to the amount of change in the other variable.

Methods of Studying Correlation

- Scatter Diagram Method
- Graphic Method
- Karl Pearson's Coefficient of Correlation
- Method of Least Squares

Scatter Diagram Method

- Scatter Diagram is a graph of observed plotted points where each points represents the values of X&Y as a coordinate. It portrays the relationship between these two variables graphically.

A Perfect Positive Correlation

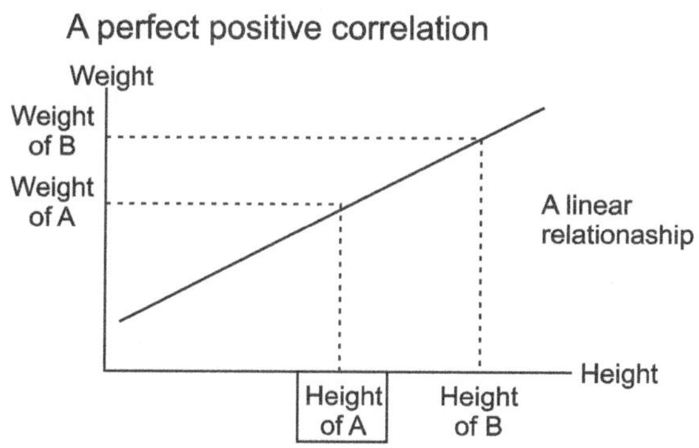

Fig. 7.4: a perfect positive correlation
(Source: based on review of literature, 2018)

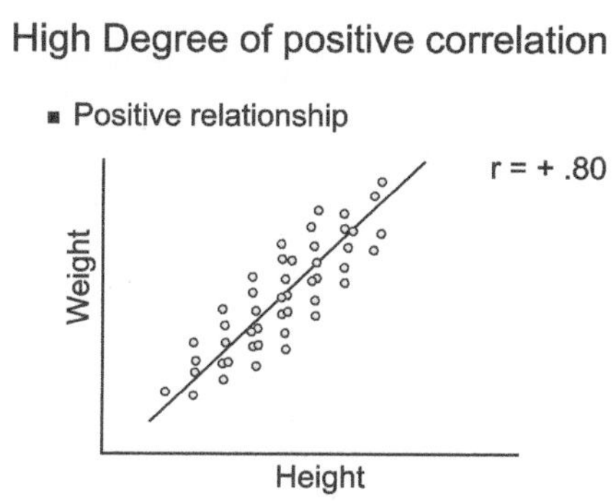

Fig. 7.5: A high degree of positive correlation
(Source: based on review of literature, 2018)

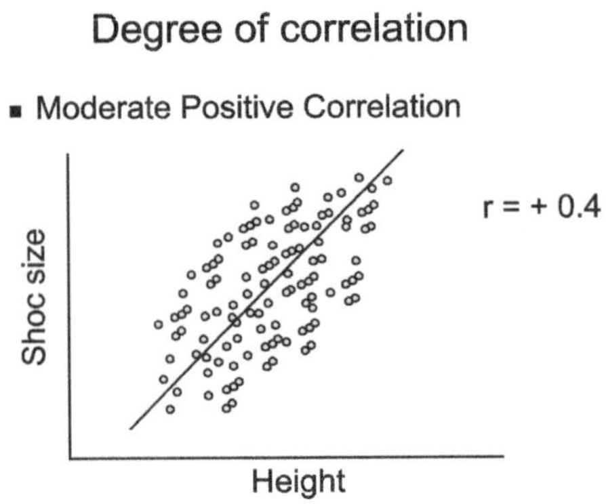

Fig. 7.6: Degree of correlation
(Source: based on review of literature, 2018)

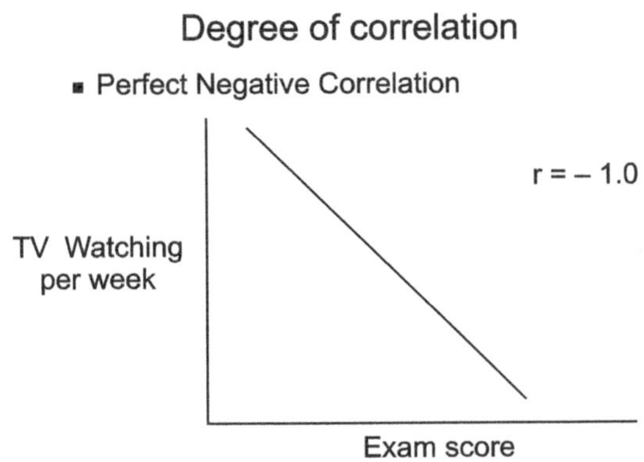

Fig. 7.7: Perfect negative correlation
(Source: based on review of literature, 2018)

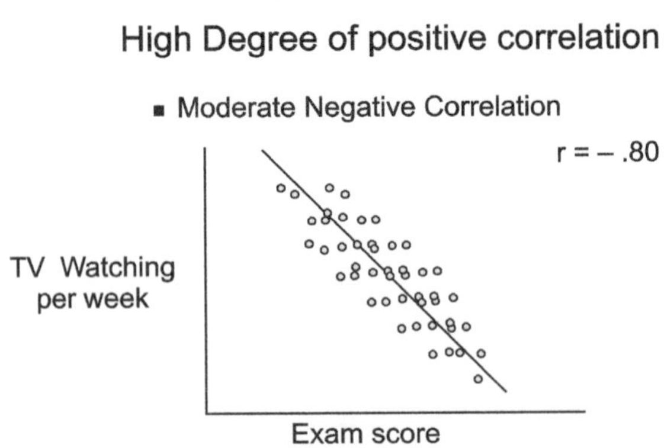

Fig. 7.8: Moderate Negative Correlation
(Source: based on review of literature, 2018)

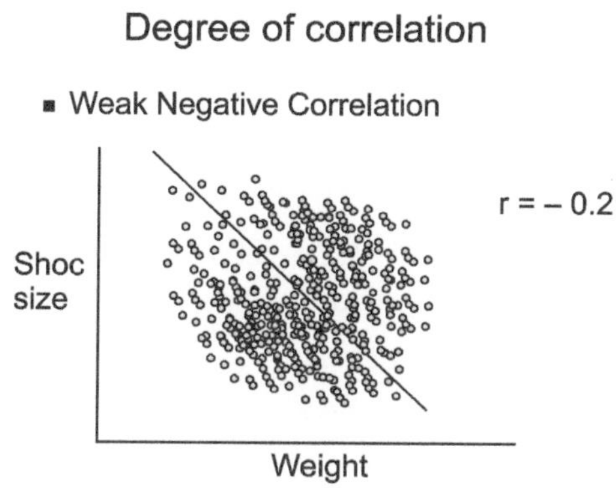

Fig. 7.9: Weak negative correlation
(Source: Based on review of literature, 2018)

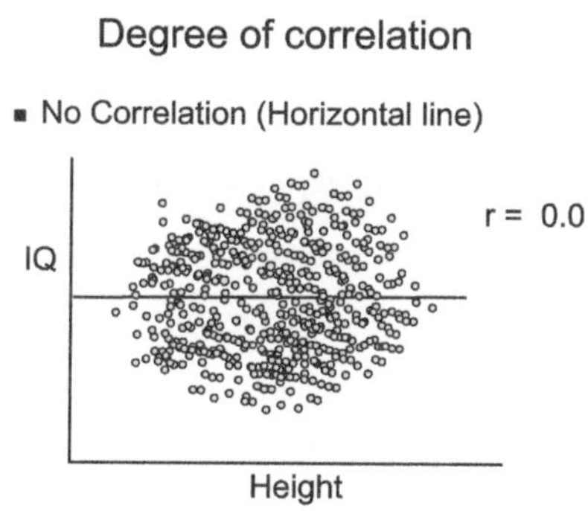

Fig. 7.10. No correlation
(Source: based on review of literature, 2018)

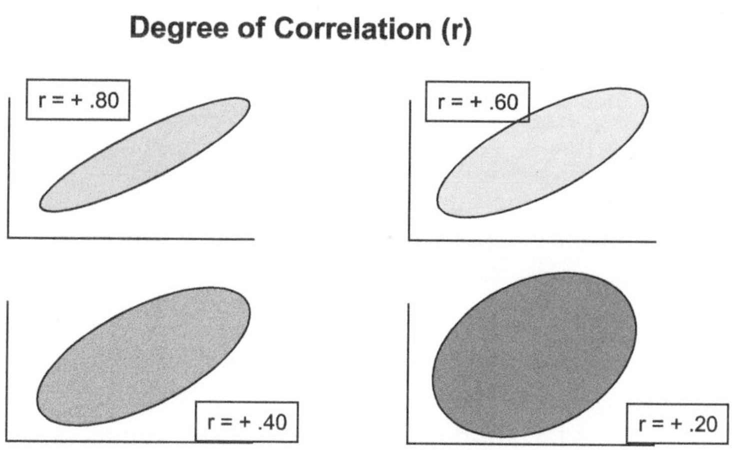

Fig. 7.11: Degree of correlation
(Source: based on review of literature, 2018)

Direction of the Relationship

- **Positive relationship** – Variables change in the same direction.
- As X is increasing, Y is increasing
- As X is decreasing, Y is decreasing
- E.g., As height increases, so does weight.
- **Negative relationship** – Variables change in opposite directions.
- As X is increasing, Y is decreasing
- As X is decreasing, Y is increasing
- E.g., As TV time increases, grades decrease

Karl Pearson's Coefficient of Correlation

- Pearson's '*r*' is the most common correlation coefficient.
- Karl Pearson's Coefficient of Correlation denoted by - '*r*' The coefficient of correlation '*r*' measure the degree of linear relationship between two variables say *x* & *y*.
- Karl Pearson's Coefficient of Correlation denoted by – r $-1 \leq r \geq +1$
- Degree of Correlation is expressed by a value of Coefficient
- Direction of change is Indicated by sign (– ve) or (+ ve)

Karl Pearson's
Coefficient of Correlation

When deviation taken from actual mean:

$r(x, y) = \Sigma xy / \sqrt{\Sigma x^2 \, \Sigma y^2}$

When deviation taken from an assumed mean :

$$r = \frac{n\Sigma dxdy - \Sigma dx \, \Sigma dy}{\sqrt{N\Sigma dx^2 - (\Delta dx)^2} \, \sqrt{N\,\Sigma dy^2 - (\Sigma dy)^2}}$$

Fig. 7.12: Karl Pearson's Coefficient of Correlation
(Source: Based on review of literature, 2018)

Procedure for Computing the Correlation Coefficient

- Calculate the mean of the two series '*x*' &'*y*'
- Calculate the deviations '*x*' & '*y*' in two series from their respective mean.
- Square each deviation of '*x*' & '*y*' then obtain the sum of the squared deviation i.e. "*x*" & . "*y*"
- Multiply each deviation under *x* with each deviation under *y* & obtain the product of '*xy*'. Then obtain the sum of the product of *x*, *y* i.e. "*xy*"
- Substitute the value in the formula.

Interpretation of Correlation Coefficient (r)

- The value of correlation coefficient 'r' ranges from –1 to +1
- If $r = +1$, then the correlation between the two variables is said to be perfect and positive
- If $r = -1$, then the correlation between the two variables is said to be perfect and negative
- If $r = 0$, then there exists no correlation between the variables

Assumptions of Pearson's Correlation Coefficient

- There is linear relationship between two variables, i.e. when the two variables are plotted on a scatter diagram a straight line will be formed by the points.
- Cause and effect relation exists between different forces operating on the item of the two variable series.

Spearman's Rank Coefficient of Correlation

- When statistical series in which the variables under study are not capable of quantitative measurement but can be arranged in serial order, in such situation pearson's correlation coefficient can not be used in such case Spearman Rank correlation can be used.
- $\mathbf{R = 1 - (6 \sum D^2) / N (N^2 - 1)}$
- R = Rank correlation coefficient
- D = Difference of rank between paired item in two series.
- N = Total number of observation.

Interpretation of Rank Correlation Coefficient (R)

- The value of rank correlation coefficient, R ranges from –1 to +1
- If R = +1, then there is complete agreement in the order of the ranks and the ranks are in the same direction
- If R = -1, then there is complete agreement in the order of the ranks and the ranks are in the opposite direction
- If R = 0, then there is no correlation

Rank Correlation Coefficient (R)

(*a*) Problems where actual rank are given.

1. Calculate the difference 'D' of two Ranks i.e. (R1 – R2).
2. Square the difference & calculate the sum of the difference i.e. $\sum D^2$
3. Substitute the values obtained in the formula.

(*b*) Problems where Ranks are not given: If the ranks are not given, then we need to assign ranks to the data series. The lowest value in the series can be assigned rank 1 or the highest value in the series can be assigned rank 1. We need to follow the same scheme of ranking for the other series. Then calculate the rank correlation coefficient in similar way as we do when the ranks are given.

Regression Analysis

- Regression Analysis is another technique for measuring the linear association between a dependent and an independent variables.
- Although simple regression and correlation are mathematically equivalent, regression is a dependence technique and correlation is an interdependence technique.
- A dependence technique makes a distinction between dependent and independent variables.
- An interdepence technique is simply concerned with how variables are related to one another.

Computing Composite Variables

- DATASET ACTIVATE DataSet1.
  COMPUTE Postsale customer service = $x9 + x18 + x16 / 3$.
  EXECUTE.
- COMPUTE Marketing = $x12 + x7 + x10 / 3$.
  EXECUTE.
- COMPUTE Techical support = $x8 + x14 / 2$.
  EXECUTE.
- COMPUTE Product value = $x6 + (11 - x13) / 2$.
  EXECUTE.

Description of HBAT Primary Database Variables

Variable	Description	Variable Type
Data Warehouse Classification Variables		
X1	Customer Type	nonmetric
X2	Industry Type	nonmetric
X3	Firm Size	nonmetric
X4	Region	nonmetric
X5	Distribution System	nonmetric
Performance Perceptions Variables		
X6	Product Quality	metric
X7	E-Commerce Activities/Website	metric
X8	Technical Support	metric
X9	Complaint Resolution	metric
X10	Advertising	metric
X11	Product Line	metric
X12	Salesforce Image	metric
X13	Competitive Pricing	metric
X14	Warranty & Claims	metric
X15	New Products	metric
X16	Ordering & Billing	metric
X17	Price Flexibility	metric
X18	Delivery Speed	metric
Outcome/Relationship Measures		
X19	Satisfaction	metric
X20	Likelihood of Recommendation	metric
X21	Likelihood of Future Purchase	metric
X22	Current Purchase/Usage Level	metric
X23	Consider Strategic Alliance/Partnership in Future	nonmetric

Fig. 7.13: HBAT Primary data base variables

(Source: based on review of literature, 2018)

Regression Analysis: Overview

- Tool: *What does it do?*
- An extension of a correlation analysis, focusing on the relationship between one Dependent Variable (DV) and one or more Independent Variables (IV's).
- How does the typical value of the DV change when any one of the IV varies, while the other IV are held fixed?

$$Y = a + b_1X_1 + b_2X_2 + b_3X_3 + \dots + E$$

All variables have to be normally distributed variables

- Use: *what problems can it solve?*
- Widely used for prediction and forecasting

Analysis of HBAT Data: Illustration

- Data
- Market segmentation study: newsprint & magazine
- Customer survey data

Customer Satisfaction (X19) - DV

- Four summated scales developed from factor analysis
- Customer Service (IV)
- Marketing (IV)
- Technical Support (IV)
- Product Value (IV)

Application

- Establish relationship among the dependent and independent variables
- Check the assumptions of running the regression analysis
- Establish the degree of the relationship among the variables

Stages 1 & 2: Objectives and Design

- Problem
- Want to use all the four factors emerged from factor analysis.
- Design
- Developed the summated scale for each of the factor.
- Customer Satisfaction (X19) is Selected as Dependent Variable.
- Post Sale Customer Service (IV), Marketing (IV), Technical Support (IV) and Product Value (IV) are selected as Independent Variables.

Stage 3: Checking Assumptions

Key Assumptions & Rationale

- To check variables are suitable for regression analysis, two steps are required to be tested
- Testing the individual dependent and independent variables
- Testing the overall relationship after model estimation.
- Three assumptions to be addressed are:
- Linearity
- Constant Variance (Homoscedasticity)
- Normality

Strength of Relationship

- Check the correlation between the variables
- What is the difference between Spearman and Pearson Correlations? And Which one you should choose?
- Depends upon type of data you have (Importance of knowing data).
- Peasrson is used when variables are approximately normally distributed.
- For ordinal or assumption of normality are markedly violated use Spearman.

Stage 3: Checking Assumptions

Correlations

		X19 - Satisfaction	ProductValue	Postsalecustomersenvice	Marketing	Technical support
Pearson Correlation	X19 - Satisfaction	1.000	.503	.633	.456	.223
	ProductValue	.503	1.000	.093	-.146	.108
	Postsalecustomersenvice	.633	.093	1.000	.294	.163
	Marketing	.456	-.146	.294	1.000	.084
	Technical support	.223	.108	.163	.084	1.000

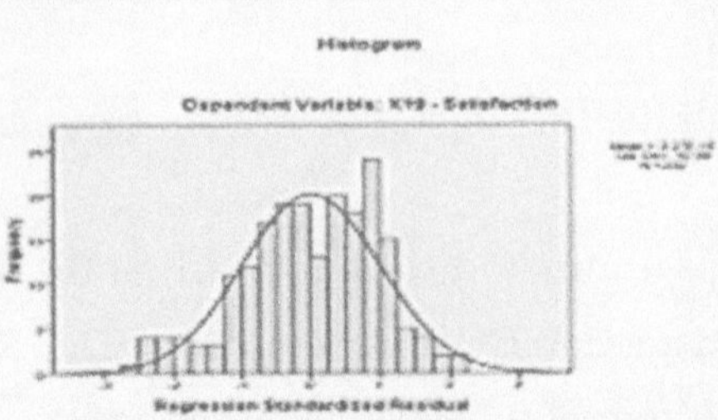

Fig. 7.14: Checking assumption

(Source: based on review of literature, 2018)

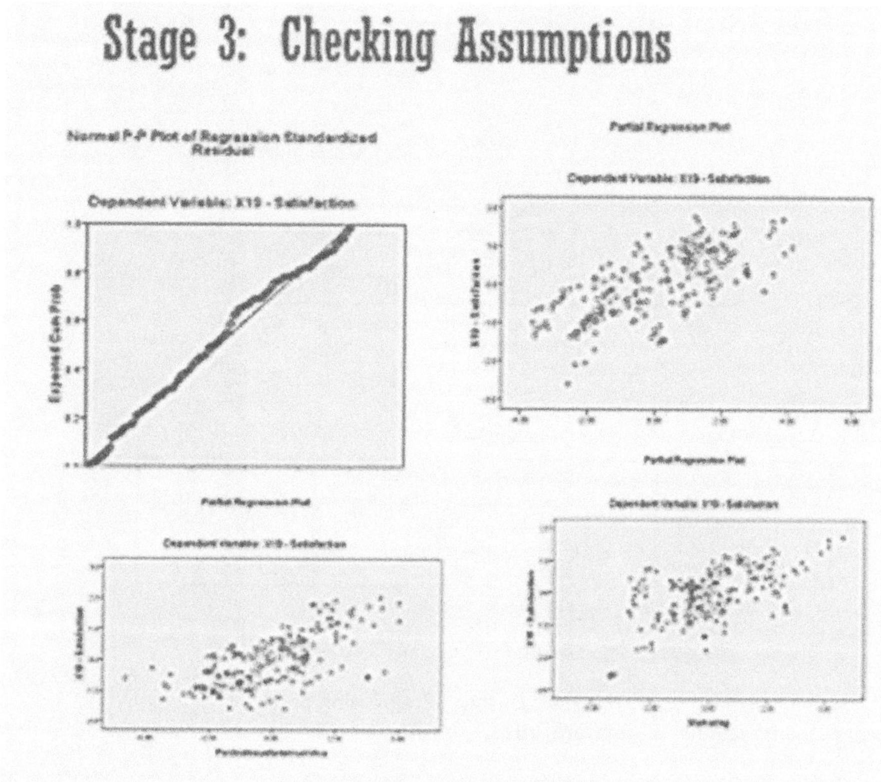

Fig. 7.15: Checking assumptions

(Source: based on review of literature, 2018)

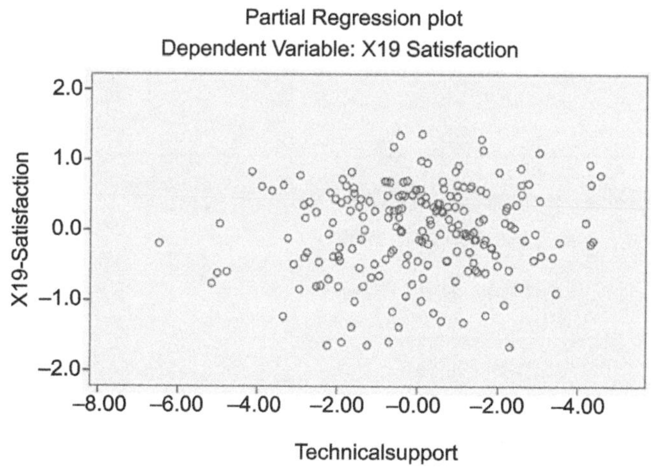

Fig. 7.16: Partial regression plot

(Source: based on review of literature, 2018)

Stage 4: Output

Adjusted R^2: Percentage of variance explained in the DV by all IV's

Model Summary[b]

Model	R	R Square	Adjusted R Square	Std. Error of the Estimate
1	.861[a]	.741	.735	.6386

a. Predictors: (Constant), Technicalsupport, Marketing, ProductValue, Postsalecustomerservice

b. Dependent Variable: X19 - Satisfaction

Is the regression model significant (can be usefully interpreted)?

ANOVA[b]

Model		Sum of Squares	df	Mean Square	F	Sig.
1	Regression	227.025	4	56.756	139.187	.000[a]
	Residual	79.515	195	.408		
	Total	306.539	199			

a. Predictors: (Constant), Technicalsupport, Marketing, ProductValue, Postsalecustomerservice

b. Dependent Variable: X19 - Satisfaction

Fig. 7.17: Output of regression data

(Source: based on review of literature, 2018)

Stage 4: Output

Coefficients[a]

Model		Unstandardized Coefficients		Standardized Coefficients	t	Sig.	Correlations			Collinearity Statistics	
		B	Std. Error	Beta			Zero-order	Partial	Part	Tolerance	VIF
1	(Constant)	-3.823	.494		-7.752	.000					
	ProductValue	.338	.025	.511	13.635	.000	.503	.699	.497	.948	1.055
	Postsalecustomerservice	.267	.022	.461	11.888	.000	.633	.648	.433	.880	1.137
	Marketing	.238	.023	.310	10.245	.000	.456	.584	.366	.881	1.136
	Technicalsupport	.038	.023	.059	1.594	.113	.223	.113	.058	.962	1.040

a. Dependent Variable: X19 - Satisfaction

- Unstandardized coefficient (*B*): How much change in the DV caused by one unit change in the IV
- Standardized coefficient (β): How much change in the DV caused by one standard deviation change in the IV.
- In most cases, we use B to interpret the result
  Sign: positive or negative?
  Effect size: small, medium, or large?
  Significance: is the result significant?

Fig. 7.18: Output of regression data

(Source: based on review of literature, 2018)

Stage 4: Output

Coefficients[a]

Model		Unstandardized Coefficients		Standardized Coefficients	t	Sig.	Correlations			Collinearity Statistics	
		B	Std. Error	Beta			Zero-order	Partial	Part	Tolerance	VIF
1	(Constant)	-3.823	.494		-7.752	.000					
	ProductValue	.338	.025	.511	13.435	.000	.503	.439	.497	.948	1.055
	Postsalecustomerservice	.267	.023	.421	11.858	.000	.633	.648	.433	.880	1.137
	Marketing	.236	.023	.360	10.545	.000	.458	.594	.366	.881	1.135
	Technicalsupport	.036	.023	.059	1.594	.113	.223	.113	.058	.962	1.040

a. Dependent Variable: X19 - Satisfaction

Interpreting unstandardized coefficients (B):

- If Post Sale Customer Service (PCS) value increased by one unit, Customer Satisfaction would increase by .26 (holding the others constant).
- One unit increase in Marketing (Mar) would increase post sale customer service by .24 (holding the others constant).
- One unit increase in Technical Support (TS) would increase post sale customer service by .04 (holding the others constant). But not significant as indicated by t value.
- One unit increase in Product Value (PV) would increase post sale customer service by .34 (holding the others constant).

Fig. 7.19: Output of regression data coefficient
(Source: based on review of literature, 2018)

Tolerance and VIF

- Variance Inflation Factor (VIF) – measures how much the variance of the regression coefficients is inflated by multicollinearity problems. If VIF equals 0, there is no correlation between the independent measures. A VIF measure of 1 is an indication of some association between predictor variables, but generally not enough to cause problems. A maximum acceptable VIF value would be 10; anything higher would indicate a problem with multicollinearity.
- Tolerance – the amount of variance in an independent variable that is not explained by the other independent variables. If the other variables explain a lot of the variance of a particular independent variable we have a problem with multicollinearity. Thus, small values for tolerance indicate problems of multicollinearity. The minimum cutoff value for tolerance is typically .10. That is, the tolerance value must be smaller than .10 to indicate a problem of multicollinearity.

Stage 5: Interpretation

- We have found that product value has a significant influence so it is the positive predictor of Customer Satisfaction.

- However the effect of product value on the customer satisfaction is higher and the other variables which qualify include marketing and post sale customer service and technical support.
- So we can accept the hypothesis that Product Value (IV), Marketing (IV), Post Sale Customer Service and Technical Service have a significant influence on Customer Satisfaction.

Removing Outliers

- Cook's Distance is a measure indicating to what extent model parameters are influenced by (a set of) influential data on which the model is based.
- Cook's distance measures the effect of deleting a given observation.
- As you know, ordinary residuals are defined for each observation, as the difference between the observed and predicted responses.

  • A studentized residual is the quotient resulting from the division of a residual by an estimate of its standard deviation.

Factor Analysis

- What comes to your mind?
- Principal Component Analysis
- Is factor analysis = Principal Component Analysis?

Exploratory Factor Analysis

- Exploratory Factor Analysis (EFA) seeks to uncover the underlying structure of a relatively large set of variables.
- The researcher's a priori assumption is that any indicator may be associated with any factor. This is the most common form of factor analysis.
- Generally there is no established (prior) theory and the one uses factor loadings to intuit the factor structure of the data.
- EFA is used for generating the hypothesis or theory building as well.
- Factors are unobservable constructs and items are the underlying dimensions.
- The identification of such underlying dimensions (factors) simplifies the understanding and description of complex constructs.
- Items are correlated with each other, some are more correlated than others, based on the correlation similarly correlated items are paired together.

Factors and Components

- Factor analysis attempts to achieve parsimony by explaining the maximum amount of common variance in a correlation matrix using the smallest number of explanatory constructs.

- These explanatory constructs are called factors.

- PCA tries to explain the maximum amount of total variance in a correlation matrix
  - It does this by transforming the original variables into a set of linear components

Terms

- Anti-image correlation matrix: Contains the negative partial covariances and correlations.
- Variance: The average of the squared differences from the mean
- Common variance: Variance in a variable that is shared with other variables.
- Communality: The proportion of a variable's variance explained by the extracted factor structure.
- Eigen Value: Represents the variance in the variables which is accounted for by a specific factor

Exploratory Factor Analysis

- Factor analysis is commonly used in:
  - data reduction
  - SCALE DEVELOPMENT
  - Assessment of the dimensionality of a set of variables

"Regardless of purpose, factor analysis is used in the determination of a small number of factors based on a particular number of inter –related quantitative variables."

Purpose

- FA helps to identify items for improvement or removal because they are:
  - Redundant
  - Unclear/irrelevant
  - Complex

How does it Help Us?

- Multivariate approach (> 1 variables) for grouping variables using redundancy (e.g., inter correlations)
- Capitalizes on *high* inter correlations with a "group" of variables
- "Clusters" or factors need not be known in advance; Often they are.
- What problems can it solve?
- Simplify the "dimensionality" of a multivariate problem

- Define "new" variables (more meaningful)
- Establish validity (usefulness) of variables (e.g., convergent and discriminant validity)

Steps Involved in Factor Analysis

1. Assess if data suitable for factor analysis
2. Decide number of "factors" (< variables) adequate to represent data
3. Decide method of extracting factors
4. Decide factor "rotation" for clear interpretation
5. Assess validity & meaningfulness of obtained "factors"
6. Recommendation for use of "factors
7. Sample size > 5-10 x Number of variables (generally)

Interval/Ratio, normally distributed variables (to use correlations to summarize data)

Large correlations: Kaiser-Meyer-Olkin (KMO) Measure of Sampling Adequacy (MSA) > 0.7

Bartlett's test of Spherecity

Bartlett test reveals that overall correlations are significant at .05 level from the correlation matrix

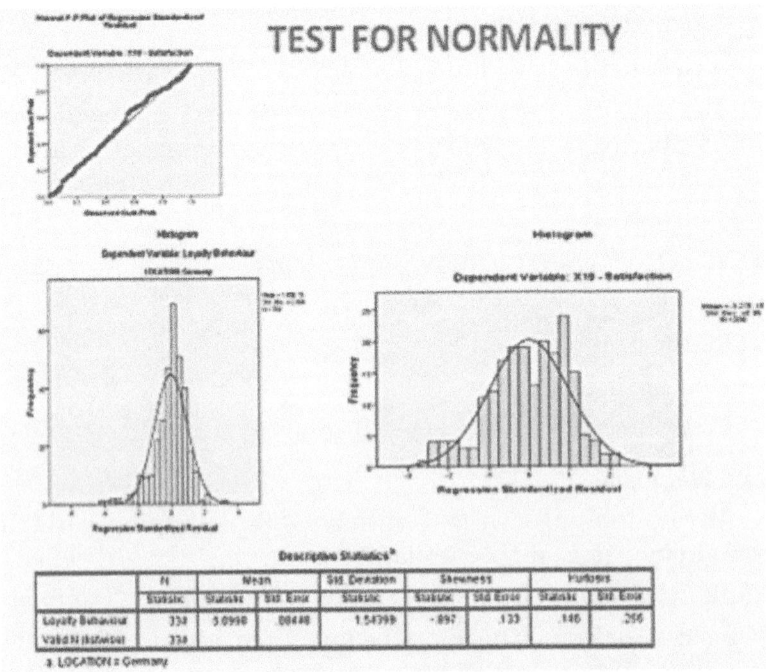

Fig. 7.20: Test for normality

(Source: Based on review of literature, 2018)

Check for assumptions.

Linearity: Plot dependent vs. independent variables.

Normality: Histogram for each variable.

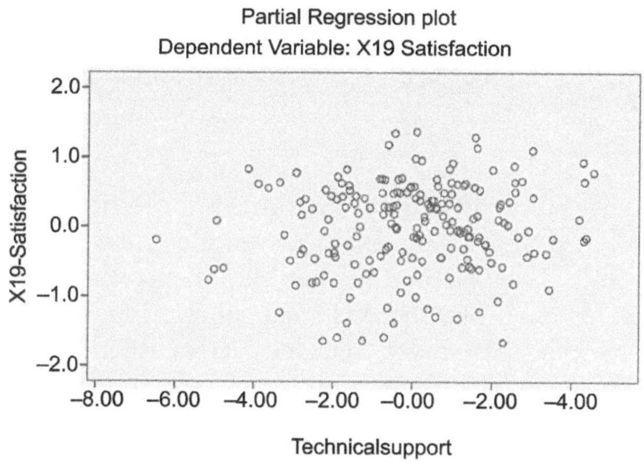

Fig. 7.21: Test for linearity
(Source: based on review of literature, 2018)

Step 3: Decide method of extracting factors

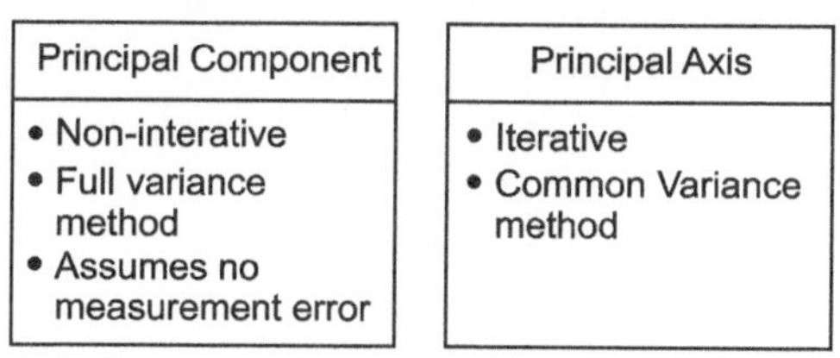

Fig. 7.22: Decide method of extracting factors
(Source: based on review of literature, 2018)

Step 4: Factor "rotation" for clear interpretation

- Doesn't change the variance explained by model

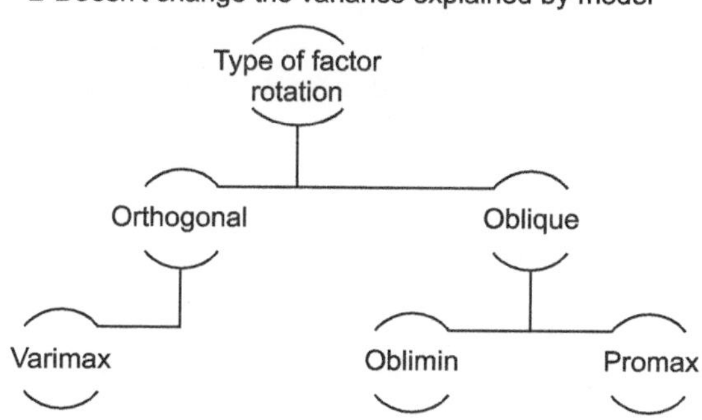

Fig. 7.23: Factor rotation for clear interpretation
(Source: based on review of literature, 2018)

- **Oblique factor rotation**: Factor rotation such that the extracted factors are correlated. Rather than arbitrarily constraining the factor rotation to an orthogonal (90 degree angle), the oblique solution allows the factors to be correlated. In SPSS, this is called Oblimin rotation.
- **Orthogonal factor rotation**: Factor rotation such that their axes are maintained at 90 degrees. Each factor is independent of, or orthogonal to, all other factors. In SPSS, this is called Varimax rotation.

Conclusion

Correlations are useful because they can indicate a predictive relationship that can be exploited in practice. For example, an electrical utility may produce less power on a mild day based on the correlation between electricity demand and weather. In this example, there is a causal relationship, because extreme weather causes people to use more electricity for heating or cooling. However, in general, the presence of a correlation is not sufficient to infer the presence of a causal relationship. In statistical modeling, regression analysis is a set of statistical processes for estimating the relationships among variables. It includes many techniques for modeling and analyzing several variables, when the focus is on the relationship between a dependent variable and one or more independent variables (or 'predictors'). More specifically, regression analysis helps one understand how the typical value of the dependent variable (or 'criterion variable') changes when any one of the independent variables is varied, while the other independent variables are held fixed.

REFERENCES

Croxton, Frederick Emory; Cowden, Dudley Johnstone; Klein, Sidney (1968) Applied General Statistics, Pitman. ISBN 9780273403159.

Dietrich, Cornelius Frank (1991) Uncertainty, Calibration and Probability: The Statistics of Scientific and Industrial Measurement 2nd Edition, A. Higler. ISBN 9780750300605.

Aitken, Alexander Craig (1957) Statistical Mathematics 8th Edition. Oliver & Boyd. ISBN 9780050013007.

Rodgers, J. L.; Nicewander, W. A. (1988). "Thirteen Ways to Look at the Correlation Coefficient". The American Statistician. **42** *(1): 59–66.* doi:10.1080/00031305.1988.10475524. JSTOR 2685263.

Dowdy, S. and Wearden, S. (1983). "Statistics for Research", Wiley. ISBN 0-471-08602-9pp 230

Francis, DP; Coats AJ; Gibson D (1999). "How High Can a Correlation Coefficient be?"Int J Cardiol. **69** *(2): 185–199.* doi:10.1016/S0167-5273(99)00028-5.

Yule, G.U and Kendall, M.G. (1950), "An Introduction to the Theory of Statistics", 14th Edition (5th Impression 1968). Charles Griffin & Co. pp. 258–270

Kendall, M. G. (1955) "Rank Correlation Methods", Charles Griffin & Co.

Mahdavi Damghani B. (2013). "The Non-Misleading Value of Inferred Correlation: An Introduction to the Cointelation Model". Wilmott Magazine. doi:10.1002/wilm.10252

Székely, G. J. Rizzo; Bakirov, N. K. (2007). "Measuring and Testing Independence by Correlation of Distances". Annals of Statistics. **35** *(6): 2769–2794. arXiv:0803.4101/.* doi:10.1214/009053607000000505.

Székely, G. J.; Rizzo, M. L. (2009). "Brownian Distance Covariance". Annals of Applied Statistics. ***3*** *(4): 1233–1303.* arXiv:1010.0297/. doi:10.1214/09-AOAS312.

Lopez-Paz D. and Hennig P. and Schölkopf B. (2013). "The Randomized Dependence Coefficient", "Conference on Neural Information Processing Systems" Reprint.

Thorndike, Robert Ladd (1947). Research Problems and Techniques (Report No. 3). Washington DC: US Govt. print. off.

Nikoliæ, D; Muresan, RC; Feng, W; Singer, W (2012). "Scaled Correlation Analysis: A Better Way to Compute a Cross-correlogram". European Journal of Neuroscience: 1–21. doi:10.1111/j.1460-9568.2011.07987.x.

Aldrich, John (1995). "Correlations Genuine and Spurious in Pearson and Yule". Statistical Science. ***10*** *(4): 364–376.* doi:10.1214/ss/1177009870. JSTOR 2246135.

Mahdavi Damghani, Babak (2012). "The Misleading Value of Measured Correlation". Wilmott. ***2012*** *(1): 64–73.* doi:10.1002/wilm.10167.

Anscombe, Francis J. (1973). "Graphs in Statistical Analysis". The American Statistician. ***27****: 17–21.* doi:10.2307/2682899. JSTOR 2682899.

Scientific Research Methodology : *Concepts and Quality*
Edited by: and Dr. Pawan Kumar 'Bharti' and Dr. Prasann Kumar
ISBN: 978-93-86841-95-7
Edition: 2019
Published by: Discovery Publishing House Pvt. Ltd., New Delhi (India)

8

Structural Equational Modeling

[1]Prasann Kumar and [2]Shweta Pathak

ABSTRACT

SEM is a procedure for estimating a series of dependence relationships among a set of constructs represented by multiple measured variables and incorporated into an integrated model. The Principles of Regression and Factor analysis provides a foundation for understanding SEM.

Keywords: Architect, Biography, Equational, Modelling

Conducting SEM

1. Define the individual Construct
2. Specify the Measurement model
3. Assess measurement model Reliability and Validity.
4. Specify the Structural Model if the measurement model is valid
5. Assess Structural model validity.
6. Draw Conclusions and make recommendations if the structural model is valid

Table 8.1: SEM & Multiple Regression

Many Dependent and many independent variables	One dependent and many independent variables
Correlation between constructs is allowed in SEM	Multicollinearity is a problem in regression analysis
Captures non linear relationships	Linear relationship is assumed between dependent and independent Variables
MLE method is used to estimate the parameters	OLS method is used to estimate the parameters

(**Source:** Based on Reviewof Literature, 2018)

[1] Department of Agronomy, School of Agriculture, Lovely Professional University, Jalandhar, Punjab, 144411, India

[2] Department of Plant Physiology, I.Ag. Sci., BHU., Varanasi, 221005, U.P., India

Construct

Unobservable or latent factors that are represented by multiple variables

Brand Loyalty

Service Quality

- Tangibility
- Reliability
- Responsiveness
- Assurance
- Empathy

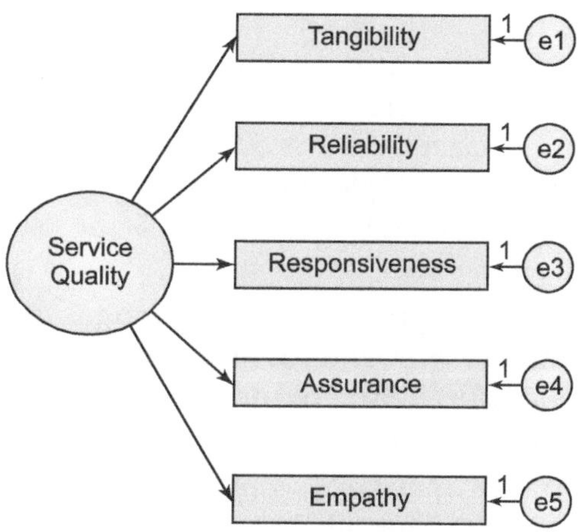

Fig. 8.1: Service quality

(Source: Based on Review of Literature, 2018)

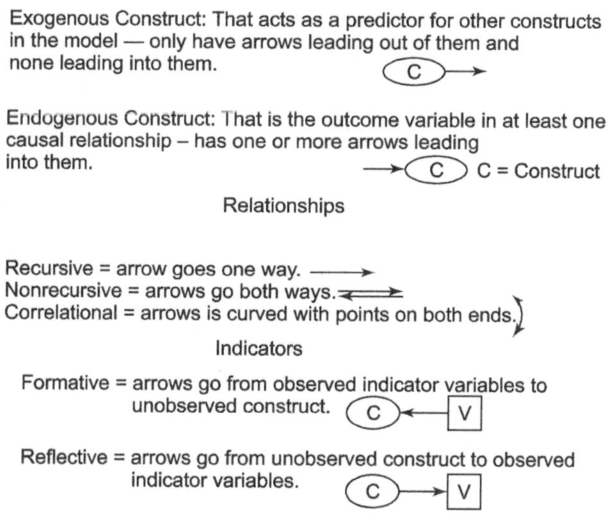

Fig. 8.2: Overview of Construct

(Source: Based on Review of Literature, 2018)

Basic Elements of CFA-SEM Models

Exogenous constructs: latent, multi-item equivalent of independent variables that are not influenced by other variables in the model.

Endogenous constructs: latent, multi-item equivalent to dependent variables – they are affected by other variables in the theoretical model.

Observed variable: known as indicator variables, this type of data is collected from respondents through various data collection methods such as surveys, interviews or observations. These are measurable variables that are used to represent the latent constructs.

Communality = total amount of variance a measured variable has in common with the construct upon which it loads. Each measured variable should load on only one construct. So it can be thought of as the variance explained in a measured variable by the construct. In CFA, the communality is referred to as the "squared multiple correlation" for a measured variable. It is similar to the idea of communality from EFA. Factor loadings are squared to get the communality of an indicator variable.

Congeneric measurement model = A model consisting of several unidimensional constructs with all cross-loadings assumed to be zero. Also, there is no covariance for between- or within-construct error variances, meaning they are all fixed at zero.

Estimated covariance matrix= A covariance matrix comprised of the predicted covariance's between all indicator variables involved in a SEM based on the equations that represent the hypothesized model. Typically abbreviated with $Ó_k$.

Fixed parameter= A parameter that has a value specified by the researcher. Most often the value is specified as zero, indicating no relationship, although there are instances in which an actual value (e.g., 1.0 or such) can be specified.

Free parameter = a parameter estimated by SEM to represent the strength of a specified relationship. These parameters may occur in the measurement model (most often denoting loadings of indicators to constructs) as well as the structural model (relationships among constructs).

Goodness-of-fit (GOF) = a measure indicating how well a specified model reproduces the covariance matrix among the indicator variables.

Maximum likelihood estimation (MLE) = an estimation method commonly employed in SEM. An alternative to OLS used in multiple regression, MLE is a procedure that improves parameter estimates in a way that minimizes the differences between the observed and estimated covariance matrices.

Observed sample covariance matrix= the typical input matrix for SEM estimation comprised of the observed variances and covariances for each measured variable. Typically abbreviated with a bold, capital letter S (**S**).

Construct reliability (CR) = a measure of reliability and internal consistency based on the square of the total of factor loadings for a construct.

Parameter = a numerical representation of some characteristic of a population. In CFA/SEM, relationships are the characteristic of interest that the modeling procedures will generate estimates for. Parameters are numerical characteristics of the SEM relationships, comparable to regression coefficients in multiple regression.

Average Variance extracted (AVE) = a summary measure of convergence among a set of items representing a construct. It is the average percent of variation explained among the items.

Validity Issues

- Content Validity (Face Validity)
- Construct Validity
    - Convergent Validity
    - Discriminant Validity
- Criteria Validity
    - Concurrent Validity
    - Predictive Validity
- Nomo logical Validity

Construct validity = is the extent to which a set of measured variables actually represent the theoretical latent construct they are designed to measure. It is made up of four components: convergent validity, discriminant validity, nomological validity and face validity.

Convergent validity= the extent to which indicators of a specific construct 'converge' or share a high proportion of variance in common.

Discriminant validity= the extent to which a construct is truly distinct from other constructs.

Face validity = the extent to which the content of the items is consistent with the construct definition, based solely on the researcher's judgment.

Nomological validity= is tested by examining whether or not the correlations between the constructs in the measurement theory make sense. The covariance matrix Phi (Φ) of construct correlations is useful in this assessment.

Measurement Theories and CFA-SEM

Reflective Measurement Theory: assumes the latent constructs cause the measured indicator variables and that the error is a result of the inability of the latent constructs to fully explain the indicators. Thus, arrows are drawn from the latent constructs to the measured indicators.

Formative Measurement Theory: assumes the measured indicator variables cause the construct and that the error is a result of the inability of the measured indicators to fully explain the construct. Therefore, the arrows are drawn from the measured indicators to the constructs. In short, "formative" constructs are not considered latent.

Measurement Model (CFA) = A visual representation that specifies the model's construct, indicator variables and interrelationships. CFA provide quantitative measures of the reliability and validity of the constructs.

Structural Model (SEM) = A set of dependence relationships linking the hypothesized model's constructs. SEM determines whether relationships exist between the constructs-and along with CFA enables you to accept or reject your theory.

In developing models to test using CFA/SEM, theory, prior experience, and the research objectives is used to identify and develop hypotheses about which independent variables predict each dependent variable.

What is the Difference Between EFA and CFA?

- In EFA we use the data to determine the underlying structure. Also, typically use an orthogonal rotation and cross-loadings are permitted, as long as they are relatively small.
- In CFA we specify the factor structure on the basis of a 'good' theory and then use CFA to determine whether there is empirical support for the proposed theoretical factor structure. Also, assumes oblique rotation and no (zero) cross-loadings.

Identification Problem

if	$k < p(p+1)/2$	$\rightarrow$	Over identified
	$k = p(p+1)/2$	$\rightarrow$	Exactly identified
	$k > p(p+1)/2$	$\rightarrow$	Under identified

If there are p measured variables, then

No of covariance $= p(p-1)/2$

No of Variances $= p$

A	B	C	D	E		
	A	x				
	B	o	x			
	C	o	o	x		
	D	o	o	o	x	
	E	o	o	o	o	x

No of covariance $= p(p-1)/2$

No of Variances $= p$

Total $= p(p-1)/2 + p = p(p+1)/2$

CFA Assumes no Cross-Loadings And Unidimensionality

- Cross-Loadings= when indicator variables on one construct are assumed to be related to another construct.
- Congeneric measurement model = All cross-loadings are assumed to be 0.
- The assumption of no cross-loadings is based on the fact that the existence of significant cross-loadings is evidence of a lack of unidimensionality and therefore a lack of construct validity, i.e. discriminant validity.

Content Validity

Construct Validity

Convergent Validity — CR > 0.7

CR > AVE

AVE > 0.5

Discriminant Validity — AVE> Inter construct correlation

Nomo logical Validity

Table 8.1: Goodness and Badness of Fit

Measure	Threshold
Chi-square/df (cmin/df)	< 3 good; < 5 sometimes permissible
p-value for the model	> .05
CFI	> .95 great; > .90 traditional; > .80 sometimes permissible
GFI	> .95
AGFI	> .80
SRMR	< .09
RMSEA	< .05 good; .05 – .10 moderate; > .10 bad
PCLOSE	> .05

(**Source:** Based on Review of Literature, 2018)

SEM GOF "Rules of Thumb"

SEM has no single statistical test that best describes the "strength" of the model's predictions. Instead, researchers have developed different types of measures that in combination assess the results.

- Multiple fit indices should be used to assess goodness of fit. For example:
  - o Normed Chi-square (χ^2 / df)
  - o One goodness of fit index (e.g., GFI, CFI, NFI, TLI)
  - o One badness of fit index (e.g., RMSEA, RMSR)
- Selecting a rigid cut-off for the fit indices is like selecting a minimum R^2 for a regression equation – there is no single "magic" value for

the fit indices that separates good from poor models. The quality of fit depends heavily on model characteristics including sample size and model complexity.

- Simple models with small samples should be held to very strict fit standards.
- More complex models with larger samples should not be held to the same strict standards.

What Does Sem Actually Test?

Can your hypothesized theoretical model be confirmed?

Three Criteria:

1. Goodness of Fit?

   Does the estimated covariance matrix

   = observed covariance matrix (absolute fit)
2. Validity and Reliability of Measurement Model?
3. Significant and Meaningful Structural Relationships?

Criteria One: Goodness of Fit (GOF)

Indicates how well the specified model reproduces the covariance matrix among the indicator variables – that is, it examines the similarity of the observed and estimated covariance matrices (absolute fit).The initial measure of GOF is the Chi-square statistic. The null hypothesis is "No difference in the two covariance matrices". Since you do not want the matrices to be different, you hope for an insignificant Chi-square (>.05) so you can accept the null hypothesis.

Table 8.2: Observed Sample Covariances for 3-Construct Model

Sample Moments (Group number 1)

Sample Covariances (Group number 1)

	AC1	AC2	AC3	AC4	OC4	OC3	OC2	OC1	EP4	EP3	EP2	EP1
AC1	1.937											
AC2	1.615	2.972										
AC3	1.364	1.687	2.009									
AC4	1.501	1.860	1.540	2.587								
OC4	.432	.601	.601	.804	4.206							
OC3	.327	.271	.302	.453	2.035	3.071						
OC2	.803	.794	.841	1.011	3.306	2.137	4.768					
OC1	.198	.452	.340	.524	2.506	1.961	2.884	6.360				
EP4	.264	.379	.247	.451	.936	.901	1.008	.803	1.936			
EP3	.345	.300	.286	.398	.792	.735	1.013	.412	1.235	1.777		
EP2	.391	.492	.378	.592	1.259	1.055	1.326	.938	1.469	1.331	2.644	
EP1	.357	.501	.406	.450	1.046	.757	1.005	.514	1.442	1.228	1.773	3.344

(**Source:** Based on Review of Literature, 2018)

Table 8.3: Implied Covariance's) (Group number 1-Default model)

Implied Covariances (Group number 1 - Default model)

	AC1	AC2	AC3	AC4	OC4	OC3	OC2	OC1	EP4	EP3	EP2	EP1
AC1	1.937											
AC2	1.619	2.972										
AC3	1.357	1.677	2.009									
AC4	1.502	1.857	1.556	2.587								
OC4	.599	.741	.621	.688	4.206							
OC3	.407	.503	.422	.467	2.025	3.071						
OC2	.660	.816	.684	.757	3.283	2.229	4.768					
OC1	.518	.641	.537	.595	2.578	1.751	2.838	6.360				
EP4	.333	.412	.345	.382	.990	.672	1.090	.856	1.936			
EP3	.299	.370	.310	.343	.889	.604	.979	.769	1.181	1.777		
EP2	.383	.473	.397	.439	1.138	.773	1.253	.984	1.512	1.358	2.644	
EP1	.367	.454	.380	.421	1.091	.741	1.201	.943	1.449	1.301	1.666	3.344

Covariances estimated by AMOS software – request Implied moments and look in Output under Estimates.

(**Source:** Based on review of Literature, 2018)

Table 8.4: Residual Covariance's

Residual Covariances (Group number 1 - Default model)

	AC1	AC2	AC3	AC4	OC4	OC3	OC2	OC1	EP4	EP3	EP2	EP1
AC1	.000											
AC2	-.003	.000										
AC3	.007	.010	.000									
AC4	-.001	.003	-.016	.000								
OC4	-.167	-.140	-.020	.116	.000							
OC3	-.080	-.233	-.119	-.014	.010	.000						
OC2	.143	-.022	.158	.254	.023	-.093	.000					
OC1	-.320	-.189	-.197	-.071	-.072	.211	.046	.000				
EP4	-.069	-.033	-.098	.069	-.054	.229	-.081	-.052	.000			
EP3	.046	-.070	-.024	.055	-.097	.131	.034	-.357	.054	.000		
EP2	.008	.019	-.018	.153	.121	.282	.073	-.046	-.043	-.026	.000	
EP1	-.010	.048	.026	.030	-.044	.016	-.196	-.429	-.007	-.073	.107	.000

Residuals = difference between observed and estimated covariances – request Residual moments.

A negative sign indicates the observed covariance (2.137) is smaller than the estimated covariance (2.229) by -.093.

(**Source:** Based on review of Literature, 2018)

Table 8.5: Standardized Residual Covariance's

Standardized Residual Covariances (Group number 1 - Default model)

	AC1	AC2	AC3	AC4	OC4	OC3	OC2	OC1	EP4	EP3	EP2	EP1
AC1	.000											
AC2	-.024	.000										
AC3	.057	.065	.000									
AC4	-.007	.020	-.116	.000								
OC4	-1.145	-.773	-.134	.689	.000							
OC3	-.645	-1.517	-.947	-.095	.048	.000						
OC2	.917	-.112	.993	1.413	.082	-.419	.000					
OC1	-1.803	-.857	-1.090	-.344	-.250	.885	.148	.000				
EP4	-.699	-.268	-.980	.609	-.354	1.809	-.504	-.290	.000			
EP3	.490	-.597	-.246	.505	-.674	1.087	.221	-2.066	.492	.000		
EP2	.071	.130	-.157	1.154	.687	1.908	.388	-.218	-.316	-.206	.000	
EP1	-.079	.298	.199	.199	-.227	.099	-.940	-1.819	-.047	-.528	.626	.000

(**Source:** Based on Review of Literature, 2018)

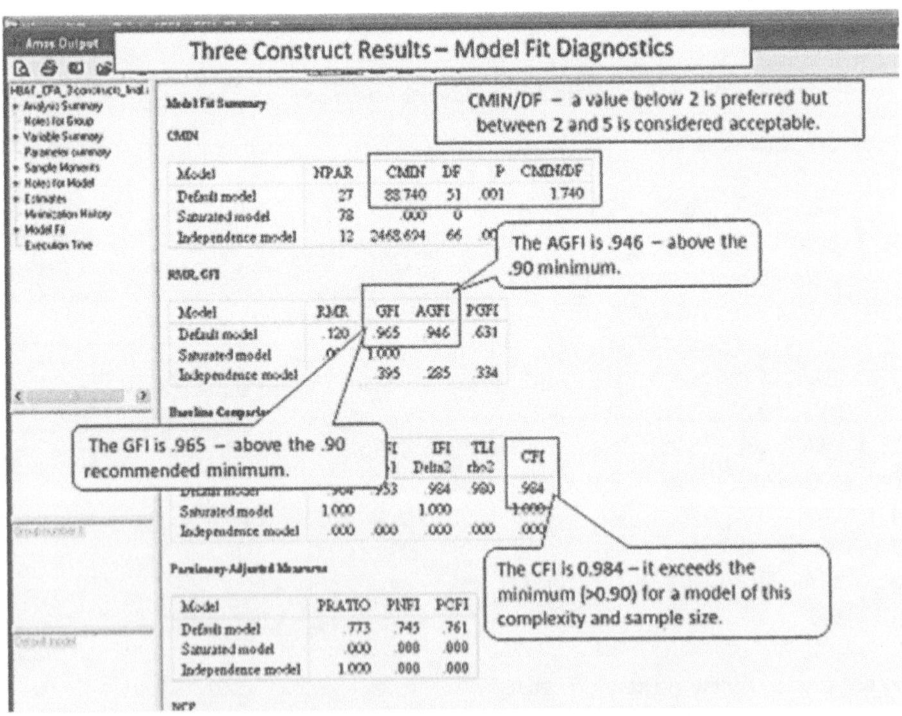

Fig. 8.3: Three construct Results-Model fir Diagnostics

(Source: Based on Review of Literature, 2018)

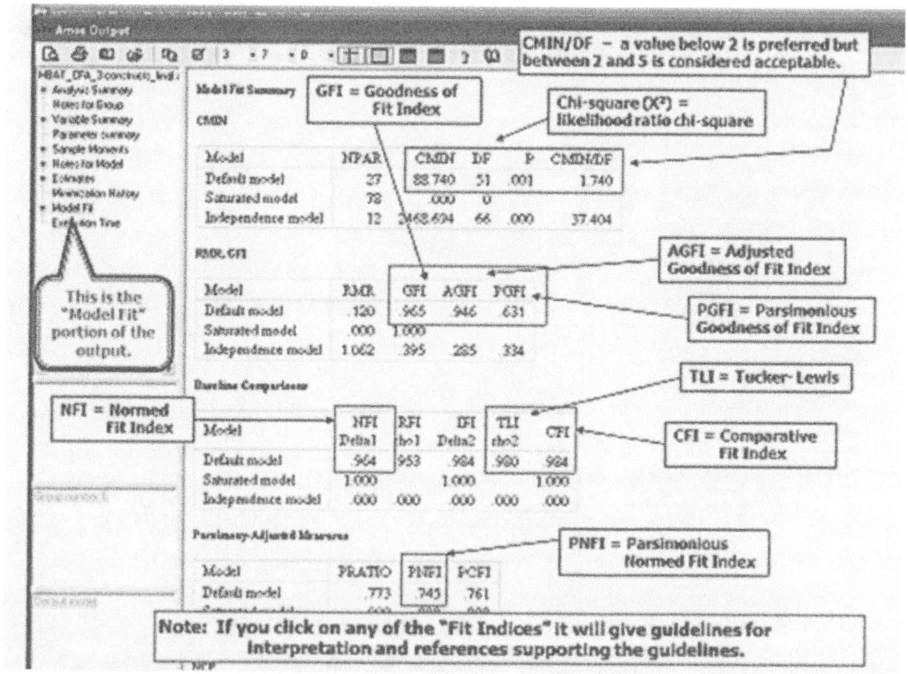

Fig. 8.4: GFI=Goodness of Fit Index

(Source: Based on Review of Literature, 2018)

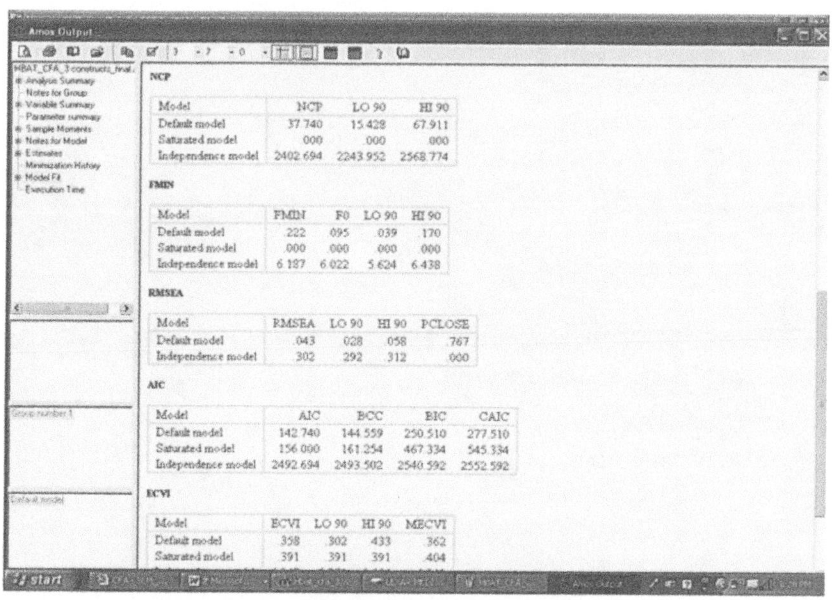

Fig. 8.5: NCP, FMIN, RMSEA, AIC, ECVI

(Source: Based on Review of Literature, 2018)

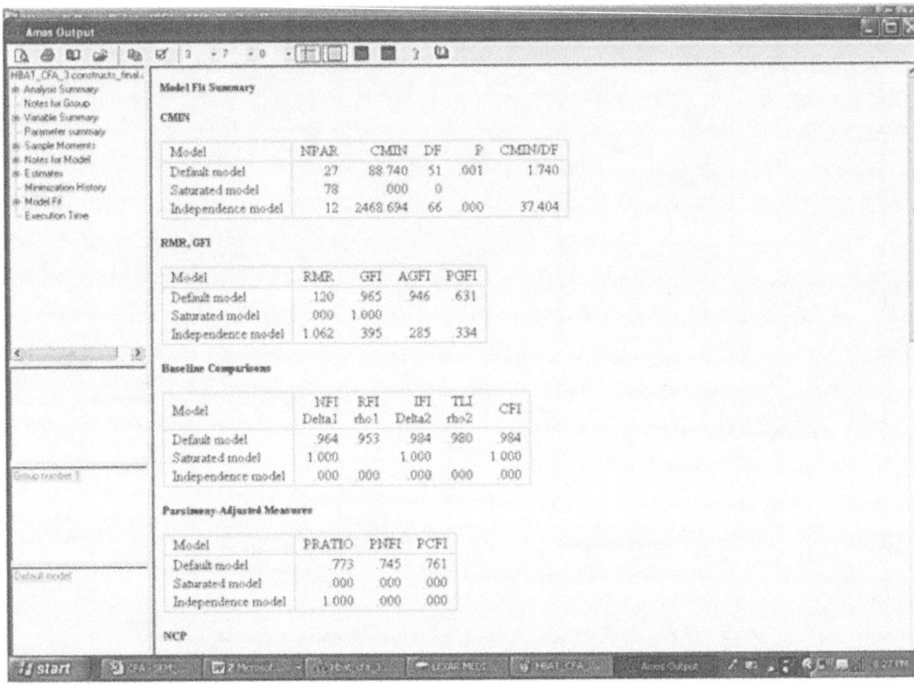

Model Fit Summary

CMIN

Model	NPAR	CMIN	DF	P	CMIN/DF
Default model	27	88.740	51	.001	1.740
Saturated model	78	.000	0		
Independence model	12	2468.694	66	.000	37.404

RMR, GFI

Model	RMR	GFI	AGFI	PGFI
Default model	.120	.965	.946	.631
Saturated model	.000	1.000		
Independence model	1.062	.395	.285	.334

Baseline Comparisons

Model	NFI Delta1	RFI rho1	IFI Delta2	TLI rho2	CFI
Default model	.964	.953	.984	.980	.984
Saturated model	1.000		1.000		1.000
Independence model	.000	.000	.000	.000	.000

Parsimony-Adjusted Measures

Model	PRATIO	PNFI	PCFI
Default model	.773	.745	.761
Saturated model	.000	.000	.000
Independence model	1.000	.000	.000

NCP

Fig. 8.6: Model Fit Summary

(Source: Based on Review of Literature, 2018)

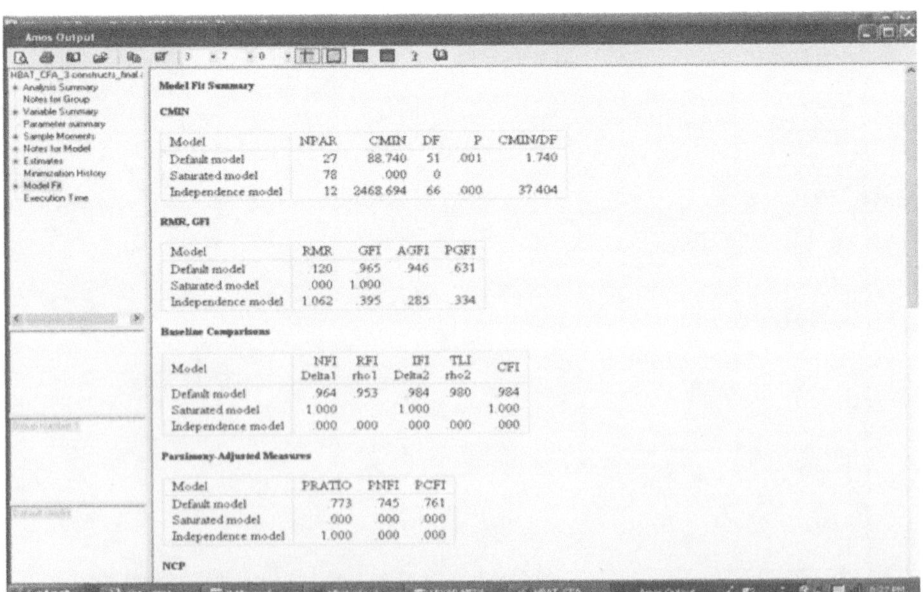

Model Fit Summary

CMIN

Model	NPAR	CMIN	DF	P	CMIN/DF
Default model	27	88.740	51	.001	1.740
Saturated model	78	.000	0		
Independence model	12	2468.694	66	.000	37.404

RMR, GFI

Model	RMR	GFI	AGFI	PGFI
Default model	.120	.965	.946	.631
Saturated model	.000	1.000		
Independence model	1.062	.395	.285	.334

Baseline Comparisons

Model	NFI Delta1	RFI rho1	IFI Delta2	TLI rho2	CFI
Default model	.964	.953	.984	.980	.984
Saturated model	1.000		1.000		1.000
Independence model	.000	.000	.000	.000	.000

Parsimony-Adjusted Measures

Model	PRATIO	PNFI	PCFI
Default model	.773	.745	.761
Saturated model	.000	.000	.000
Independence model	1.000	.000	.000

NCP

Fig. 8.7: Model Fit Summary

(Source: Based on Review of Literature, 2018)

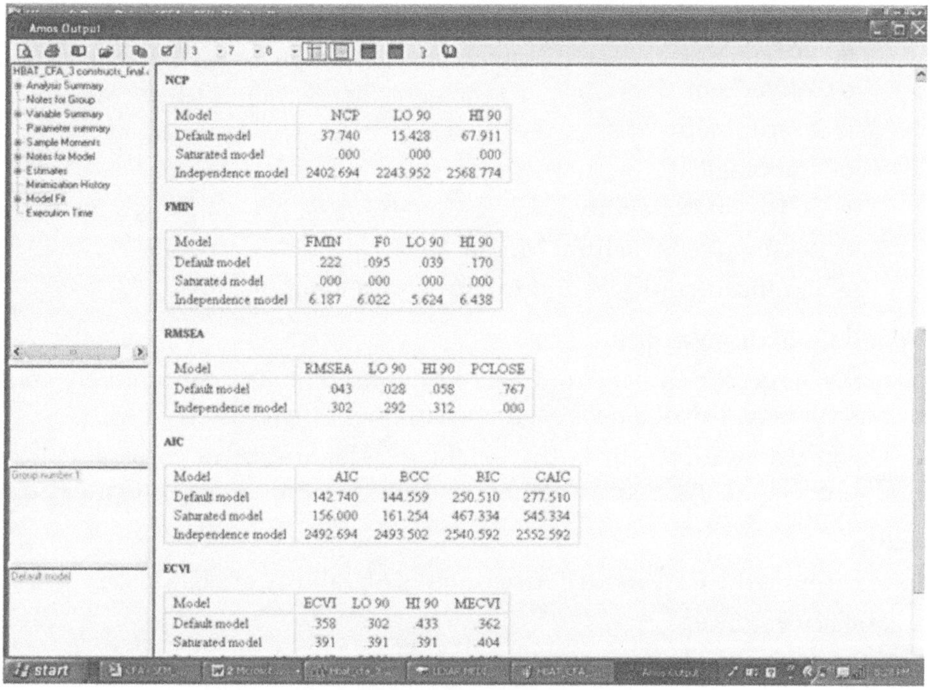

NCP

Model	NCP	LO 90	HI 90
Default model	37.740	15.428	67.911
Saturated model	.000	.000	.000
Independence model	2402.694	2243.952	2568.774

FMIN

Model	FMIN	F0	LO 90	HI 90
Default model	.222	.095	.039	.170
Saturated model	.000	.000	.000	.000
Independence model	6.187	6.022	5.624	6.438

RMSEA

Model	RMSEA	LO 90	HI 90	PCLOSE
Default model	.043	.028	.058	.767
Independence model	.302	.292	.312	.000

AIC

Model	AIC	BCC	BIC	CAIC
Default model	142.740	144.559	250.510	277.510
Saturated model	156.000	161.254	467.334	545.334
Independence model	2492.694	2493.502	2540.592	2552.592

ECVI

Model	ECVI	LO 90	HI 90	MECVI
Default model	.358	.302	.433	.362
Saturated model	.391	.391	.391	.404

Fig. 8.8: Amos Output

(Source: Based on Review of Literature, 2018)

Guidelines for Establishing Acceptable Fit

- Use multiple indices of differing types.
- Adjust the index cutoff values based on model characteristics, e.g., number of constructs and indicators, sample size. Simpler models and smaller samples sizes require stricter evaluation.
- Remove indicator variables that do not meet established criteria.
- Use GOF indices to compare models.
- The pursuit of better fit at the expense of testing a true model is not a good trade-off.

What does SEM actually test?

Three Criteria

1. Goodness of Fit? estimated covariance matrix = observed covariance matrix
2. Validity and Reliability of Measurement Model?
3. Significant and Meaningful Structural Relationships?

Second & Third Criteria

2. Assessing the Measurement Model

- Construct Validity
  - o Face
  - o Convergent
  - o Discriminant
  - o Nomological
- Construct Reliability

3. Assessing the Structural Model
   - Significant and Meaningful Structural Relationships

CFA and Construct Validity

One of the biggest advantages of CFA/SEM is its ability to quantitatively assess the construct validity of a proposed measurement theory.

Construct validity . . . is the extent to which a set of measured items actually reflect the theoretical latent construct they are designed to measure.

Validity

Before running the CFA model, assessments of validity are based on:

- Face validity.
- Published results from previous studies.
- Pre-test or pilot study findings.

A major objective of applying CFA is to empirically estimate validity using more rigorous approaches; e.g., construct validity.

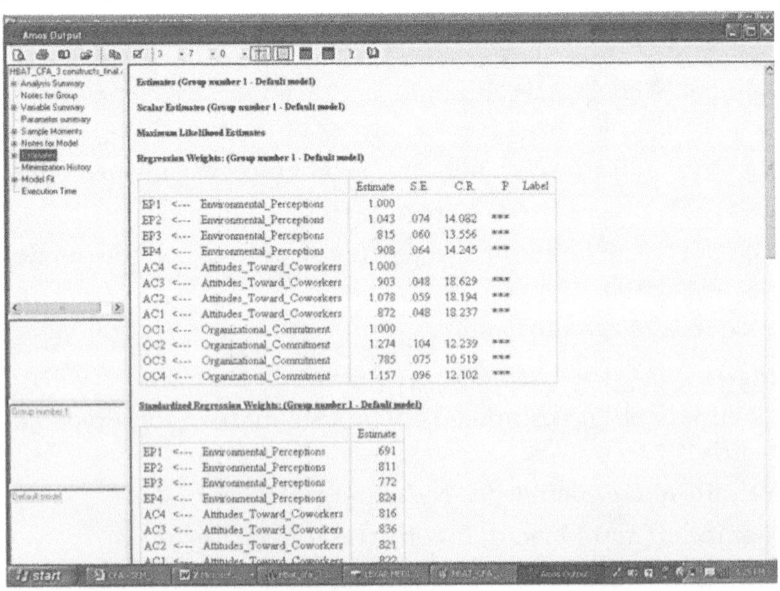

Fig. 8.9: CFA model Assessments

(Source: Based on Review of Literature, 2018)

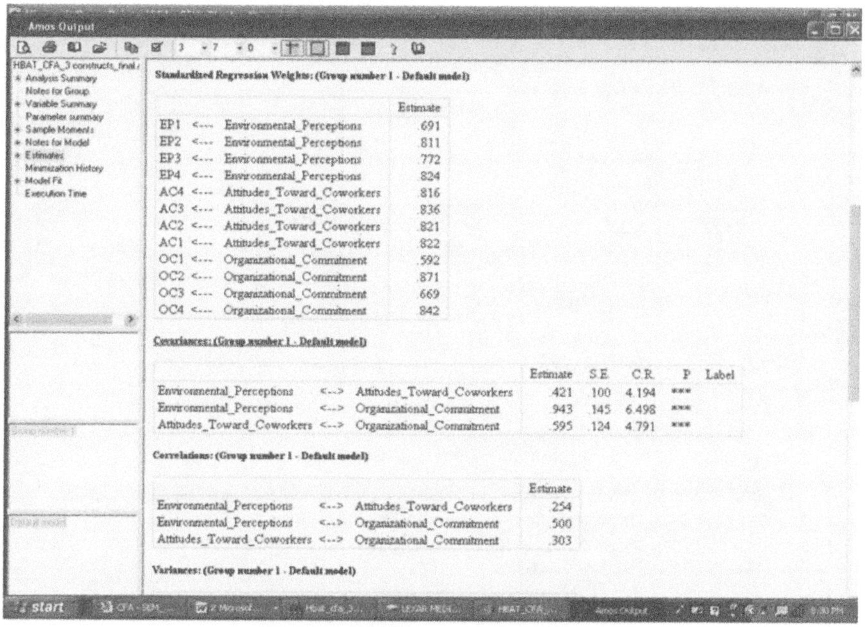
Standardized Regression Weights: (Group number 1 - Default model)

			Estimate
EP1	<---	Environmental_Perceptions	.691
EP2	<---	Environmental_Perceptions	.811
EP3	<---	Environmental_Perceptions	.772
EP4	<---	Environmental_Perceptions	.824
AC4	<---	Attitudes_Toward_Coworkers	.816
AC3	<---	Attitudes_Toward_Coworkers	.836
AC2	<---	Attitudes_Toward_Coworkers	.821
AC1	<---	Attitudes_Toward_Coworkers	.822
OC1	<---	Organizational_Commitment	.592
OC2	<---	Organizational_Commitment	.871
OC3	<---	Organizational_Commitment	.669
OC4	<---	Organizational_Commitment	.842

Covariances: (Group number 1 - Default model)

			Estimate	S.E.	C.R.	P	Label
Environmental_Perceptions	<-->	Attitudes_Toward_Coworkers	.421	.100	4.194	***	
Environmental_Perceptions	<-->	Organizational_Commitment	.943	.145	6.498	***	
Attitudes_Toward_Coworkers	<-->	Organizational_Commitment	.595	.124	4.791	***	

Correlations: (Group number 1 - Default model)

			Estimate
Environmental_Perceptions	<-->	Attitudes_Toward_Coworkers	.254
Environmental_Perceptions	<-->	Organizational_Commitment	.500
Attitudes_Toward_Coworkers	<-->	Organizational_Commitment	.303

Variances: (Group number 1 - Default model)

Fig. 8.10: Standardized Regression

(Source: Based on Review of Literature, 2018)

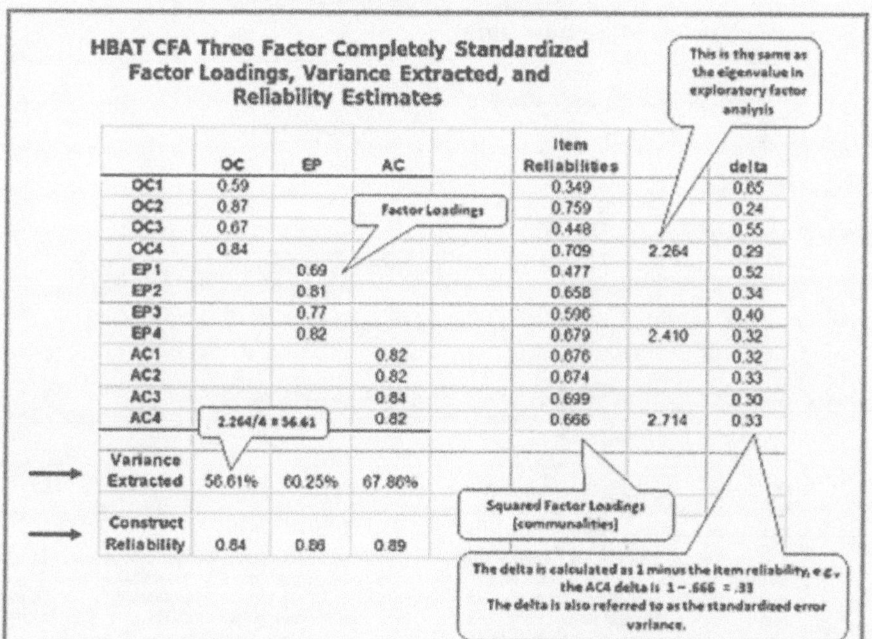
HBAT CFA Three Factor Completely Standardized Factor Loadings, Variance Extracted, and Reliability Estimates

	OC	EP	AC		Item Reliabilities		delta
OC1	0.59				0.349		0.65
OC2	0.87				0.759		0.24
OC3	0.67				0.448		0.55
OC4	0.84				0.709	2.264	0.29
EP1		0.69			0.477		0.52
EP2		0.81			0.658		0.34
EP3		0.77			0.596		0.40
EP4		0.82			0.679	2.410	0.32
AC1			0.82		0.676		0.32
AC2			0.82		0.674		0.33
AC3			0.84		0.699		0.30
AC4			0.82		0.666	2.714	0.33
Variance Extracted	56.61%	60.25%	67.86%				
Construct Reliability	0.84	0.86	0.89				

Fig. 8.11: HBAT CFA three Factor completely Standardized

(Source: Based on a review of literature, 2018)

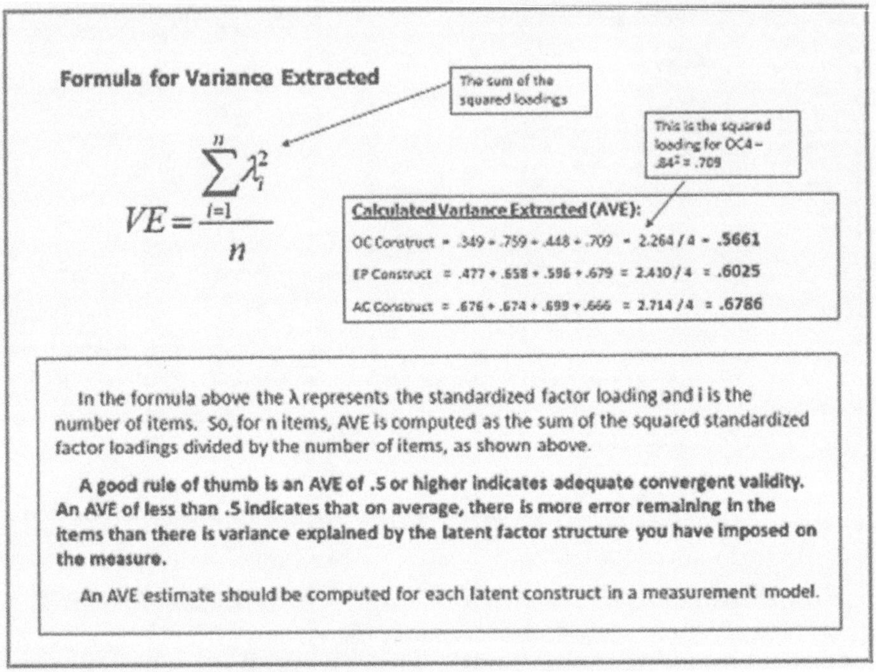

Fig. 8.12: Formula for Variance Extracted

(Source: Based on a review of literature, 2018)

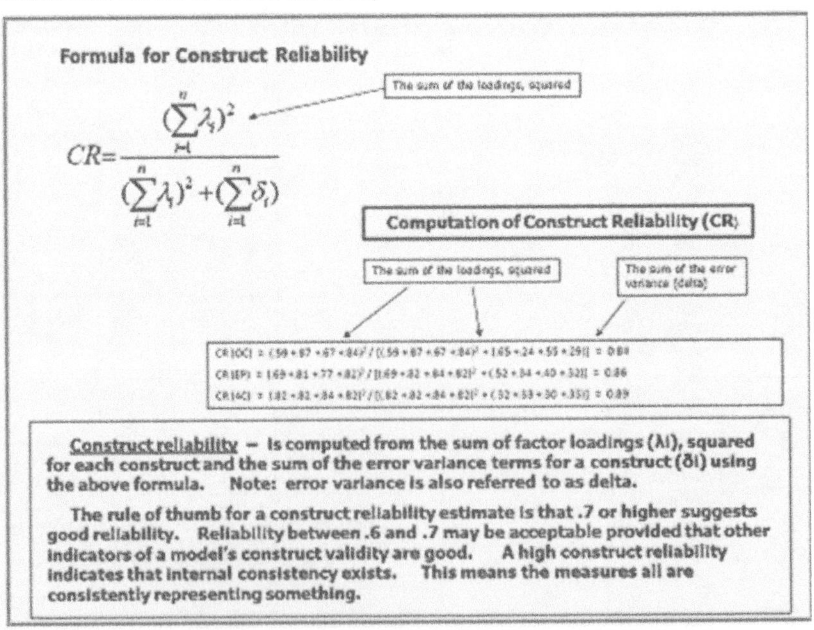

Fig. 8.13: Formula for Construct Reliability

(Source: Based on a review of literature, 2018)

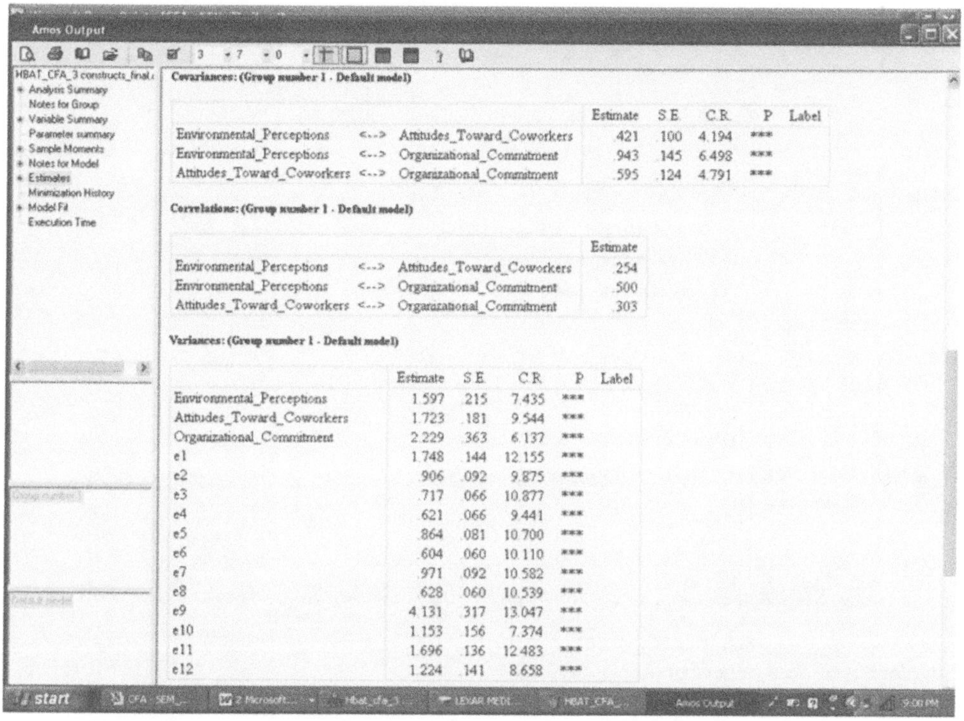

Covariances: (Group number 1 - Default model)

			Estimate	S.E.	C.R.	P	Label
Environmental_Perceptions	<-->	Attitudes_Toward_Coworkers	.421	.100	4.194	***	
Environmental_Perceptions	<-->	Organizational_Commitment	.943	.145	6.498	***	
Attitudes_Toward_Coworkers	<-->	Organizational_Commitment	.595	.124	4.791	***	

Correlations: (Group number 1 - Default model)

			Estimate
Environmental_Perceptions	<-->	Attitudes_Toward_Coworkers	.254
Environmental_Perceptions	<-->	Organizational_Commitment	.500
Attitudes_Toward_Coworkers	<-->	Organizational_Commitment	.303

Variances: (Group number 1 - Default model)

	Estimate	S.E.	C.R.	P	Label
Environmental_Perceptions	1.597	.215	7.435	***	
Attitudes_Toward_Coworkers	1.723	.181	9.544	***	
Organizational_Commitment	2.229	.363	6.137	***	
e1	1.748	.144	12.155	***	
e2	.906	.092	9.875	***	
e3	.717	.066	10.877	***	
e4	.621	.066	9.441	***	
e5	.864	.081	10.700	***	
e6	.604	.060	10.110	***	
e7	.971	.092	10.582	***	
e8	.628	.060	10.539	***	
e9	4.131	.317	13.047	***	
e10	1.153	.156	7.374	***	
e11	1.696	.136	12.483	***	
e12	1.224	.141	8.658	***	

Fig. 8.14: Covariance (Group number 1)
(Source: Based on Review of Literature, 2018)

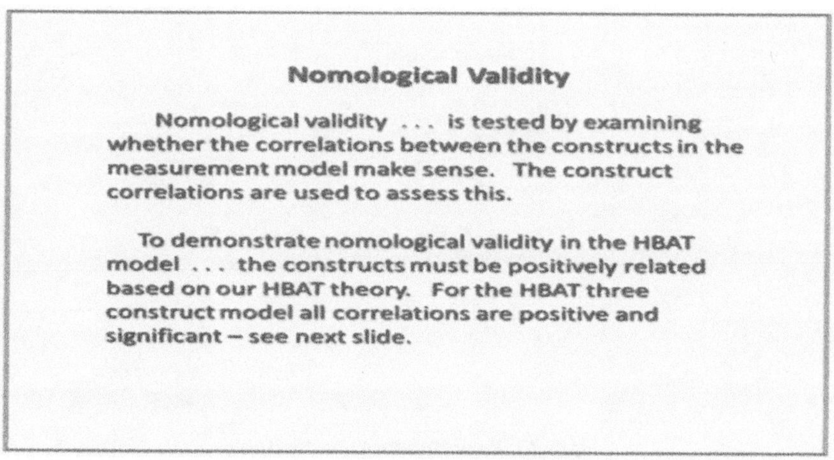

Fig. 8.15: Nomological validity
(Source: Based on Review of Literature, 2018)

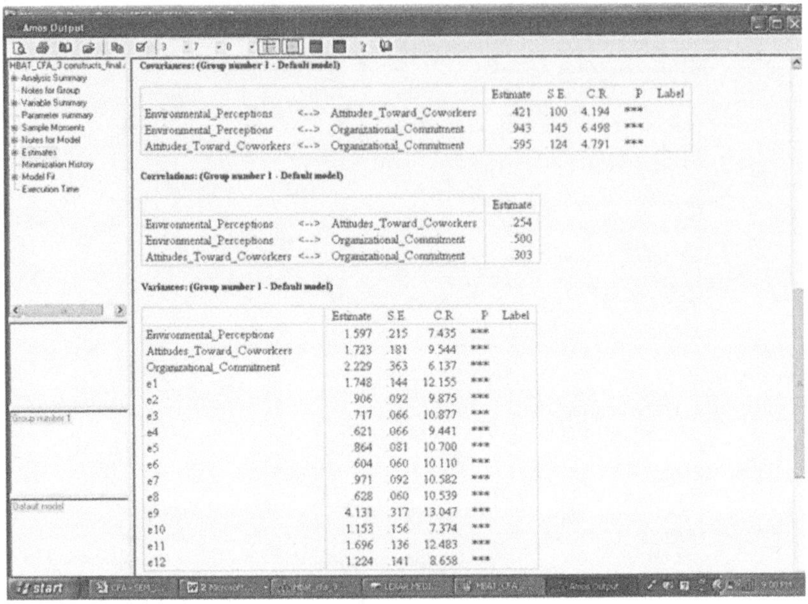

Covariances: (Group number 1 - Default model)

			Estimate	S.E.	C.R.	P	Label
Environmental_Perceptions	<-->	Attitudes_Toward_Coworkers	.421	.100	4.194	***	
Environmental_Perceptions	<-->	Organizational_Commitment	.943	.145	6.498	***	
Attitudes_Toward_Coworkers	<-->	Organizational_Commitment	.595	.124	4.791	***	

Correlations: (Group number 1 - Default model)

			Estimate
Environmental_Perceptions	<-->	Attitudes_Toward_Coworkers	.254
Environmental_Perceptions	<-->	Organizational_Commitment	.500
Attitudes_Toward_Coworkers	<-->	Organizational_Commitment	.303

Variances: (Group number 1 - Default model)

	Estimate	S.E.	C.R.	P	Label
Environmental_Perceptions	1.597	.215	7.435	***	
Attitudes_Toward_Coworkers	1.723	.181	9.544	***	
Organizational_Commitment	2.229	.363	6.137	***	
e1	1.748	.144	12.155	***	
e2	.906	.092	9.875	***	
e3	.717	.066	10.877	***	
e4	.621	.066	9.441	***	
e5	.864	.081	10.700	***	
e6	.604	.060	10.110	***	
e7	.971	.092	10.582	***	
e8	.628	.060	10.539	***	
e9	4.131	.317	13.047	***	
e10	1.153	.156	7.374	***	
e11	1.696	.136	12.483	***	
e12	1.224	.141	8.658	***	

Fig. 8.16: Covariance: (Group number 1-Default Model)

(Source: Based on a review of literature, 2018)

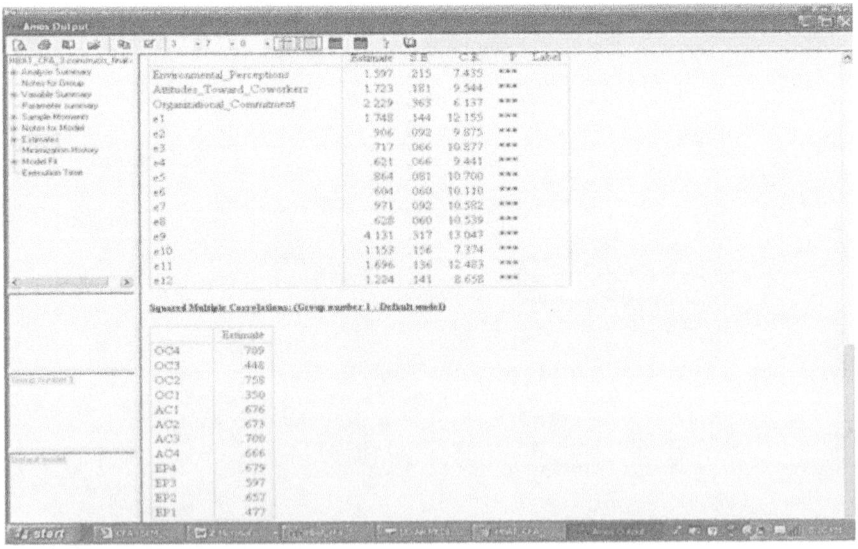

	Estimate	S.E.	C.R.	P	Label
Environmental_Perceptions	1.597	.215	7.435	***	
Attitudes_Toward_Coworkers	1.723	.181	9.544	***	
Organizational_Commitment	2.229	.363	6.137	***	
e1	1.748	.144	12.155	***	
e2	.906	.092	9.875	***	
e3	.717	.066	10.877	***	
e4	.621	.066	9.441	***	
e5	.864	.081	10.700	***	
e6	.604	.060	10.110	***	
e7	.971	.092	10.582	***	
e8	.628	.060	10.539	***	
e9	4.131	.317	13.047	***	
e10	1.153	.156	7.374	***	
e11	1.696	.136	12.483	***	
e12	1.224	.141	8.658	***	

Squared Multiple Correlations: (Group number 1 - Default model)

	Estimate
OC4	.709
OC3	.448
OC2	.758
OC1	.350
AC1	.676
AC2	.673
AC3	.700
AC4	.666
EP4	.679
EP3	.597
EP2	.657
EP1	.477

Fig. 8.17: Environmental Perceptions

(Source: Based on Review of Literature, 2018)

Diagnosing Measurement Model Problems

In addition to evaluating goodness-of-fit statistics, the following diagnostic measures for CFA should be checked:

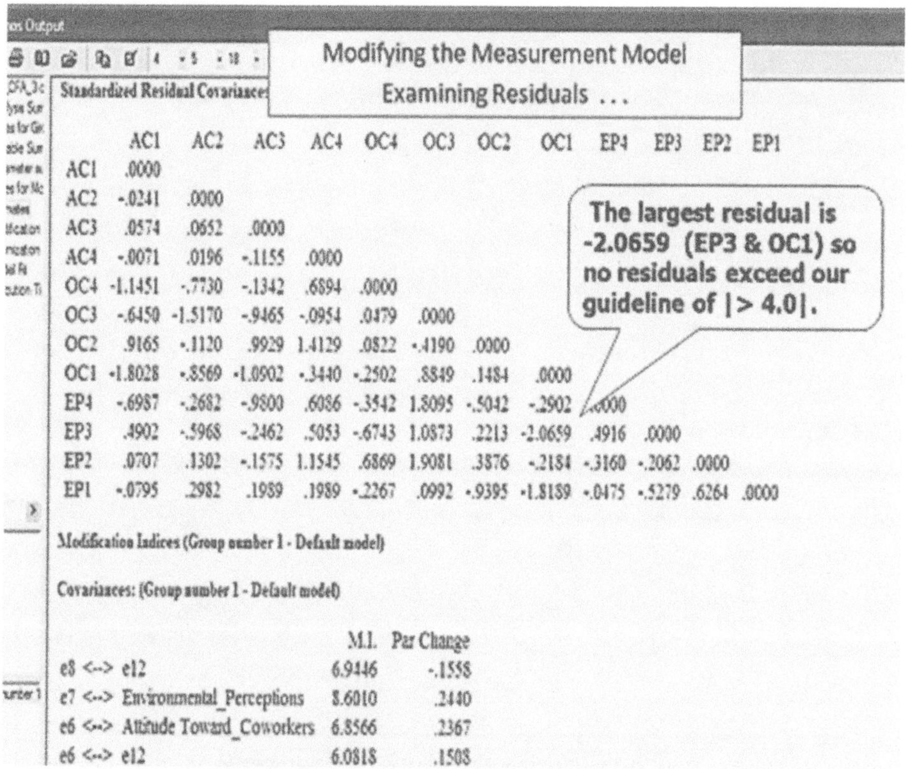

Standardized Residual Covariances

	AC1	AC2	AC3	AC4	OC4	OC3	OC2	OC1	EP4	EP3	EP2	EP1
AC1	.0000											
AC2	-.0241	.0000										
AC3	.0574	.0652	.0000									
AC4	-.0071	.0196	-.1155	.0000								
OC4	-1.1451	-.7730	-.1342	.6894	.0000							
OC3	-.6450	-1.5170	-.9465	-.0954	.0479	.0000						
OC2	.9165	-.1120	.9929	1.4129	.0822	-.4190	.0000					
OC1	-1.8028	-.8569	-1.0902	-.3440	-.2502	.8849	.1484	.0000				
EP4	-.6987	-.2682	-.9800	.6086	-.3542	1.8095	-.5042	-.2902	.0000			
EP3	.4902	-.5968	-.2462	.5053	-.6743	1.0873	.2213	-2.0659	.4916	.0000		
EP2	.0707	.1302	-.1575	1.1545	.6869	1.9081	.3876	-.2184	-.3160	-.2062	.0000	
EP1	-.0795	.2982	.1989	.1989	-.2267	.0992	-.9395	-1.8189	-.0475	-.5279	.6264	.0000

Modification Indices (Group number 1 - Default model)

Covariances: (Group number 1 - Default model)

	M.I.	Par Change
e8 <--> e12	6.9446	-.1558
e7 <--> Environmental_Perceptions	8.6010	.2440
e6 <--> Attitude Toward_Coworkers	6.8566	.2367
e6 <--> e12	6.0818	.1508

Fig. 8.18: Modifying the measurements model Examining Residuals (Source: Based on review of Literature, 2018)

Is the Measurement Model Valid?

- No – refine measures and design a new study.
- Yes – proceed to test the structural model with stages 5 and 6.

Assessing the Structural Model Validity

To do so . . .

- Assess the goodness of fit (GOF) of the structural model. Should be essentially the same as with the CFA model.
- Evaluate the significance, direction, and size of the structural parameter estimates.

AMOS Practice: Drawing a Three Construct HBAT SEM Model

Constructs:

- Exogenous
  - ➢ Environmental Perceptions (EP)
  - ➢ Attitudes towards Coworkers (AC)

- Endogenous
  - ➢ Organizational Commitment (OC)

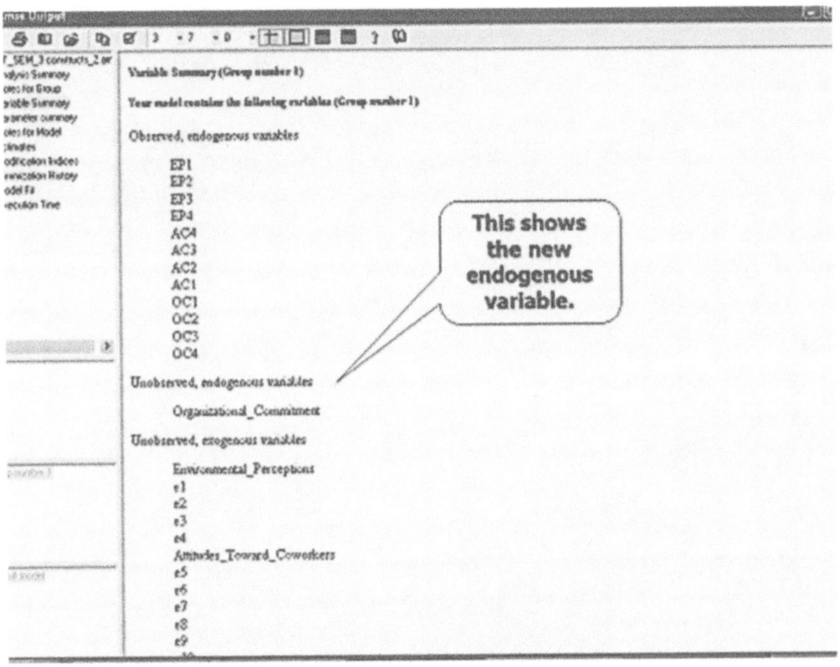

Fig. 8.19: Variable summary (Group number 1)

(Source: Based on Review of Literature, 2018)

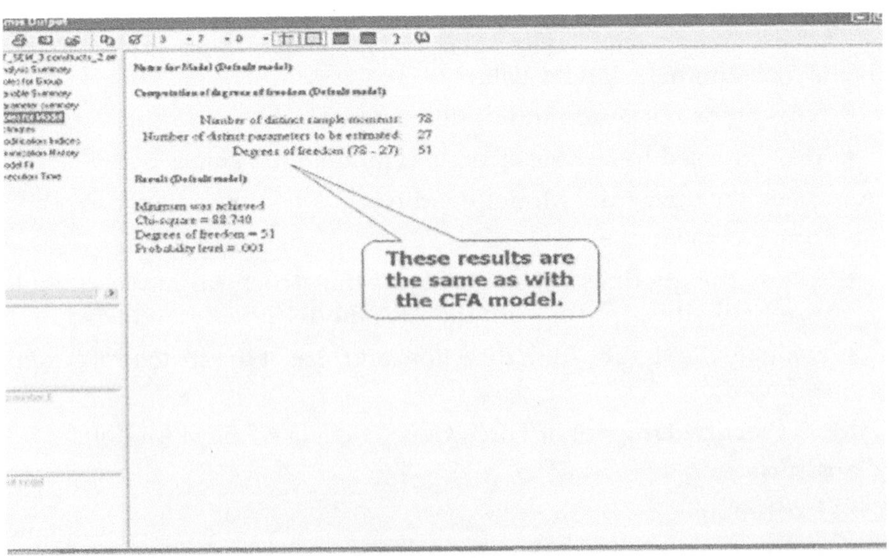

Fig. 8.20: Nature for model

(Source: Based on Review of Literature, 2018)

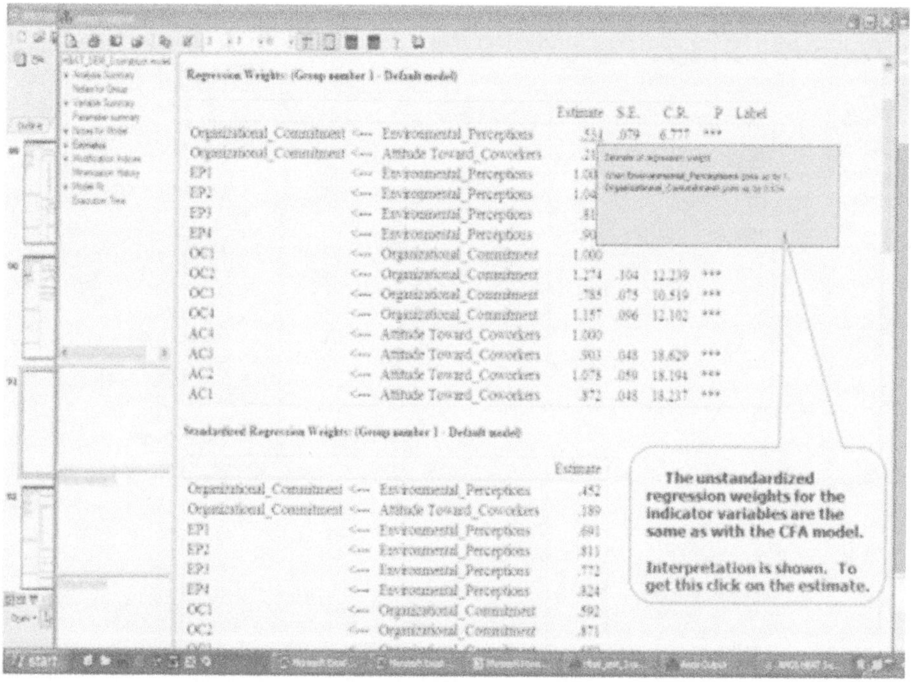

Fig. 8.21: Regression weight

(Source: Based on a review of Literature, 2018)

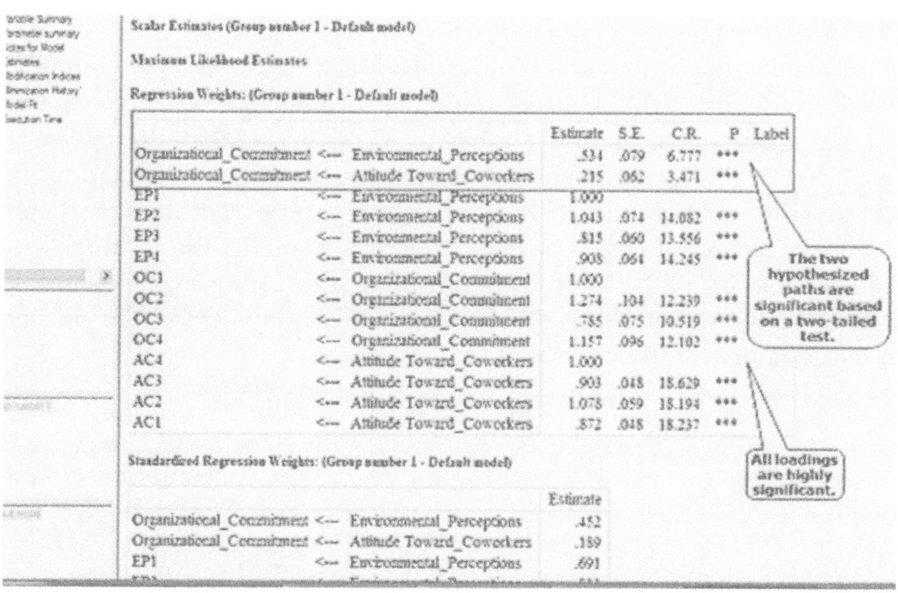

Fig. 8.22: Scalar Estimates(Group number 1-Default model)

(Source: Based on the review of literature, 2018)

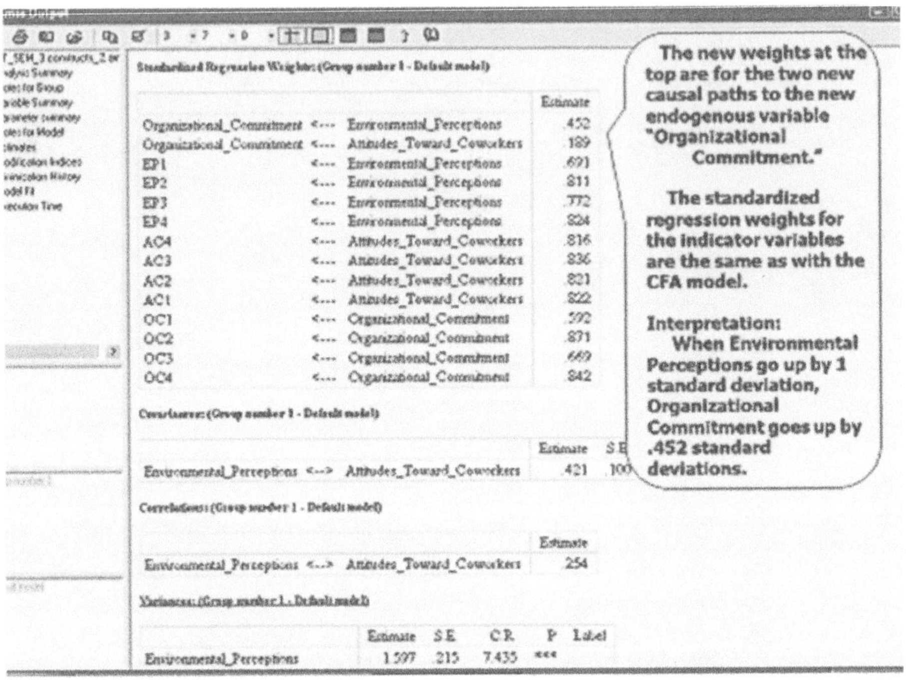

Fig. 8.23: Structural Regular Weight (Group number 1)
(Source: Based on a review of literature, 2018)

CONCLUSION

Path estimates – the completely standardized loadings (AMOS = standardized regression weights) that link the individual indicators to a particular construct. The recommended minimum = .7; but .5 is acceptable. Variables with insignificant or low loadings should be considered for deletion. Standardized residuals – the individual differences between observed covariance terms and fitted covariance terms. The better the fit the smaller the residual – these should not exceed |4.0|. Modification indices – the amount the overall Chi-square value would be reduced by freeing (estimating) any single particular path that is not currently estimated.

REFERENCES

Bagozzi, Richard P; Yi, Youjae (2011). "Specification, Evaluation and Interpretation of Structural Equation Models". Journal of the Academy of Marketing Science. **40** (1): 8–34. doi:10.1007/s11747-011-0278-x.

Bartholomew, D. J., and Knott, M. (1999) Latent Variable Models and Factor Analysis Kendall's Library of Statistics, vol. 7, Edward Arnold Publishers, ISBN 0-340-69243-X.

Bentler, P.M. & Bonett, D.G. (1980), "Significance Tests and Goodness of Fit in the Analysis of Covariance Structures", Psychological Bulletin, 88, 588-606.

Bollen, K. A. (1989). Structural Equations with Latent Variables. Wiley, ISBN 0-471-01171-1.

Byrne, B. M. (2001) Structural Equation Modeling with AMOS - Basic Concepts, Applications and Programming. LEA, ISBN 0-8058-4104-0.

Goldberger, A. S. (1972). Structural Equation Models in the Social Sciences. Econometrica 40, 979- 1001.

Haavelmo, Trygve (January 1943). "The Statistical Implications of a System of Simultaneous Equations". Econometrica. **11** (1): 1–12. doi:10.2307/1905714. JSTOR 1905714.

Hoyle, R H (ed) (1995) Structural Equation Modeling: Concepts, Issues and Applications. SAGE, ISBN 0-8039-5318-6.

Hu, Litze; Bentler, Peter M (1999). "Cutoff Criteria for Fit Indexes in Covariance Structure Analysis: Conventional Criteria Versus New Alternatives". Structural Equation Modeling: A Multidisciplinary Journal. **6**: 1. doi:10.1080/10705519909540118.

Jöreskog, Karl G.; Yang, Fan (1996). "Non-linear Structural Equation Models: The Kenny-Judd Model with Interaction effects". In Marcoulides, George A.; Schumacker, Randall E. Advanced Structural Equation Modeling: Concepts, Issues, and Applications. Thousand Oaks, CA: Sage Publications. pp. 57–88. ISBN 978-1-317-84380-1.

Kaplan, D. (2000), Structural Equation Modeling: Foundations and Extensions SAGE, Advanced Quantitative Techniques in the Social Sciences Series, Vol. 10, ISBN 0-7619-1407-2

Scientific Research Methodology : *Concepts and Quality*
Edited by: and Dr. Pawan Kumar 'Bharti' and Dr. Prasann Kumar
ISBN: 978-93-86841-95-7
Edition: 2019
Published by: Discovery Publishing House Pvt. Ltd., New Delhi (India)

9

Origin of Food Plants
Research with Special Reference to Geographical Regions

[1]Prasann Kumar, [2]Shweta Pathak, [1]Lamneivah Misao

ABSTRACT

Research into the origins of food plants has led to the recognition that specific geographical regions around the world have been of particular importance to the development of agricultural crops. Yet the relative contributions of these different regions in the context of current food systems have not been quantified. Here we determine the origins ('primary regions of diversity') of the crops comprising the food supplies and agricultural production of countries worldwide.

Keywords: Agricultre, Biotic, Crop, Density, Energy, Forage, Gap.

Introduction

We estimate the degree to which countries use crops from regions of diversity other than their own ('foreign crops'), and quantify changes in this usage over the past 50 years. Countries are highly interconnected with regard to primary regions of diversity of the crops they cultivate and/or consume. Foreign crops are extensively used in food supplies (68.7% of national food supplies as a global mean are derived from foreign crops) and production systems (69.3% of crops grown are foreign). Foreign crop usage has increased significantly over the past 50 years, including in countries with high indigenous crop diversity. The results provide a novel perspective on the ongoing globalization of food systems worldwide, and bolster evidence for the importance of international collaboration on genetic resource conservation and exchange.

Crop Origin

The origins of agriculture and domesticated crops are intertwined, and the change from a hunter-gatherer mode to tillage, sowing and harvesting was one of the major technological innovations of humankind. There is good evidence that this occurred some 10,000 years ago in several different locations, and involved the domestication of wild-relatives of the major crops.

[1] Department of Agronomy, School of Agriculture, Lovely Professional University, Jalandhar, Punjab, 144411, India
[2] Department of Plant Physiology, I.Ag. Sci., BHU., Varanasi, 221005, U.P., India

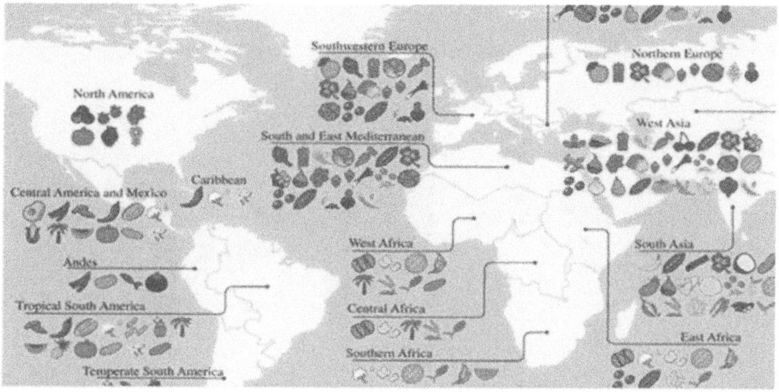

Fig. 9.1: Origin place of different crops

(Source: Review of Literature)

Domestication involves changes in the genetic makeup and morphological appearance of plants. These changes occur because people select the variations of a wild plant that best suit their needs. If the desired features can be passed to offspring, over generations of planting and harvesting, the strains of plants grown change. Despite the fact that these domesticated varieties of plants are preferred over their original forebears, the wild-relatives of crop plants continue to be an important resource. Reserves of wild plants offer a pool of genetic diversity. Traits of plants that might have been lost in domestication, sometimes become crucial for protection of domesticated crops from stress and disease. Maintaining wild strains for their gene pool helps ensure food security.

Center of origin: A **center of origin** (or **centre of diversity**) is a geographical area where a group of organisms, either domesticated or wild, first developed its distinctive properties. Centers of origin are also considered **centers of diversity**. For crop plants, Nikolai Vavilov initially identified 8 of these, later subdividing them into 12 in 1935.

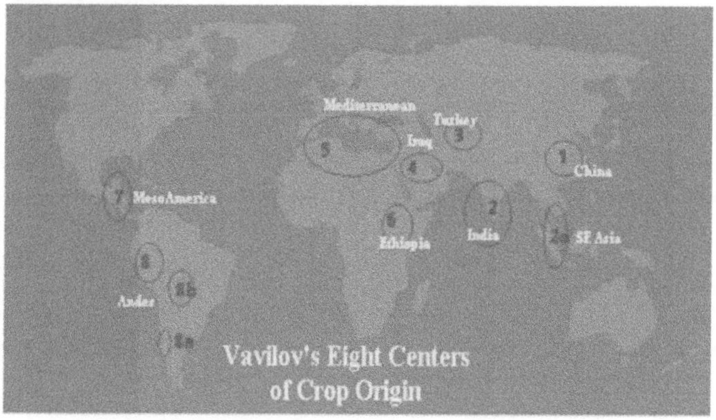

Fig. 9.2: Vavilov's Eight Centers of Crop Origin

(Source: Review Literature)

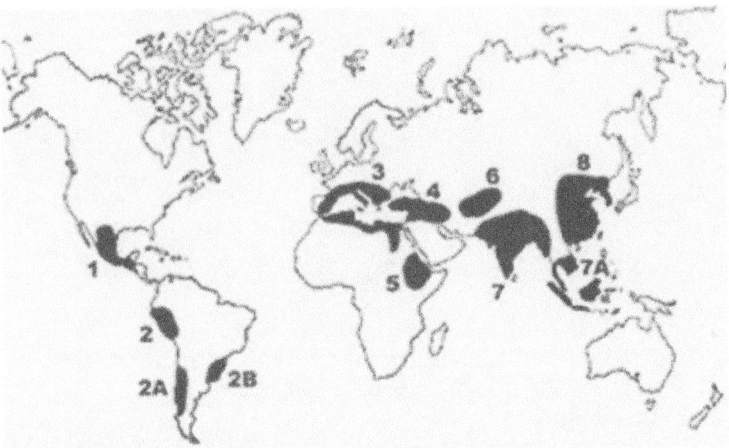

Fig. 9.3: Schematic Diagram of Vavilov Eight Centers of Origin
(Source: Based on Review of Literature)

where,

(1) Mexico –Guatmala, (2) Peru-Ecuador-Bolivia, (2A) Southern Chile, (2B) Southem Brazil, (3) Mediterranea, (4) Middle East, (5) Ethiopa, (6) Central Asia, (7) Indo-Burma, (7A) Siuam –Malaya- Java, (8) China and Korea.

Plants

Locating the origin of crop plants is basic to plant breeding. This allows one to locate wild relatives, related species, and new genes (especially dominant genes, which may provide resistance to diseases). Knowledge of the origins of crop plants is important in order to avoid genetic erosion, the loss of germplasm due to the loss of ecotypes and landraces, loss of habitat (such as rainforests), and increased urbanization. Germplasm preservation is accomplished through gene banks (largely seed collections but now frozen stem sections) and preservation of natural habitats (especially in centers of origin).

Vavilov Centers

A VavilovCenter (of Diversity) is a region of the world first indicated by Nikolai Vavilov to be an original center for the domestication of plants. Vavilov developed a theory on the centers of origin of cultivated plants. He stated that plants were not domesticated somewhere in the world at random but there are regions where the domestication started. The center of origin is also considered the center of diversity. Vavilovcenters are regions where a high diversity of crop wild relatives can be found, representing the natural relatives of domesticated crop plants. Later in 1935 Vavilov divided the centers into 12, giving the following list:

1. Chinese center
2. Indian(Hindustan) center

3. Indo-Malayan center
4. Central Asiatic center
5. Persian center
6. Mediterranean center
7. Abyssinian center
8. South American center
9. Central American center
10. Chilean center
11. Brazilian center
12. North American center

Table 9.1: World Centers of Origin of Cultivated Plants

Center	Plants
1. South Mexican and Central American Center	Includes southern sections of Mexico, Guatemala, Honduras and Costa Rica.
	• Grains and Legumes: maize, common bean, lima bean, tepary bean, jack bean, grain amaranth
	• Melon Plants: malabar gourd, winter pumpkin, chayote
	• Fiber Plants: upland cotton, bourbon cotton, henequen (sisal)
	• Miscellaneous: sweetpotato, arrowroot, pepper, papaya, guava, cashew, wild black cherry, chochenial, cherry tomato, cacao.
2. South American Center	62 plants listed; three subcenters
	2. Peruvian, Ecuadorean, Bolivian Center:
	• Root Tubers: Andean potato, Other endemic cultivated potato species. Fourteen or more species with chromosome numbers varying from 24 to 60, Edible nasturtium
	• Grains and Legumes: starchy maize, lima bean, common bean
	• Root Tubers: edible canna, potato
	• Vegetable Crops: pepino, tomato, ground cherry, pumpkin, pepper
	• Fiber Plants: Egyptian cotton
	• Fruit and Miscellaneous: cocoa, passion flower, guava, heilborn, quinine tree, tobacco, cherimoya, coca
	2A) Chiloe Center (Island near the coast of southern Chile)
	• Common potato (48 chromosomes), Chilean strawberry
	2B) Brazilian-Paraguayan Center
	• manioc, peanut, rubber tree, pineapple, Brazil nut, cashew, Erva-mate, purple granadilla.

3. Mediterranean Center	Includes the borders of the Mediterranean Sea. 84 listed plants
	• Cereals and Legumes: durum wheat, emmer, Polish wheat, spelt, Mediterranean oats, sand oats, canarygrass, grass pea, pea, lupine
	• Forage Plants: Egyptian clover, white clover, crimson clover, serradella
	• Oil and Fiber Plants: flax, rape, black mustard, olive
	• Vegetables: garden beet, cabbage, turnip, lettuce, asparagus, celery, chicory, parsnip, rhubarb,
	• Ethereal Oil and Spice Plants: caraway, anise, thyme, peppermint, sage, hop.
4. Middle East	Includes interior of Asia Minor, all of Transcaucasia, Iran, and the highlands of Turkmenistan. 83 species
	• Grains and Legumes: einkorn wheat, durum wheat, poulard wheat, common wheat, oriental wheat, Persian wheat, two-row barley, rye, Mediterranean oats, common oats, lentil, lupine
	• Forage Plants: alfalfa, Persian clover, fenugreek, vetch, hairy vetch
	• Fruits: fig, pomegranate, apple, pear, quince, cherry, hawthorn.
5. Ethiopia	Includes Abyssinia, Eritrea, and part of Somaliland. 38 species listed; rich in wheat and barley.
	• Grains and Legumes: Abyssinian hard wheat, poulard wheat, emmer, Polish wheat, barley, grain sorghum, pearl millet, African millet, cowpea, flax, teff
	• Miscellaneous: sesame, castor bean, garden cress, coffee, okra, myrrh, indigo.
6. Central Asiatic Center	Includes Northwest India (Punjab, Northwest Frontier Provinces and Kashmir), Afghanistan, Tadjikistan, Uzbekistan, and western Tian-Shan. 43 plants
	• Grains and Legumes: common wheat, club wheat, shot wheat, peas, lentil, horse bean, chickpea, mung bean, mustard, flax, sesame
	• Fiber Plants: hemp, cotton
	• Vegetables: onion, garlic, spinach, carrot
	• Fruits: pistacio, pear, almond, grape, apple.
7. Indian Center	Two subcenters
	7) Indo-Burma: Main Center (India): Includes Assam and Burma, but not Northwest India, Punjab, nor Northwest Frontier Provinces, 117 plants
	• Cereals and Legumes: rice, chickpea, pigeon pea, urd bean, mung bean, rice bean, cowpea,
	• Vegetables and Tubers: eggplant, cucumber, radish, taro, yam

	• Fruits: mango, orange, tangerine, citron, tamarind
	• Sugar, Oil, and Fiber Plants: sugar cane, coconut palm, sesame, safflower, tree cotton, oriental cotton, jute, crotalaria, kenaf
	• Spices, Stimulants, Dyes, and Miscellaneous: hemp, black pepper, gum arabic, sandalwood, indigo, cinnamon tree, croton, bamboo.
	7A) Siam-Malaya-Java: statt Indo-Malayan Center: Includes Indo-China and the Malay Archipelago, 55 plants
	• Cereals and Legumes: Job's tears, velvet bean
	• Fruits: pummelo, banana, breadfruit, mangosteen
	• Oil, Sugar, Spice, and Fiber Plants: candlenut, coconut palm, sugarcane, clove, nutmeg, black pepper, manila hemp.
8. Chinese Center	A total of 136 endemic plants are listed in the largest independent center
	• Cereals and Legumes: e.g. broomcorn millet, Italian millet, Japanese barnyard millet, Koaliang, buckwheat, hull-less barley, soybean, Adzuki bean, velvet bean
	• Roots, Tubers, and Vegetables: e.g. Chinese yam, radish, Chinese cabbage, onion, cucumber
	• Fruits and Nuts: e.g. pear, Chinese apple, peach, apricot, cherry, walnut, litchi
	• Sugar, Drug, and Fiber Plants: e.g. sugar cane, opium poppy, ginseng camphor, hemp.

Importance

In 2016, researchers linked the origins and primary regions of diversity ("areas typically including the locations of the initial domestication of crops, encompassing the primary geographical zones of crop variation generated since that time, and containing relatively high species richness in crop wild relatives") of food and agricultural crops with their current importance around the world in modern national food supplies and agricultural production. The results indicated that foreign crops were 68.7% of national food supplies as a global mean, and their usage has greatly increased in the last fifty years.

Agriculture Classification of Crops

There are many systems of classification of crops for example, commercial, taxonomical and agricultural among the **agricultural classification of crops** are more widely accepted because it is commonly it covers the taxonomical and commercial and other aspects.

- Taxonomical classification
- Commercial classification
- Agricultural classification

Taxonomical classification

Taxonomical classification deals with the taxonomical aspects of classifying aspects of crops — that is their morphology and economical parts and agro-botanical characters. Advantage: understanding of the morphological characters of any particular family. Disadvantage: crops with different economic uses and morphological and other agro-botanical peculiarities when brought under one family do not generally bring out the economic importance of the individual crops.

Commercial Classification

Plants are classified according to the commercial purposes as Food crops, Industrial crops, Food adjuncts.

Food crops - cereals – Rice, wheat, maize, sorghum, ragi, Pulses, legumes, fruits, vegetables and nuts.

Industrial crop - Cotton, Sugarcane, tobacco, groundnut, castor, gingelly, tapioca, etc.

Food adjuncts - No distinct demarcation – food and Industrial usage. spices and condiments, beverages and narcotics.

Disadvantage: It is possible that one crop which has been included as a food crop may figure also as an industrial crop. e.g. maize or tapioca.

A better classification is the agricultural classification.

Agricultural classification

Use of plants and plant products to man, viz. Cereals, Pulses, Vegetables, Fruits, Nuts, Oilseeds, Sugars and Starches, Fibres, Beverages, Narcotics, Spices, Condiments, Rubber Forages, Green and Green leaf manure.

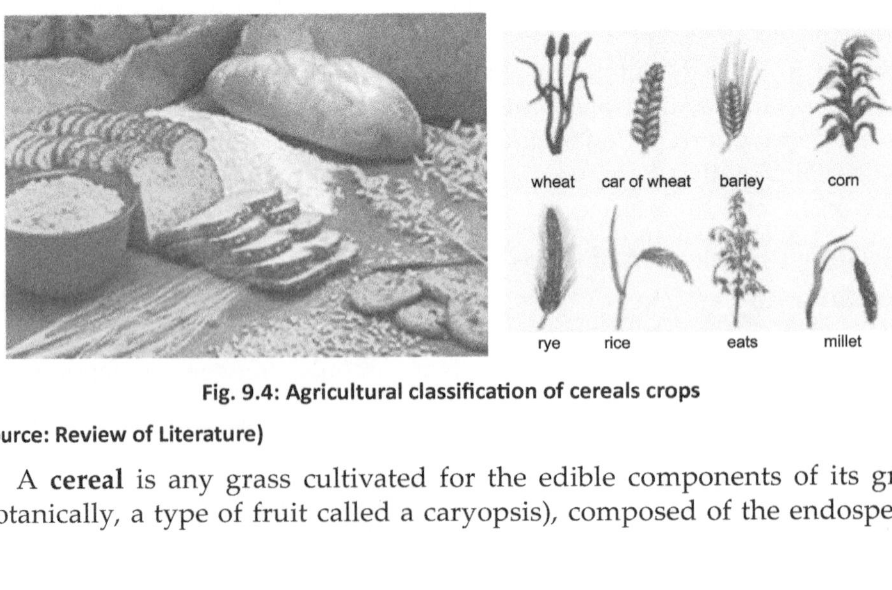

Fig. 9.4: Agricultural classification of cereals crops

(Source: Review of Literature)

A **cereal** is any grass cultivated for the edible components of its grain (botanically, a type of fruit called a caryopsis), composed of the endosperm, germ, and bran. Cereal grains are grown in greater quantities and provide more food energy worldwide than any other type of crop and are therefore staple crops. Edible grains from other plant families, such as buckwheat (Polygonaceae), quinoa (Amaranthaceae) and chia (Lamiaceae), are referred to as pseudocereals. In their natural form (as in *whole grain*), cereals are a rich source of vitamins, minerals, carbohydrates, fats, oils, and protein. When refined by the removal of the bran and germ, the remaining endosperm is mostly carbohydrate. In some developing nations, grain in the form of rice, wheat, millet, or maize constitutes a majority of daily sustenance. In developed nations, cereal consumption is moderate and varied but still substantial.

Pulses are one of the important food crops globally due to higher protein content. Pulses are an important group of crops in India, which is also responsible for yielding large financial gains by amounting for a large part of the experts. Pulses are the major sources of protein in the diet. India is the largest producer of pulses in the world. Pulses are 20 to 50 per cent protein by weight which is double the protein content of wheat and three times that of rice. Pulses are the dried seeds of the legume plants. Hundreds of different varieties of pulses are grown around the globe.

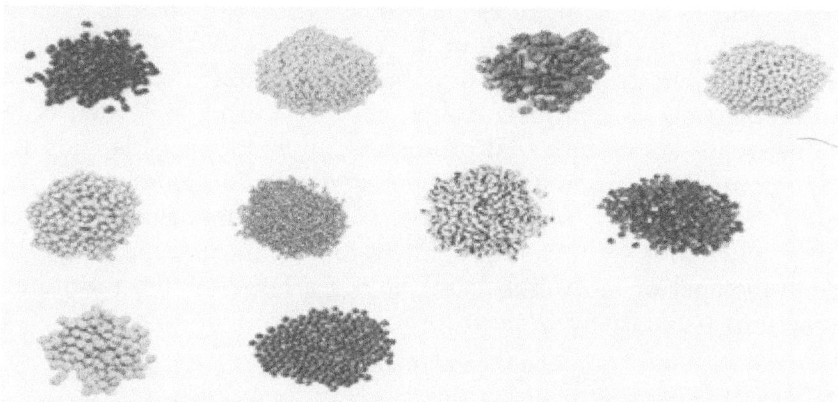

Fig. 9.5: Different types of pulse in India

(Source: Review Literature)

Seed oil

A **seed oil** is a vegetable oil that is obtained from the seed (endosperm) of some plant, rather than the fruit (pericarp). Most vegetable oils are seed oils. Some common examples are sunflower oil, canola oil, and sesame oil. Some important vegetable oils are not seed oils. Some examples are olive oil and peanut oil (Figure 9.6).

Fig. 9. 6: Example of oil seed crop

(Source: Review of Literature)

Natural rubber, also called **India rubber** or ***caoutchouc***, as initially produced, consists of polymers of the organic compound isoprene, with minor impurities of other organic compounds, plus water. Malaysia and Indonesia are two of the leading rubber producers. Forms of polyisoprene that are used as natural rubbers are classified as elastomers. Currently, rubber is harvested mainly in the form of the latex from the rubber tree or others. The latex is a sticky, milky colloid drawn off by making incisions in the bark and collecting the fluid in vessels in a process called "tapping". The latex then is refined into rubber ready for commercial processing. In major areas, latex is allowed to coagulate in the collection cup. The coagulated lumps are collected and processed into dry forms for marketing. Natural rubber is used extensively in many applications and products, either alone or in combination with other materials. In most of its useful forms, it has a large stretch ratio and high resilience, and is extremely waterproof (figure 9.7).

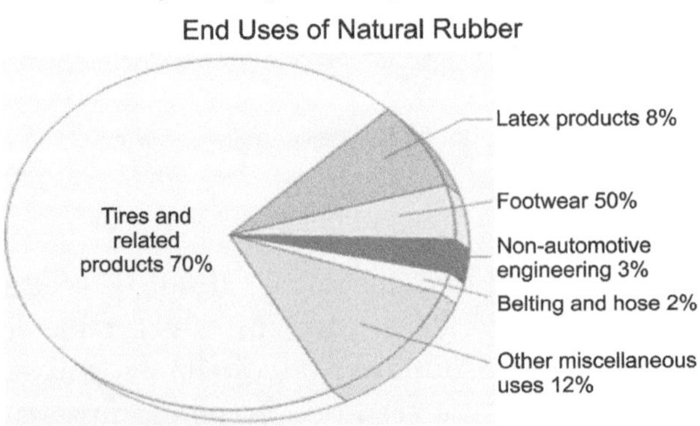

Fig. 9.7: End Uses of Natural Rubber

(Source: Review of Literature)

Fiber or **fibre** is a natural or synthetic substance that is significantly longer than it is wide. Fibers are often used in the manufacture of other materials. The strongest engineering materials often incorporate fibres, for example carbon fiber and ultra-high-molecular-weight polyethylene. Synthetic fibers can often be produced very cheaply and in large amounts compared to natural fibers, but for clothing, natural fibers can give some benefits, such as comfort, over their synthetic counterparts. Vegetable **fibers** are generally based on arrangements of cellulose, often with lignin: examples include cotton, hemp, jute, flax, ramie, sisal, bagasse, and banana. Plant **fibers** are employed in the manufacture of paper and textile (cloth), and dietary **fiber** is an important component of human nutrition.

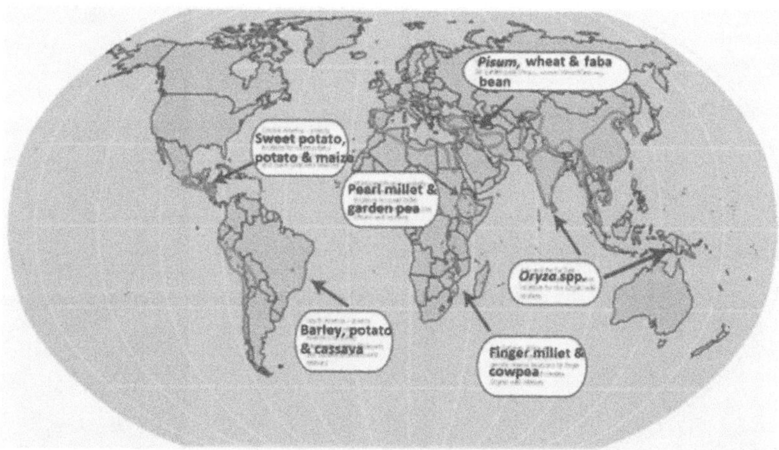

Fig. 9.8: Global Priority genetic reserve locations for wild relative of 12 food crops (Source: Based on Review of Literature, 2018)

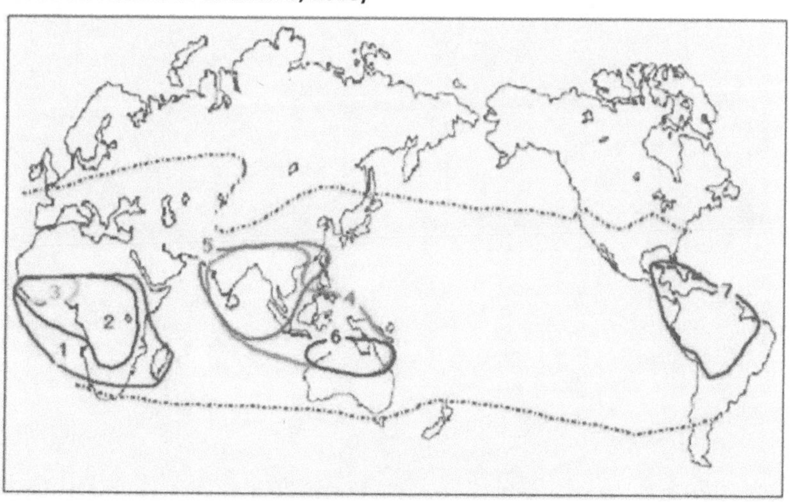

Fig. 9.9: *Oryza sativa* complex (AA Genome) (Source: Based on Review of Literature, 2018)

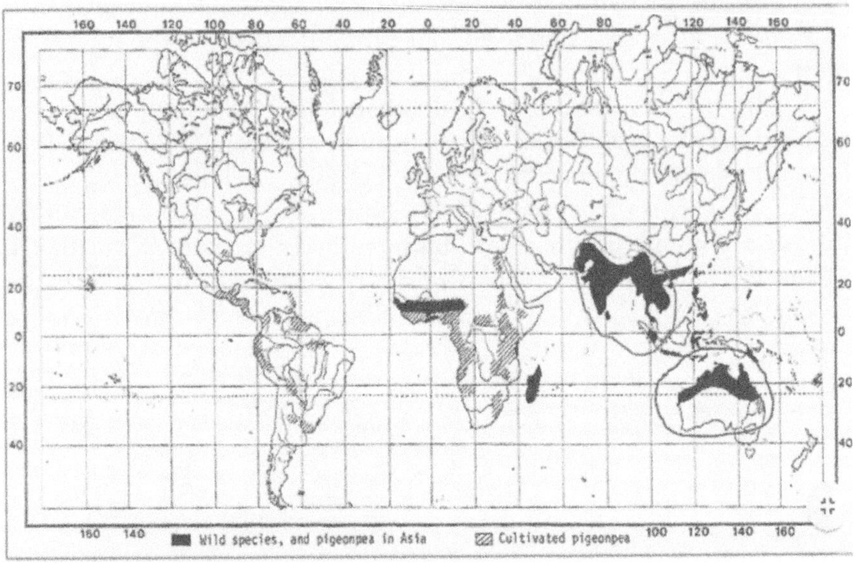

Fig. 9.10: Origin and Distribution of *Cajanus cajan*
(Source: Based on Review of Literature)

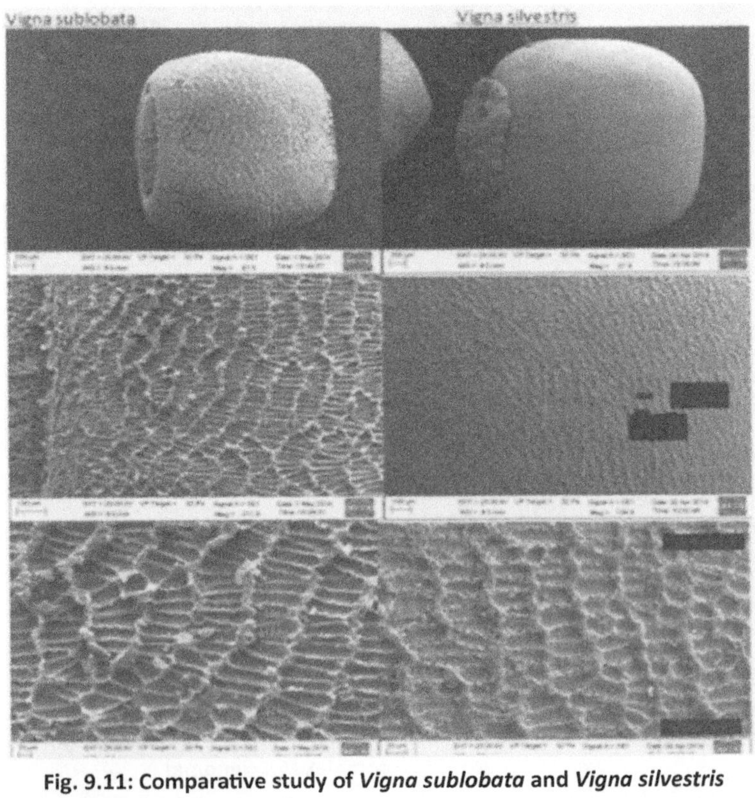

Fig. 9.11: Comparative study of *Vigna sublobata* and *Vigna silvestris*
(Source: Based on Review of Literature)

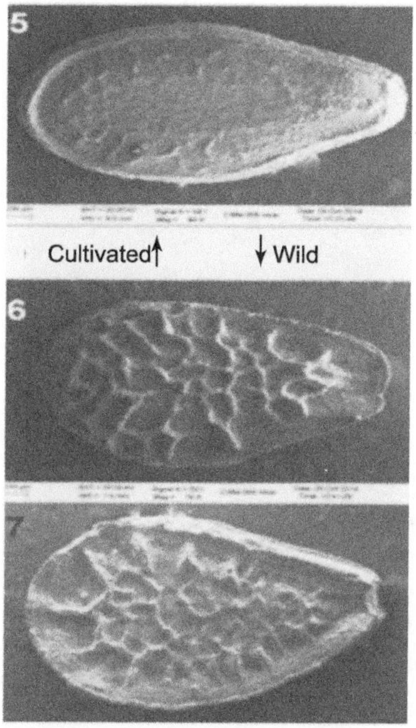

Fig. 9.12: Study of Sesamum
(Source: Based on Review of Literature)

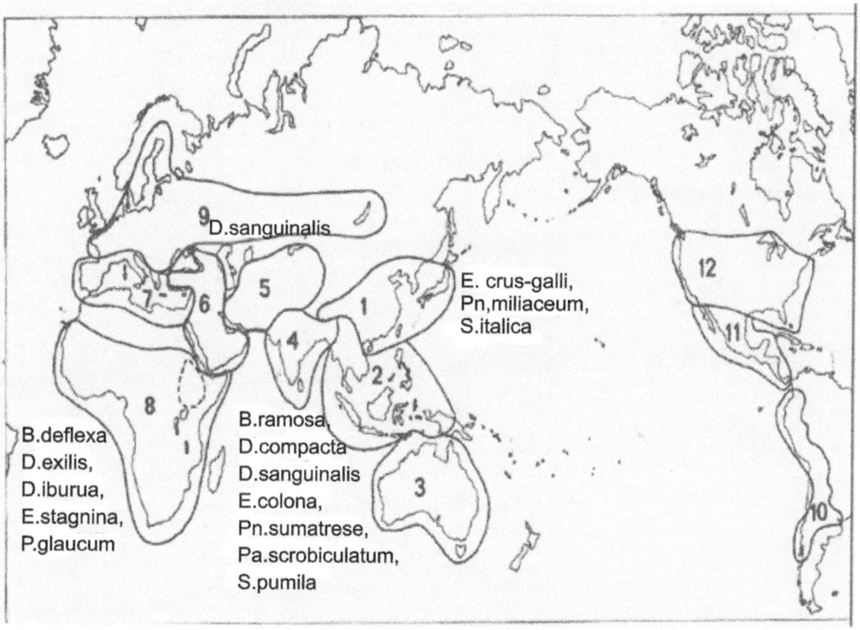

Fig. 9.13: Crop origin and their center of origin
(Source: Based on Review of Literature)

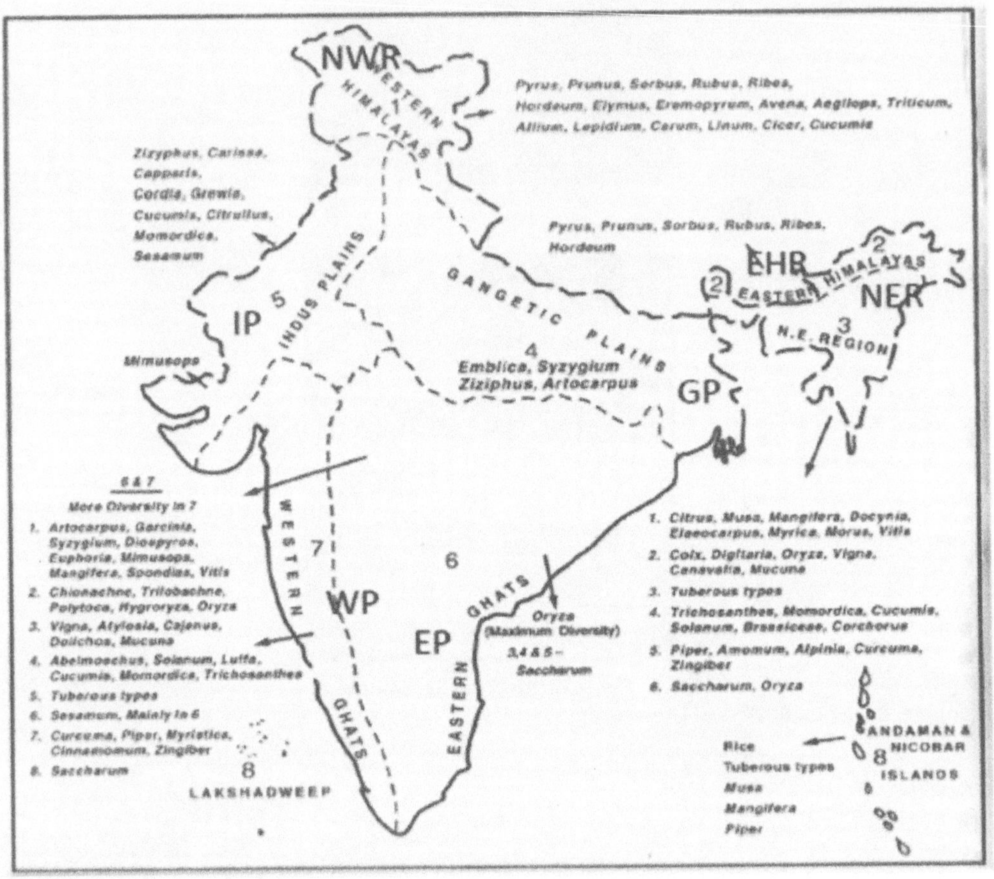

Fig. 9.14: Indian centre of diversity

(Source: Based on Review of Literature)

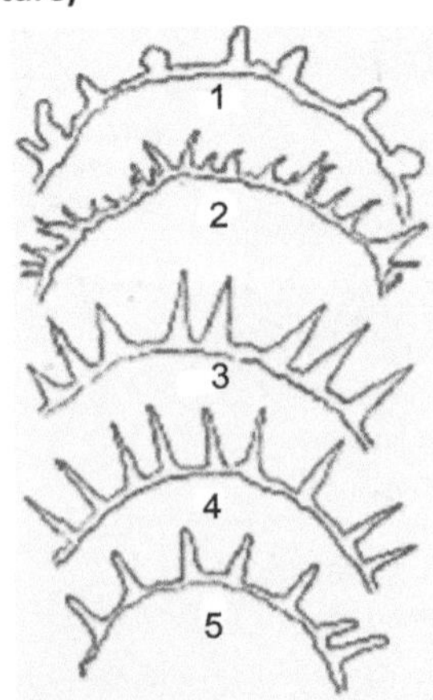

Fig. 9.15: South Africa Okra

(Source: Based on Review of Literature)

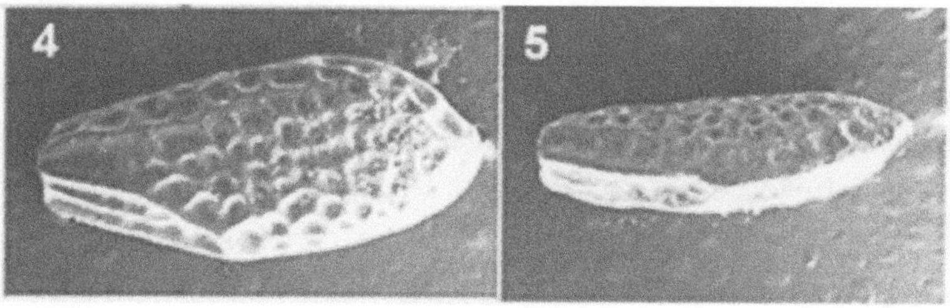

Fig. 9.16: Gene Pool
(Source: Based on Review of Literature)

Crop Origin with Special Reference to Vegetables

As recently as the mid-1800s relatively little was known about the origin of our important economic crops. For many scientists at that time, their origin was thought to be an "impenetrable secret." Alphonse de Candolle's classic work, *Origin of Cultivated Plants,* published in 1886 and more recent studies of the Russian botanist/geneticist Nikolai Vavilov and the many efforts of other scientists contributed to identifying likely centers of origin, diversity, and/or domestication of most of the world's important crops. Also deserving recognition are the early plant explorers and observers such as von Humboldt and Captain James Cook, and more recent scientists Carl Sauer, Jack Harlan, and Jack Hawkes for their theories and studies concerning crop evolution and domestication of many useful plants. Although full agreement about the theories proposed is lacking, the contributions of these people were essential for our knowledge about many plant species. Continuing studies using new technologies should reveal further information and possibly close some existing gaps about the origin and development of certain crop plants.

Humans and Agriculture

To understand the origin and evolution of crop plants, it is useful to also understand the processes that are believed to have occurred during the development of agriculture. Humans have existed on earth for over two million years, and as early inhabitants they were food gathers and hunters. Early humans followed a nomadic or seminomadic existence in their search for food. It is reasonable to assume that where and when the food supply was adequate, a somewhat sedentary life form could be followed, with various plants supplementing food obtained from hunting and fishing. This premise is supported by discoveries found in many archaeological sites.

Plant Cultivation and Domestication

It is generally believed that *in situ* cultivation of plants began about 8-10 thousand years ago-only a fraction of the human existence period. Why did it take so long? Probably because there were no examples or few experiences to follow and upon which to build. Because food searching was a major survival activity, to which much time and effort was devoted, there probably was little time to think about crop cultivation, even if aware of cultivation practices. Furthermore, experience and knowledge about plant cultivation could not be widely disseminated because travel between settlements and communication was minimal. However, within communities, plant cultural knowledge could be passed to subsequent generations.

Conditions Considered Necessary for Early Plant Domestication

Areas with an abundant supply of game and a marked diversity of edible food plants were where early agriculture started. These conditions allowed for some degree of permanence of settlements. With less effort required to roam and search for food, more effort and thought could be directed to the domestication and management of plants and animals. Geographer botanist Carl Sauer theorized that certain conditions had to be present in order for plant domestication to have occurred. He proposed that the first cultivated lands would have been those that required little preparation. Not all land required clearing, and relatively flat well-drained land was more appropriate for early cultivation than situations that might require drainage or other modifications. Another required condition would be the control of fire, necessary for cooking, warmth, and protection from predators, but also useful for land clearing. Even today in some regions, "slash and burn" practices continue to be widely practiced to prepare land for cultivation. Continuing conversion of rain forests and other land for arable cropping or animal grazing that use slash and burn procedures are causing serious regional and international environmental and sociological concerns. Early experiences would have shown that river valleys that faced periodic flooding or arid areas were less desirable. Agriculture is one of the most momentous inventions of humanity. It generated a surplus of food as a consequence of which a sizable fraction of societies were able to engage in economic activities other than agriculture. Thus, agriculture is considered to have been a prerequisite for the development of many civilizations throughout the world. It originated independently and at similar times (around 10 000 years ago) in different areas on several continents, notably Mesoamerica and South America, the Near East, the Sahel and Ethiopia, China, and Southeast Asia. Selection resulting from the cultivation and harvesting of plants by humans induced genetic modifications in these plants resulting in their domestication. In contrast to their wild progenitors, crop plants are unable to disperse their seeds and lack seed dormancy. They also have smaller plants but larger harvested organs (fruits, seeds, leaves) and contain lower amounts of toxic compounds. Flowering time is also less susceptible to environmental influences, mainly day-length. Following their domestication crop plants were widely dispersed across the globe, chiefly after the conquest of the Americas by the Europeans from 1492 on (the "Columbian exchange"). As a consequence of this dispersal, the assemblage of crops in any agricultural region is actually an assemblage originating throughout the world. During their evolution under cultivation, plants have been subjected to three reductions in genetic diversity. Therefore, wild progenitors and primitive cultivars in the areas of origin are a source of additional genetic diversity to further improve elite cultivars of our major crop plants. In the evolution of humankind, agriculture is a fairly recent activity, having originated some 10 000 years ago after the last glaciation, more or less simultaneously in a limited number of regions of the world, principally the Near East or southwest Asia, east Asia, Africa, Mesoamerica, and South America. In contrast to other, more recent technological advances, agriculture was invented multiple times and independently in these different regions. From the limited number of hearths of invention, agriculture spread relatively quickly over the entire world and is now practiced on the five major continents. Prior to agriculture, food acquisition by humans depended on hunting game animals and gathering wild plants. The importance of the transition from hunter-gatherer to agricultural societies cannot be overstated. This transition, often referred to as the Neolithic revolution, saw the appearance of a sedentary lifestyle in villages, the domestication of our major crops and farm animals, and the development of ceramics and grain storage technologies. Although these individual technologies did not all appear concurrently with domestication of plants and animals, and some actually prepared domestication, there is no doubt that the introduction of agriculture led to a much-changed world. First and foremost, because agriculture led to a surplus of food, a significant proportion of societies could devote its energies to activities other than food acquisition, including commerce, administration, and warfare. Egalitarian societies evolved into hierarchical, centralized societies. Thus, agriculture is widely considered to be a prerequisite of the subsequent development of civilizations. Indeed, one of the definitions of civilization is precisely a society that relies on agriculture for its food procurement. Striking examples of this feature are the development of the Mesopotamian civilizations such as Sumer, Ur, and Babylon and the Mesoamerican civilizations such as the Olmecs, Mayas, and Aztecs. These civilizations would not have been possible without the existence of a more or less reliable system of food supply provided by agriculture. Differences in the degree of success and hegemony among these civilizations and the ones derived from them have been related to the domestication of cereals and farm animals. The reliance of major civilizations on agriculture and particularly specific crops for their development is mirrored by the reliance of our major crops on humankind for their continued survival. As will be explained below, fully domesticated crops have lost their means to disperse seeds. In addition, these crops have often lost seed dormancy, the requirement for vernalization, and photoperiod sensitivity—three mechanisms assuring they will grow and mature during the favorable part of the year (either the warm or the wet season). In the absence of human intervention, crops would therefore not survive in the long term. This mutual dependence of humankind and domesticated plants represents a striking example of a symbiosis or mutually beneficial relationship. It would be impossible to feed the six billion inhabitants of this planet without this relationship. Agriculture has had other major consequences. The sedentary lifestyle and the higher labor requirements of agricultural practices have led to an increase in population growth. After having reached the carrying capacity in the centers of origin, the excess population overflowed into neighboring areas leading to a dispersal of agriculture by demic rather than cultural diffusion. Accompanying this dispersal was a diffusion of some (but not all) of the major human language families. For example, from the Near Eastern center of agricultural origin, the Indo-European, Turkic, Elamo-Dravidian, and Afro-Asiatic (particularly Semitic) families were dispersed. From the Chinese center, the Sino-Tibetan, Austroasiatic, Austronesian-Tai, and Hmong-Mien families were dispersed. The success of agriculture was generally so overwhelming that, except in the most remote and inhospitable areas, it replaced hunting and gathering as the dominant food procurement type and lifestyle. Hunter-gatherers are found nowadays only in a few regions with extreme conditions, either in rain forests (Indians in the Amazon or Pygmies in central Africa) or steppes (Kung in southern Africa or Aborigines in Australia). Concurrently, native vegetation has largely been displaced by agricultural ecosystems, not only in areas of dispersal but also in the centers of origin. For example, agriculture accounts for 80% of the annual world deforestation. Some of the most famous landscapes on our planet, such as the golden wheat fields of Montana, the windmill-studded pastures and flower fields of the Low Countries, the rolling hills of Tuscany, and the terraced rice fields of eastern Asia are typical agricultural landscapes in which native species play only a minor role. The displacement of hunter-gatherer societies by agricultural societies is somewhat paradoxical. Studies of contemporary hunter-gatherer groups have shown that they generally have a desirable lifestyle at least for certain aspects. Food gathering and hunting takes up only part of their time, leaving ample opportunities for leisure time. In addition, their diet is usually quite diverse. Because of the low population density, epidemics of infectious diseases are rare but parasitic diseases are more frequent. In contrast, early agricultural societies are characterized by a heavy labor investment. This includes child labor, which may be one of the reasons for marked increases in population growth following the transition to agriculture. Their diet is much less diverse and subject to variation in availability. Years of abundant harvests can be followed by lean years, hence periodic starvation and malnutrition are frequent. Because of the higher population densities in agricultural societies, infectious diseases may have been more prevalent. It appears that the overall level of well-being was higher in hunter gather societies than in the agricultural societies that followed them. This observation further raises the question as to why the transition to agriculture took place in the face of a deterioration of living conditions. The disappearance of natural vegetation is of particular importance in centers of agricultural origins because of the presence of wild relatives of crop species. These wild relatives are sources of genes to improve crops for higher yield and disease and pest resistance, among other traits. Their loss threatens the continued improvement of the crop by plant breeding. This loss is of special concern given the narrow genetic base of most major crops as a consequence of genetic bottlenecks following domestication, dispersal from centers of origin, and twentieth century plant breeding. An additional concern is the loss of wild (i.e. non-domesticated) species altogether, whether related or not to crop plants. Some 250 000 plant species have been described, of which 75 000 are considered to provide edible products. Whether edible or not, at most 2000–3000 have been subject to at least the initial stages of domestication. It is unlikely that most undomesticated species remain so because they proved to be refractory to domestication efforts. This would have required massive efforts to bring each species under cultivation for a substantial period of time. Rather, for reasons that are not understood, domestication focused on a limited number of species. Whether these species were particularly predisposed for domestication is not known. If they were not, other plant species could be domesticated that would provide useful food or other products to humankind (Figure 9.17).

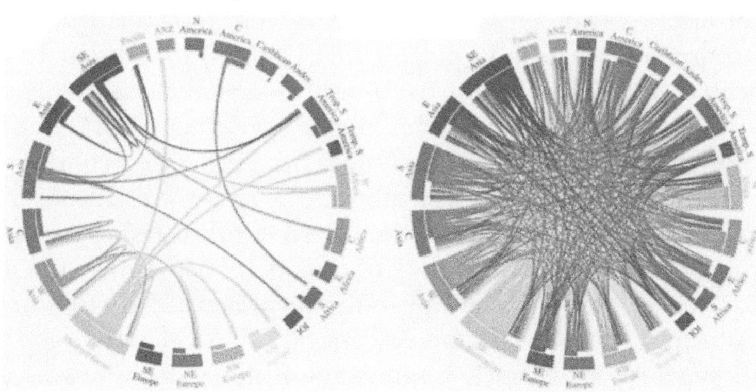

(a) (b)

Fig. 9.17: Origin of Food crops connects world wide
(Source: Based on Review of Literature)

Molecular Markers as Tools to Study Domestication

The development of increasingly informative molecular markers has allowed for detailed investigations of the evolution and domestication of a number of crops. Moreover, with the increasing ease and decreasing cost of molecular tools, the resources necessary for investigating the genetic underpinnings of phenotypic traits are now in place for most major crops. These advances not only allow for an investigation of the overall genetic architecture of the wild-crop transition, but also make possible the identification of genomic regions and genes that were subjected to selection during the evolution of various crops. In some cases, researchers have been able to pinpoint the exact nucleotide changes responsible for the production of key crop-related trait. Kilian *et al.* in the year 2018, stated that the keys to obtain deeper insights to plant domestication using molecular biology are (i) a comprehensive germplasm collection covering the whole distribution area for each species; (ii) the comparison of many wild and domesticated accessions for each species; (iii) the identification of the wild progenitor in the wild gene pool and its comparison with domesticated descendants; (iv) the use of new molecular fingerprinting techniques at many loci and the access to new generation high throughput sequencing technologies; and (v) improvement of analytical methods capable of treating domestication issues based on mathematical and statistical models. Molecular information has for almost two decades provided new insights on genetic diversity of crop plants; in relation to wild relatives, identification of crop progenitors, centers of domestication, time frame of the domestication process and specific alleles supporting domesticated traits. This is due largely to the rapid accumulation of genomic resources that provided genome-wide markers for population and molecular analyses of crops and their wild relatives. One of the leading studies in this area of research was done by Brubaker and Wendel, who used the DNA markers derived from nuclear restriction fragment length polymorphisms (RFLPs) to reevaluate the origin of domesticated cotton. Matsuoka, used multi-locus microsatellite genotyping to identify a single domestication for maize. Wills and Burke, used hyper-variable chloroplast simple-sequence repeat markers to search for evidence of a possible Mexican origin of domestication for sunflowers. The data provided further evidence that the extant domesticated sunflowers are the product of a single domestication event somewhere outside of Mexico. In the mean time Konishi *et al.* used single nucleotide polymorphism (SNP) to elucidate loss of seed shattering during rice domestication. The localization and timing of domestication events and the demographics of domestication was addressed by Liu and Burke. Further important contributions using molecular markers for other species include the works on barley; einkorn wheat; maize and rice. The most popular of the molecular approaches is the AFLP, a PCR-based procedure that resolves radioactively labeled electrophoretic bands (polymorphic loci) on sequencing gels or in gene sequencing machines. The AFLP approach became feasible in the 1990s, when the development of hight hroughput methods made it possible to type multiple markers in many individual plant.

For the AFLP fingerprinting, DNA is digested with EcoRI and MseI and specific doublestranded adapters with sequence complementary to newly formed ends of fragments, labeled with fluorescent dye moiety, are used to amplify AFLP fragments using PCR that is then separated in polyacrylamide gel or using automated DNA sequencing machine. The presence (1) or absence (0) of amplified fragments, in the range of 50–500 bp long is scored for data analyses. This multi-locus analysis was first applied to einkorn wheat, through typing of 288 amplified fragment length polymorphisms (AFLP) in 338 wild and cultivated accessions. Phylogenetic trees constructed from the AFLP data showed that domesticated einkorn is monophyletic, all modern crop plants rooting back to a single point, indicative of their common descent from a single progenitor population of early domesticate. The early domesticates were genetically most similar to wild plants from the Karacadag region of southeast Turkey. Similar AFLP analyses subsequently revealed an origin for barley in N Israel – NW Jordan area and the tetraploid emmer wheat that was also found in Karacadag mountains region of southeast Turkey questioned the use of AFLP markers in phylogenetic studies addressing crop domestication. Subsequently, Salamini *et al.* cited several dozens of papers that correctly addressed domestication issues based on AFLP markers. The monophyletic and localized event detected by AFLP typing in wheat and barley was thus interpreted as emergence of a 'superior landrace' possibly one possessing a major domestication phenotype such as the tough rachis. This scenario is compatible with a lengthy period of plant utilization before domestication, but the difficulty remained that the tight affinity between each modern crop and a single wild population was consistent with a gradual transition only if during this transition the plants ancestral to the superior landrace either did not cross-hybridize with wild plants or only cross-hybridized with their parent population. Brown *et al.* argued that neither scenario is likely unless the early cultivators possessed the ability to isolate their crops from wild plants or if these pre-Neolithic communities were much less mobile than previously thought. They suggested that archaeo-botanical studies are showing that acquisition of the full set of traits observed in domesticated cereals was a protracted process, intermediate stages being seen at early farming sites throughout the Fertile Crescent. These authors favor a multiregional nature of cereal domestication, in contrast to a previous view that each crop was domesticated by a rapid, unique and geographically localized process. Olsen and Gross pointed out that a multi-locus cluster analyses can generate a monophyletic grouping for a hybrid species even if that species has evolved multiple times independently. This scenario potentially parallels that of independent domestication events followed by admixture of events. Thus, in assessing whether a crop's monophyletic grouping is real, it is critical to examine whether the alleles in the crop are truly a subset of those in the wild populations with which the crop is most closely clustered, as would be expected in a progenitor/derivative relationship (Figure 9.18).

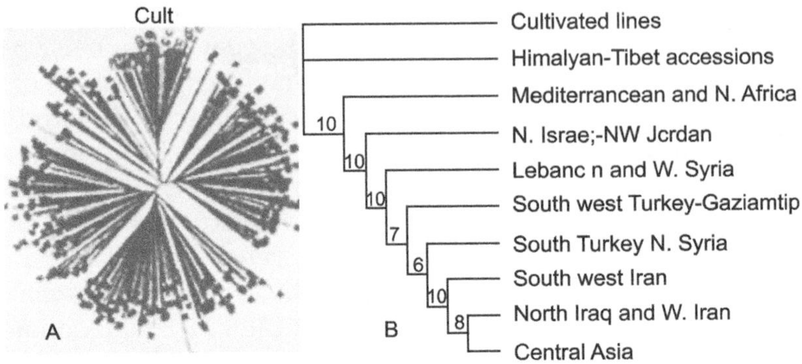

Fig. 9.18: Polygenic tress for Barley

(Source: Based on Review of Literature)

Molecular Approaches to Clover Ancestry and Domestication

The Egyptian clover (*Trifolium alexandrinum* L.) belongs to section *Trifolium* of the genus Trifolium L., which comprises 242 species, of World-wide distribution, and includes 16 cultivated species all as forage crops. The Egyptian clover (Berseem) has been widely cultivated, as a forage crop, in western Asia and North Africa for a long time. Its cultivation was extended to Middle Asia, particularly Pakistan and India and also the United States of America since the beginning of the 20th century. In their comprehensive monograph on the whole genus, Zohary and Heller recognized two varieties of *T. alexandrinum*; Var. alexandrinum with the local name Fahli and Var. serotinum with the local name Muscavi. The Fahli variety gives basal branching and one crop per cultivation, whereas the Muscavi variety gives apical branching and 4–6 crops per cultivation. A third variety, the Saidi, produces both basal and apical branching and gives 2–3 crops per cultivation (Figure 9.19).

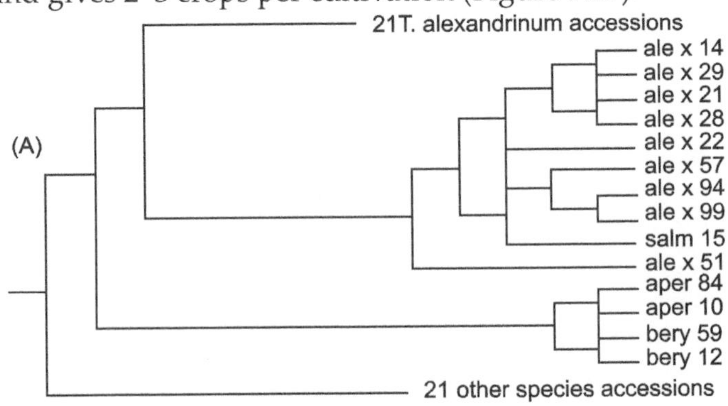

Fig. 9.19: Phylogenetic tress of T. ***alexandrium***

(Source: Based on Review of Literature)

Conclusion

The development of increasingly informative molecular markers has allowed for detailed investigations of the evolution and domestication of a number of crops. Moreover, with the increasing ease and decreasing cost of molecular tools, the resources necessary for investigating the genetic underpinnings of phenotypic traits are now in place for most major crops.

REFERENCES

A.H. Abdel-Ghani, H.K. Parzies, A. Omary, H.H. Geiger, Theor. Appl. Genet. 109 (2004) 588–595. [2] R.G. Allaby, T.A. Brown, Genome 46 (2003) 448–453.

A.M. Casas, S. Yahiaoui, F. Ciudad, E. Igartua, Genome 48 (2005) 41–45.

A.R. Delile, Histoire des plantes cultive´es en Egypte (Description de Egypte, Second ed., 19). Paris, 1824.

A. Badr, K. Mueller, R. Schaeffer-Pregl, H. El-Rabey, S. Efgen, H.H. El-Shazly, C. Pozzi, W. Rhoda, F. Salamini, Mol. Biol. Evol. 14 (2000) 499–510.

A.J. Ammerman, L.L. Cavalli-Sforza, Princeton Univ. Press, Princeton, NJ, 1984.

C.L. Brubaker, J.F. Wendel, Am. J. Bot. 81 (1994) 1309–1326.

D.Q. Fuller, Ann. Bot. (Lond.) 100 (2007) 903–924.

D.R. Given, Principles and Practices of Plant Conservation, Chapman & Hall, London, 1994.

E.G. Bobrov, Acta Inst. Bot. N. Acad. Sci. USSR Ser 1 (6) (1947) 164–336 (cited from Putiyevski *et al.* 1975).

G. Hegi, Illustrierte Flora von Mittle Europa, Vol. 4, Munchen, 1923 (cited from Oppenheimer, 1959).

G. Hillman, Plant Food Economy of Abu Hureyra, in: A. Moore, G. Hillman, T. Legge (Eds.), Village on the Euphrates from Foraging to Farming at Abu'Hureyra, Oxford University Press, New York, 2000, pp. 372–392.

G. Becker-Dellingen, Handbuch des Hulsenfruchtterbaues und Futterbaues, Berlin, 1922 (cited from Oppenheimer, 1959).

J.C. Burger, M.A. Champan, J.M. Burke, Am. J. Bot. 95 (2008) 113–122.

J. Diamond, Nature 418 (2002) 700–707.

J.F. Doebley, B.S. Gaut, B.D. Smith, Cell 127 (2006) 1309–1321.

J. Felsenstein, Cladistics 5 (1989) 164–166.

J. Harlan, J. de Wet, G. Price, Evolution 27 (1973) 311–325.

J.R. Harlan, Crops and Man, American Society of Agronomy, Madison, WI, 1992.

K. Hammer, Kulturpflanze 32 (1984) 11–34.

M. Heun, R. Schafer-Pregl, D. Klawan, R. Castagna, M. Accerbi, B. Borhi, F. Salamini, Science 278 (1997) 1312–1314.

M.W. Blair, G. Iriarte, S. Beebe, Theor. Appl. Genet. 112 (2006) 1149–1163.

P. Azhaguvel, T. Komatsuda, Ann. Bot. 100 (2007) 1009–1015.

P. Gepts, Crop Domestication as a Long-term Selection Experiment. Plant Breeding Reviews, 24 Part 2, J. Janick (ED), Plant Breeding Reviews, Vol. 24, John Wiley & Sons Inc., 2004.

R.G. Allaby, D.Q. Fuller, T.A. Brown, Proc. Natl. Acad. Sci. USA 105 (2008) 13982–13986.

R. Bothmer von, T. van Hintum, H. Knupffer, K. Sato (Eds.), Diversity in Barley (Hordeum vulgare), Elsevier, Amsterdam, 2003.

T.A. Brown, M.K. Jones, W. Powell, R.G. Allaby, Trends Ecol. Evol. (2008), doi:10.1016/j.tree.2008.

INDEX

D

E

L

M